PRAISE FOR
TOUCHED BY ETERNITY

As a lifelong believer in Christ, I experienced a surge of passion following my mother's death to better understand heaven and the dying experience of Christ-followers. Along with Scripture, I read books and articles that recount visions and unusual deathbed happenings, either witnessed by observers or explained by those who had, like the author, one or more near-death experiences. This book clearly serves as witness to a truth of which I have become ever more solidly convinced: the other side of eternity lays barely a whisper from us—as immediate as our breath, as certain as that kind Spirit which constantly draws the impassioned believer ever closer to our good, good Father. By her testimony, though at the cost of repeated bouts of ill-health, God has shown Susan Harris treasures in hidden places. Her impeccably detailed recounting of her visions and their interpretations both fascinates and invites. I gladly add *Touched By Eternity* to my collection.

KATHLEEN GIBSON, *faith columnist, broadcaster of Simple Words, author of Practice by Practice and West Nile Diary*

Unapologetic and assured of the veracity of her experiences, Susan Harris is convinced that her spiritual being was indeed in Heaven during specific health crises. However, she encourages her readers to delve into the biblical scriptures for themselves and make up their own minds. Ms. Harris's Caribbean background and faith heritage, along with her Canadian work experience and Christian service, and also her knowledge of biblical scripture, give texture and colour to her 'life-fabric'. She processes and interprets her experiences from the wealth of this milieu, and that ultimately informs how she expresses them. This work may challenge certain long-held assumptions about life and death, and life beyond death. And yet, the spiritually hungry and those who experience severe suffering, and who struggle with their faith in a loving God, may well gain understanding and receive comfort and insight through a thoughtful reading of *Touched By Eternity: A True Story of Heaven, Healing, and Angels.*

REV. PETER A. BLACK, *pastor, freelance writer and columnist, author of Raise Your Gaze and Mindful Musings of a Grateful Heart*

Touched By Eternity gives readers accounts by author Susan Harris of her experiences with the supernatural, including angels and Jesus Christ. Susan lays bare her encounters without hesitation to encourage readers that there is indeed another life and world beyond this one. *Touched By Eternity* also offers an introduction to Near Death Experiences (NDE) for those unfamiliar with them. Susan's excitement and enthusiasm about her encounters is evident from page to page. In this day of "spirituality," *Touched By Eternity* shines a light on questions people may have regarding this life and what lies ahead.

ALAN ANDERSON, *M.A., Christian Studies, retired pastor and chaplain, co-author of Good Grief People*

An eye-opening and thought-provoking account of the reality of life after death. It challenges us to take stock of what we believe and, more so, who we believe in. It drives us to consider the true purpose of life and how we live it. It follows, what is life without God? Why not live for Him and meet Him one day in Eternity?

DR. ANDEL ROBERTS, *MBBS (UWI) DM Psychiatry, Consultant Psychiatrist*

From the moment I started reading *Touched By Eternity*, Susan Harris's words transported me to her presence. I felt I was an invisible witness—wanting to reach out and end her suffering, to protect and nurture her. Her succinct description of her "outer world" experiences enveloped me like a warm cocoon and I immediately felt reassured that, if one were to leave her earthly body, she'd be loved and cared for far better than on earth. In the darkest of times with my own illnesses, I have had similar occurrences even though I do not belong to a fixed religion. As a healer with both Western medicine and holistic medicine qualifications, the author's words spoke volumes regarding how closely entwined our spiritual and physical beings are. In my opinion, society, with the "assistance" of social media, has lost the vital connection between spirit and body. Written accounts such as Harris's perfectly describe this connection.

BELINDA DENNISS, *AES, Owner/Operator, INK Fitness and Health*

Susan Harris is frank and honest as she leads her readers through remarkable experiences. Some of us have perhaps ushered loved ones to the gates of heaven, but few of us have had the privilege to personally visit and return to earth. In being obedient to tell and encourage others to take seriously the surety of life beyond the grave, Susan has stepped out in faith and vulnerability. You will not regret reading her story.

RUTH SMITH MEYER, *Author & Speaker, Out of the Ordinary and Not Easily Broken*

Courageously written, Susan's personal, powerful story of overcoming painful health and life issues is beautifully interwoven with her vivid spiritual encounters. Her encouraging testimony is passionately engaging and thought-provoking. Susan's experiences are truly unique and her perspectives interesting. For those of us who yearn for heaven and hope... get ready to be edified

IRISH BETH MADDOCK - *Award Winning Children's Author, "The Great Carp Escape"*

TOUCHED BY
ETERNITY

A True Story of
Heaven, Healing, and Angels

SUSAN HARRIS

WHITE LILY PRESS

Cover design by Yvonne Parks
Author photo by Tracy Kerestesh

Legal deposit with Library and Archives Canada
ISBN 978-0-9949869-4-8 (pbk)
ISBN 978-0-9949869-6-2 (ebook)

Contact Susan Harris at:

Website :	https://www.susanharris.ca
Facebook:	https://www.facebook.com/SusanHarrisAuthor
Twitter :	https://twitter.com/SusanHarris20
Amazon:	https://www.amazon.com/Susan-Harris/e/B007XMP4QS

For those who long for Heaven

∾

I will not die, but live,
and tell of the works of the LORD.
(Psalm 118:17 NASB)

CONTENTS

INTRODUCTION

MOST PEOPLE IMAGINE THE afterlife. I do not have to imagine—I've been there.

I have always believed in Heaven, but for the most part considered it a pleasant, faraway place where we would sing all day and night long. Over the three decades that I've preached the gospel, not once did I speak exclusively of Heaven. But then something unexpected took place. I knew what had happened to me, but I did not have a name for it. It wasn't until the summer of 2017 when I shared my third experience on social media that my good friend and chaplain, Alan Anderson, put a name to it—near-death experience (NDE), a term coined by Dr. Raymond Moody in 1975.[1] The term refers to an experience originating through the natural process of being on the brink of death or in death itself. I've had three such experiences over twenty years.

My first NDE occurred on October 16th, 1998 in my OB/GYN's presence in Toronto.

My second NDE happened on November 3rd, 2015 at a hospital.

My third NDE took place on June 24th, 2017 at home following a tooth extraction. My story starts with this episode and is told with flashbacks.

Touched By Eternity overflows with dramatic and engaging experiences, encounters and anecdotes, revelations and comprehension, theology and reflection, encouragement and inspiration, wrapped up in a 112-pound adventurer touring this life and the next. My descriptions and facts are supported by medical records, a childbirth diary, observation, memory, research, and Scripture. Most significant are the insights from God as promised in Jeremiah 33:3- "Call to me and I will answer you and tell you great and unsearchable things you do not know" (NIV). I called, and God told.

Imagining life after death is at best frustrating. Considering that the death rate is 100%, the life to come holds universal fascination that crosses cultures and beliefs. I've written this book for such audiences, even if their belief systems are different from mine, for the religious and non-religious. Our souls transit to the other world following the process we call death. Eternity is a concept that includes both Heaven and Hell, and there are routes to get there. This book addresses each aspect.

Touched By Eternity is my story, but it could be yours. A story of faith and healing, forgiveness and restoration, a trophy of grace. It's a story of everyday living. If you've had health complications, been pregnant, extracted a tooth, or been castigated for a life choice, join me and let's walk together. God will use any people who make themselves available to Him, who long for the joyous hope of being in His presence one day.

Sure there may be some who won't believe unless it happened to them. And had it not happened to me, I may not have given NDEs the credence I now do either. Eternity is beyond the imagining of any experience on earth, and since people process experiences through the five senses, the default position is to dismiss what cannot be contained in the senses. Those senses, however, must be deadened to the physical world in order to be made alive for the spiritual one. I could not have fabricated the things I've written, because I do not have the imaginative power to do so nor do I watch sci-fi movies or read fiction. And when I think of the clarity and details of my NDEs and visions, I can only wish that my memory would be as concise in everyday matters. Yet we have a sixth sense, a "gut feeling" or instinct, and this intangible aspect ties us to Eternity. Fortunately, millions have experienced NDEs like mine, and even more know of someone who had a comparable actuality, and although our stories bear similarities and may hold differences, they validate life after death.

We were created for eternity. I did not want to come back to earth after my NDEs, but had I not come back, I'd never have known I had been healed of hyperemesis gravidarum or another condition in 1998. Those secrets would have mildewed with my childbirth diary. Now I want to travel the world and tell men and women and children about the secrets of the glorious future that awaits us and how we can prepare for it. I do not have all the answers, and each day new questions pop up, but I have faith, and I know what happened to me did indeed happen, and I know the plan of salvation. I may not have proof with photos or memorabilia of my trips to Eternity, but I have evidence through Scripture as I understand it, and of healing through medical records. After all, the spiritual does not require proof, it necessitates faith. Belief in the unseen. I believed long before I saw, ever since I was a child. As Jesus said to Thomas in John 20:29, "…blessed are those who have not seen and yet have believed" John 20:29b (NIV). Many of you have likewise believed without seeing, and for you is the inherent blessing of John 20:29. Only faith in God's Son will qualify us for Eternity, and it is my prayer that you will believe what you read in the pages of this book.

I want to reassure the dying and comfort the fearful and lead them to Jesus. For when they have Jesus, they have Heaven. My testimony will build faith in the one crumbling under hopelessness and pain. It will gladden those who believe and stimulate thought in those who question. Seeing the Bible come alive through my eyes, through the miracles and encounters in my ordinary life, made from the same dust as theirs, will impact the reader deeply. For I am remarkably ordinary – born in the Caribbean and living on the snowy prairies, a mom and wife trying out recipes, a former teacher and health care employee, a preacher and a writer, posting too many pictures of kittens on social media, and using capital letters for emphasis.

For twenty years I grieved for Heaven. I longed to go back. But now I don't want to go back. Not yet. For my pleasure is to talk about death, the one subject that makes me feel as alive as I felt in Eternity.

PROLOGUE

I've been touched by Eternity over five decades through:

- 2 encounters with angels
- 3 near-death experiences with visits to Heaven
- 3 supernatural healings
- 4 visions, including one of Hell.

It was frustrating returning to earth after my first experience in the glorious life to come.

It was downright despairing the second time.

And the third seemed a cruel taunt.

When the last transition was snatched, I knew God was keeping me here for a reason: to carry peace, compassion, and the message that Heaven is gained only through Jesus Christ. But it was not an easy commission. What would have been easy would be for me to exit this life and carry with it my privacy. Instead, I'm driven to forego my pride and lay open my vulnerabilities.

So, here's my story. (Wait, have you read the Introduction?)

CHAPTER 1

COME HOME!

*"…I am with you always, even unto the end of the world…" Matthew 28:20
(KJV).*

COME HOME!
My cryptic text message galvanized my husband into action.
A shrill ping signaled his immediate reply: *Sure, I'm close by.*

June 24th, 2017 dawned as an ordinary day, a sunny Saturday that unfolded in anything but an ordinary way. Less than five minutes before asking Tim to come home, I had texted, *Upped the dose to 300 mg Gabapentin so I'm going back to sleep. Too much pain.*

His message came back: *Do you need me to take you to the ER?*

Me: *No, I might overdose if I take more medication.*

Tim: *Hopefully the afternoon is better.*

The texting ended at 9:34 a.m. At that point we both thought our communication was finished for the morning. That I'd be safe in bed snuggled into pillows and creeping into dreamland, as I had been over the last three days. But instead I was slumped on the dining table, my teeth chattering.

I was unsteady, partly because of the pain and partly because of the side effects of the medication. 100 mg of Gabapentin at 5:00 a.m., another 200 mg at 9:30 a.m. with an extra-strength Tylenol, had left me dazed.

In the seconds following his encouragement for a better afternoon, the chattering started. My teeth were in control and I was helpless to stop them. As the pain increased, so did my weakness, and my jaw muscles could not clench enough to stop the movement. I was more than Woozy Suzy, as Tim referred to me when I was medicated.

I unplugged my iPhone from the socket on the kitchen island where it was being charged, and hanging on to the island, dragged myself to the dining area where I plunked down on a chair. *Is chattering teeth normal? I must research this.*

The phone dropped from my hands onto the green damask tablecloth. Forget research. Panic surged as my body sagged.

I must text Tim. I have to text Tim. He thinks I'm asleep, but I'm getting worse. Oh Jesus, help me!

"You can do it, you can do it, you can do it." The sounds were those of a wounded animal, not words even but ragged breaths. I pressed the button on my iPhone and the screen lit up, blue with a patch of brown. The image in the lower left corner resembles waves. Sky and water. Thankful that I had chosen fingerprint recognition to unlock my phone, I pressed my thumb on the small circle. The screen brought up the Messages icon in the top corner. Slowly but surely my pointer finger typed *Come home!*

The SOS dispatched, the chattering gained dominance. *This can't be real. I must lie down. Help me, Lord.*

Thrusting the electronic lifeline into the pocket of my housecoat, I gripped the table in an effort to stand. Ahead of me, next to the window in the living room, sat the daybed, serene and inviting. On a regular day I'd walk twenty steps to get to it. Today it looked like a 20-kilometer Olympian obstacle course. Shortly before, amid the pain, Reason had been assertive. Reason had cautioned against taking more pills, because I might overdose. Now Reason guided me.

Hold on to the table and grasp the chair on the left. I did.

Drag to another chair. I dragged.

Reach for the island. Hunched over, I shuffled and reached it. The irony was not lost on me. I had been born on an island five decades earlier, and here I was holding on to an island for dear life.

Inch towards the living room. I inched, my robe falling open to reveal my coral nightgown.

Reach for the bookshelf. After what seemed like hours, I finally let go of the island and leaned against the black bookshelf.

DO NOT TOUCH THE FRENCH CAFÉ!

The caution rose in crescendo in my brain. My French Café, situated between the kitchen and the corridor, with its Lennox French Perle place setting on the little bistro, could not take my weight without fine china shattering in a thousand pieces. I kept my distance from the delicate crockery and hugged the bookshelf, grateful for shelves at varying heights. I had only made it halfway to the living room, and I was panting and drained.

Jesus, Jesus. I puffed. *Help me.*

Reason continued: *Lean on the wall and move. You can do it, you can do it, you can do it.*

A box sat in front of me. If I could reach it, I'd have more support. My breathing was loud and labored, but I pushed one slippered foot a few centimeters ahead, gaining ground. Tim had said he was close by but how near "close by" was I did not know.

I held on to the Monarch Specialties box with the replacement chair for the one that had broken in transit, and whispered my one-word prayer, *Jesus.* The rocker beckoned me, but I could not sit. I had to lie down. Seven more steps to the daybed—seven kilometers on my obstacle course.

Help me, Lord. Help me to get to the daybed.

You're almost there, you're almost there, you're almost there. Reason urged me on. *You can do it.*

I shuffled to the sofa. Usually I'd sit on it and enjoy a kilometer-length view of the highway, its happenings and cars as they zoomed by. Not today. Leaning against the beige backrest, I summoned every ounce of strength to drag myself towards the window. With tortoise pace, I pushed on, and with a final heave I flopped my limp body onto the soft green cushions of the daybed. A satin pillow cradled my head. It had been there five days now since I first experienced the toothache.

How long this marathon from dining room to daybed actually took I cannot say. I heard the key in the door and my husband's anxious face rushed in view. He took in my inert frame, dull eyes, and agonized countenance.

"What can I do for you?" His hazel eyes can change from green to brown. That day they were green. Those eyes, which had captured my heart years ago, contemplated my brown ones. They were filled with worry. Pain prohibited me from speaking fully, so through dry lips I mouthed the syllables, "Pay–pa" in my accented tones. That was my last word for a while. He grabbed a notepad and a pen and handed it to me. I jotted "research if chattering teeth is normal". I felt reassured now that he was here, that we could try some self-help. I did not consider my condition a medical emergency yet.

He dove into a Google search on his iPhone. No sooner had he typed "chattering wisdom", than he responded with "Dang!" Autocomplete had brought up suggestions, and such suggestions only popped up if someone else had searched using the same words.

"If other people are asking about chattering teeth, it's got to be a concern," he yelped. "I'm going to change."

He marched into the bedroom. Obviously he suspected I was getting worse and might need emergency treatment, and the gray shirt and dusty khaki trousers were not suitable for the ER. Even more pressing, dust bothered me. Later he told me he had been in the farmyard working with the Kubota tractor, moving hay wagons a kilometer away. When he got my text he jumped in the tractor as it was the quickest way to get home. But although I could hear the tractor pull up on a regular day, noisy as tractors could be, I had not noticed it that day.

I had heard nothing other than the voice of Reason in my head, urging me not to give up.

CHAPTER 2

HEALTHLINE

"I will not die; instead, I will live to tell what the LORD has done"
Psalm 118:17 (NLT).

TIM EMERGED FROM THE bedroom in jeans and a white T-shirt, his biceps bulging through the thin merino. The rest of his bare arms are equally muscled, and veins protrude blue on his fair skin. The white showed off his tanned face well and, in spite of the pain, I could appreciate how strong and wiry he looked, with not an ounce of fat on his medium frame.

I felt safe now that he was there, as I've always felt with him. That confidence had led me to give up the city life with its conveniences and go-to services, because I knew he could take care of me in the country-side. I could not have known how soon I would need that care, though, for it had only been eleven weeks since we had moved to the acreage. Placing my forefinger and thumb together as if holding a pen, I gestured and he passed me the writing materials again.

Call healthline I jotted. HealthLine is designed to serve non-emergency situations, thereby freeing up the ER for real emergencies. I was naïve as to the magnitude of my situation. This was my first tooth removal and I didn't want to overreact.

Tim dialed the number and activated speakerphone for my benefit. The automated voice advised us to have our health cards ready, which Tim had already fished out. I believe he'd have produced the land deed, too, if it was needed.

My dentist had suggested that I buy extra-strength Tylenol and extra-strength Advil to deal with any discomfort I may experience.

"Don't I need stronger prescriptions?" I had asked. Tylenol and Advil were over-the-counter pills and may not be strong enough for pain. My daughter had been prescribed narcotics and opioids after her wisdom teeth surgery in 2015, and the pain had been intolerable even with those, offering relief for half the time instead of the full hours between dosages.

"No, you'll be fine." The dentist had sounded certain, and with my gums still heavy with the localized anesthesia, I'd felt somewhat assured. People had their teeth extracted every day and were fine. But I had not been fine, or anything even remotely resembling fine, so had rummaged through the old prescriptions like a beggar looking for morsels in a trash can.

The HealthLine's wait was long. My brain felt as though it was on overdrive. I motioned for water and Tim brought the straw and glass to my cracked, parched lips. I slurped the water. It leaked from the side of my mouth and down my neck on to my robe. I scribbled *Kleenex* and a box appeared as if conjured from air.

About ten minutes later the receptionist came on the line, and after briefing her on my condition, Tim was queued for the nurse.

He sat next to me on a chair with textured fabric in blue and orange. The chair was one of the set we had used prior to purchasing the script design for the French theme of our new house, and an oddity around the table, but he had voted to keep it to use when wearing farm clothes.

Meanwhile, I was sinking lower, grappling with the torment. About five minutes later, I scribbled, "*Call hospital + talk to nurse.*" Grammar was inconsequential, and my normally legible handwriting looked like a four year old's.

Except for when searching the Internet and reading health card numbers, Tim had not taken his eyes off me. I was moaning, lying on my back with my head towards the window. I had not showered nor had I brushed my hair or teeth. The coral satin nightgown, which lent some semblance to the real me, was hidden under the woolly red robe. If he looked ahead to the china cabinet in the dining room, in stark contrast he'd see me smiling in white, holding his hand amid the golden elegance of Trump International Hotel where we had taken the wedding photo. I didn't have the energy upon waking to hobble to the closet and pull out the matching coral negligée with its lilac embroidered collar and cuffs.

If I had known what was to follow, I might have asked Tim to fetch it for me.

CHAPTER 3

A FACE, A CASTLE, AND A LIGHT

"...I am the light of the world..." John 8:12 (KJV).

THE WAIT ON THE phone with HealthLine was too long. My eyes could no longer stay open, and the lids met in a line of long black lashes. I could not focus on the reminders not to hang up, or the old red robe, or how pathetic I looked. The pain was excruciating. My little body, just 112 pounds, could not bear it. Oh, to be relieved of this agony.

Remove this torment, Jesus.

Eyes closed, I moaned quietly. Suddenly a man's face flashes before me. It's a headshot, and he's wearing glasses. He has short, dark hair and appears to be near middle age, healthy and vigorous. I do not put a name to his face just then, but I recognize him as a computer magnate. There are two very famous ones in the field, Bill Gates and Steve Jobs, but it's the one who died that I see. He is smiling and happy.

His face disappears and in the distance I see the most incredible sight. A spectacular castle with towers and turrets rising high above its walls. They are edged with delicate craftsmanship, patterns with fine details of peaks, curves, and circles. The castle is blue, a luminescent, glorious, amazing shade that I haven't seen on earth. The sides and edges are trimmed with gold, and more strips of gold run vertically down the walls. The gold gleams white at some angles. It is breath-taking, stunning, beautiful like no other building I've seen. I've been to Paris and have seen the Palace at Versailles, one of the most opulent castles in history, but Versailles does not compare to this castle in the sky. The castle walls are an opaque, shimmery blue. The best way I can describe it is to think of the rainbow, stark and intense before it begins to dissipate, when the bands of color shimmer but are not transparent. The castle is elegant and taller than it is wide.

The vision faded and I opened my eyes. Tim was still on hold with the HealthLine. I picked up the pad and pen and wrote in spidery handwriting:

Blue, gold, with gold gleaming white. Castle heaven.

Eager to share the wonder with him in words, I made a heroic effort to utter the words. They came out in monosyllables, "Pree ... ty. So ... pree ... ty."

Count one, two, three, four ... and I began to gasp. Suddenly I was gurgling and panting for air. Air, the breath God breathed into Adam, was leaving my body. My breath came from deep inside my abdomen. I was aware that from way down in my belly I was exhaling huge bursts of fresh clean air, but they were more like powerful shoots of water than air. I was also aware of my un-brushed teeth. Surely my breath ought to be smelly, but instead it was pure, and the air-water was clean and fresh.

As from a distance, I heard my husband cry out. He grabbed my hand and shouted, "I'm calling 911! I'm calling 911!" as if to involve me in the decision. Or maybe it was to keep me there, with him. But I was unresponsive.

He hung up on HealthLine and dialed 911. Frustration and exasperation mixed with desperation in the words he uttered, "The call dropped."

He fidgeted with the phone, but no connection was made. A few seconds later it rang.

"Hello!" Tim spoke rapidly, and somewhat shrilly, no doubt panicked by what he had just witnessed with me. The 911 operator was on the phone, wanting to know our emergency.

"My wife is semi-conscious. She is gasping and can't breathe. Her wisdom tooth was extracted on Wednesday, and she is not doing well. I need an ambulance." The information tumbled out. I caught snatches of the conversation and heard him giving her our land location, even as I tethered to my next location in Eternity. In the countryside addresses are not cut and dried as in cities. There are no streets or house numbers. Instead, the land location is given, and verbal directions and GPS locate homes.

The interruption had brought me back to earth. I opened my eyes, caught a glimpse of Tim's dear face, then closed them again. I was aware of this world and I was aware of the other world, moving in and out of consciousness.

I see a bright orange light in a circle coming towards me. The orange lightens to an amber color of the most beautiful gold. It is soft, the color of champagne. Then there is no orange, only a circle with deep browny-gold on the perimeter, radiating in umbra style to the color of champagne then becoming white at the core. This exquisiteness defies imagination. The deeper gold on the circumference is likewise indescribable, not like the yellow-gold we see on earth (I tried to capture the light on the cover of the book). The light is more stunning than anything I have ever seen, brighter than the sun, yet it does not hurt or dazzle my eyes, nor do I squint.

As I watch the light come towards me, I think of Jesus' words, "I am the light of the world. If you follow me, you won't have to walk in darkness, because you will have the light that leads to life" (John 8:12 NLT). Jesus is there to lead me to eternal life as I depart my body. He is moving towards me as I exhale earth and inhale Eternity. John the Divine describes this light in Revelation 21:23, "And the city has no need of sun or moon, for the glory of God illuminates the city, and the Lamb is its light" (NIV).

In spite of my dazed, pain-filled state, I knew one thing with absolute certainty. I had seen Jesus, the Light of the World.

CHAPTER 4

PARAMEDICS

"For the wages of sin is death..." Romans 6:23a (KJV).

T IM TALKED TO THE 911 dispatcher for a long time. Then solu-
tion-mode kicked in and I stuttered, "Put down the phone and drive
me to the ER." We might get there quicker.

"They've dispatched an ambulance and it will arrive soon," he whispered. "I can't drive right now, anyway."

I hadn't realized how shaken up he was by everything that was happening. His eyes darted to the window, watching the highway for the
ambulance. A mere 135 meters to the south, Highway 15 runs in an
east-west direction. With Herculean effort I begged him in garbled frag-
ments not to tell my almost-adult child, should anything happen to me.
Graduation was only four days away, and I didn't want anything to take
away from the joy of that momentous occasion.

"Sometimes graduation never happens." My husband's voice was
grim. There was no way ceremonies and pageantry were going to silence
my death if it should occur.

As we waited for the ambulance, I became aware that I did not feel
pain. It was gone. In Revelation, the Bible states that there is no pain in
Heaven. I had just glimpsed Heaven—not entered it, merely glimpsed it—
and my pain was gone.

I was touched by Eternity!

Tim went out to move our cars to make a place for the ambulance.
The door clicked and I imagined him going down the makeshift steps,
which had been built hastily so the movers could bring our furniture
in. The permanent steps would be built with the deck later in summer.
The garage had been deemed the more urgent project before hail hit the
"Princess Mobile" as Tim had christened my CRV. But the rickety steps

alongside the sleek new house were inconsequential today as he made his way back into the house and to my side.

About fifteen minutes later he exclaimed, "This can't be!" He rushed to the door as a car pulled into the spot he had cleared for the ambulance. My pain had de-escalated, but my body was still weak and it was difficult to focus. Who was it? A chance visit from a neighbor was unlikely, since we had moved here so recently. Was this the help the 911 dispatcher had promised? Was it a grain buyer? Where was the ambulance?

"It's a woman," he informed me.

Why was she here? Tim greeted the visitor and ushered her into the living room. The dark-haired woman wore a white T-shirt and came across as jolly. She perched herself on the French script footstool, face level with me, and introduced herself.

"My name is Patricia and I am a first responder. How are you feeling? Are you experiencing pain? Can you show me where?"

The rapid-fire questions overwhelmed my already heightened sense of un-wellness. I mumbled unintelligibly and pointed at my husband. A swollen mouth did not allow the leisure of conversation. I did not want to talk. But Patricia's role was to keep *me* alert, and she took that role seriously. I closed my eyes.

"Don't fall asleep on me, Susan, don't fall asleep. Open your eyes, Susan," she cantillated.

I was tired, drowsy, and weak. My eyelids dropped against my will while Patricia talked and cajoled, begging me not to fall asleep. She had to keep me conscious until the ambulance arrived, but the small talk was not going well. I wanted quiet, and I couldn't speak comfortably.

Let me close my eyes. Let me go to my peace, to the place I don't have words to describe.

But Reason willed me to blink my eyes and respond to this good lady whose only motive was to keep me alive. *To keep me here to write this book.*

Reason had cautioned earlier in the morning, or rather commanded, *Do not take another pill because you will overdose.* Reason had interjected seventeen months earlier when I was in torturous pain. *Do not take another pill. You will overdose. Go back to the ER.* So I had moaned and fought the pain alone, with Reason cheering me on, and when I could no longer stand the torment, and it was not time for the next dose, that voice inside me had directed me to the ER.

Patricia was Reason in person.

"Look at me, Susan. Talk to me, Susan. Look at me …"

"Don't tell me this!" Tim interrupted the first responder's voice. "The ambulance passed our road. It slowed down, then picked up speed and is heading east."

Thankfully, the driver realized the mistake and rerouted, finally turning into our driveway. The ambulance bill stated the arrival time as 12:06 p.m., thirty minutes after the initial call had been placed.

Tim told me afterwards that he had been livid when the female Emergency Medical Technician (EMT) gushed to him, "We took a wrong turn. What's up?" followed by a chuckle. Really? What's up? His wife was slipping in and out of consciousness and could have left this world anytime, and the ambulance driver was joking about a wrong turn? My husband did not find that funny.

Tim ushered two EMTs into our house. The male EMT was tall and big, or perhaps he appeared bigger because he loomed over my prostrate form. Both paramedics wore navy uniforms, shirts with short sleeves tucked into trousers and belted at the waist.

The tall man seemed to be in charge. I noticed his blue gloves immediately, the kind worn in hospitals but not as thin as the surgical ones I used for penny magic, as I called the lemon and salt concoction I use when I shine pennies for school children. His were turquoisey-blue, and the uniforms were dark blue, neither color as beautiful as the castle in the air, but still significant. Behind them I noticed a young man. He wore a white T-shirt and was dressed as a civilian, like Patricia. He was quiet the entire time.

"How are you feeling?" the big EMT asked me.

"Good," I replied. He stood at right angles to me and I could not focus fully on him. Turning to Tim, the man directed, "You'll have to give her health card to the driver." He waved a hand at the female EMT.

My speech may have been stilted, but my cognizance was intact in that moment, and a warning bell went off in my brain. Health cards, social insurance cards, passports … such things one does not hand over to strangers. And strangers the paramedics were to me.

Still slurring, I piped up, my gaze fixed on Tim who held the coveted card in his hand. "Do not give her my health card. Don't give anyone my health card." My words continued to come out in monosyllables. Handing over my health card didn't make sense to me. I thought that, since the danger was over, they would pronounce me fine and go their way. The EMT explained that my health card would be going with me, but his partner would hold on to it.

Going with me? Where am I going?

He explained more, "When we get to the hospital the driver will give the card to the nurse and you will get it back when they are finished."

"Why am I go-ing to the hosp-tal?" I stuttered on the word *hospital*.

"We want to make sure you don't have an infection or a fever. We don't have any equipment to check it here." That sounded like proper procedure. But I must have looked doubtful, for he added with a bright smile, "They have a really nice doctor on call."

I looked at Tim, still standing in the middle of the room with the card in his hand. Even a tornado would have a hard time ripping it from his hand without my permission. Blue-collar farmer that my husband is, his day job is a white-collar professional at the same hospital we were going to. He knows and respects patients' wishes.

"Your health card will be safe, I promise." The EMT's assurance resonated and I felt I could trust him. Later I wondered why he didn't take the card, but emphasized that the driver had to have it. My gaze went from him to his colleague's face and then to Tim. I did not look at Patricia or the quiet man in the white T-shirt, although I knew they were absorbing it all. But there was still one confirmation to make.

"He has to come with me."

No way I was going without my husband.

"He can accompany you, but he's not coming in the ambulance," the EMT explained in gentle tones.

Tim was quick to reassure me. "I'll drive my car so I can bring you back home." That made sense.

"Give her the card," I conceded.

Tim handed it over, and I allowed Patricia to help me into a sitting position. I solved the problem of getting to the ambulance by saying, "I - can - walk. I - don't- need - 'strchr'." I garbled the word *stretcher*. Those *e* vowels were so frustrating!

I was conscious of my appearance, mismatched red coat over a coral nightgown. The old pair of blue slippers I had been shuffling around in lay on the floor next to the daybed. I couldn't do much about the coat, but I was going to ensure those slippers remained right where they were. In the simplest of language and motions, I conveyed to my husband my desire for him to fetch me my red ones. My teeth hadn't been cleaned, my hair hadn't been brushed, I had not taken a shower, and there I was, surrounded by strangers. If I was going to the ER to be surrounded by more strangers, the least I could do was wear matching slippers.

Tim brought the soft velvet pair with the red satin bows and placed my feet into them. My toes, polished in Baby Lavender, peeked through the openings in the front. My fingers were the same glossy mauve, a small consolation given the sorry picture I presented. From previous experiences in the ER, we knew how easily a visit could turn into a stay, so when Tim suggested he pack a bag, I outlined what I wanted him to bring in brief, broken words.

The ambulance driver and Patricia helped me off the daybed and we inched our way to the front door, then down the makeshift treaders to the gurney waiting at the bottom. The two EMTs and Patricia positioned me on the gurney.

"Thank you for coming," I whispered to the first responder. She smiled and said a few words I couldn't really process. I had no idea where the quiet man was.

I closed my eyes against the dazzling light of a golden sun on a June summer day. It was hot and bright and the glare was harsh, a startling contrast to the champagne brilliance I had looked at earlier and had been fully able to withstand. Tim bent and kissed my left cheek. I struggled to keep my eyes open, but I lost the battle. The blinding sun was too much and I could only see my husband's outline. When one is as close the death as I had been, every moment, every look, every syllable, is treasured.

"I love you," he whispered.

My muffled sound bite of "I love you, too," was our last exchange before I was wheeled into the ambulance. The report indicated we departed at 12:19 p.m.

It was my first ride ever in an ambulance. In fact, it was the closest I'd been to one in spite of the six years I'd worked in health care. The male EMT sat on a seat to my left with a clipboard and pen.

"I thought you would be driving," I observed in broken speech.

"My partner is driving," he replied.

The ride was bumpy. The first leg of the trip was an eight-kilometer stretch of pavement from the junction of Bangor Road along Highway 15, and it was chipped, pitted with holes and erosion. *Broken like I am.* With tax dollars scarce, the much-needed repairs might not happen for a long time. Nausea swept over me at the jerky motions, and I whimpered. I knew the driver was doing her best to get me to the ER as quickly as possible, and navigating potholes was no dream job, but that didn't stop a headache from developing. The kilometers stretched to infinity, it seemed.

Are we there yet? No! I asked and answered my own question silently. It was another thirty-four kilometers once we had cleared the 15 West and reached the intersection of the Number 9 highway. From there, we turned north en route to the hospital in Yorkton. The Number 9 had been repaved the year before and was normally a joy to drive on, but not today while lying down. I could feel the vibrations of the vehicle as it turned the corners and my jaw seemed to bounce, producing a different kind of anguish than I had experienced earlier.

My EMT companion was reading his clipboard, and when he saw me turn my head he asked me a few questions. He jotted down the answers while I spoke. I don't remember all the questions he asked me or the order of any, but they were things like my date of birth, the date I had my wisdom tooth removed, what medication I had taken, when I started to feel really ill, what symptoms I was experiencing, and what had happened. Even though we had given that information, except my date of birth, earlier, I had to repeat it again.

I had an uncontrollable urge to tell everyone about my transiting to the other world and what I saw. I started with the man beside me.

"I saw Heaven." I did not look at him, as turning made me more nauseated in the moving vehicle.

The EMT laughed. "The medicine could make you hallucinate," he replied politely. I could see he was trying to be respectful to me and my experience. In his clinical profession one is not supposed to give factors merit unless they can be proven or measured.

"I'm not saying it didn't happen," he underscored. "Because people have strange experiences when the Vagus nerve is touched. I'm just saying there is another explanation for the things a person sees."

I made a sound that was supposed to be one of assent and continued speaking in my painfully slow way. "I was lying on the daybed and I saw a castle in the air. It was blue with gold trim and the gold gleamed white in some places. I saw Heaven."

He was writing, but I couldn't be sure what he was writing at that point. Two months later, when I requested my health records, the copy was faint and not legible in parts, but one note read, "Patient crying frequently, but would not disclose reason." I was not aware of crying, but I certainly remember moaning in pain from the drive.

I did not ask him if he believed in Heaven, because I felt he did not. But I needed to let everyone know that Heaven is real, so I said to him, "We all need to live in such a way that we will be reunited with Jesus when we die."

He didn't reply. I continued with my story. "I felt as if my body was convulsing and the air was being squeezed out from my belly. I was wavering between Heaven and earth. Heaven is so beautiful."

His notes on my medical record stated, "Patient strongly religious." I pray his encounter with me will remain with him forever and change his life.

He looked up from his chart. "I've had experiences that I thought were real, but they turned out to be hallucinations. I remember when I was a teen I was really sick and felt that I was in a deep, dark basement when I was really on the top floor. Some medicine, and sickness and pain, lead us to believe we are in places when we aren't actually there. So I'm not saying it's not real and it didn't happen, because it happened to me too. But it's an effect of the Vagus nerve." Making a mental note to research the Vagus[1] nerve when I returned home, and to give his theory credence, I asked him to spell the word. He did.

"Where is the Vagus located?"

From what he described, I understood it as running from the brain down close to the heart and into the stomach. I was honestly interested in his theories, because the more I could understand the clinical world, the more I could disprove it with my experience. The writing finished, the EMT put away his pen and conversed in a more relaxed manner. He asked me a few more questions, but did not take any notes.

"Did you go to the bathroom a few minutes before the experience?"

"No."

"Did you have a fever?"

"No."

"Were you sweating?"

"No."

"Did you throw up?"

"No."

He explained how, if the Vagus nerve is stimulated, a person can feel sweaty and nauseated, even become unconscious. But I had not been sweating and the nausea had started after I got in the ambulance and it turned and swung around corners and bumped on the rough highway.

"They'll check all of this in the ER," he informed me.

I wanted everything to be checked and looked forward to it. I had been unconscious to this world when I saw Heaven, but whether it was due to my Vagus nerve being stimulated, or the side effects of the Gabapentin, I wasn't sure. Whichever it was, I had indeed drifted into the next world.

The ambulance slowed down as we entered the city limits then crawled its way to the compound of the Yorkton Regional Health Center. We entered the enclosed area adjacent to the emergency department through a dark, narrow space.

"We're here," my companion announced. It was 12:50 p.m. according to the report. The drive had taken thirty-one minutes.

CHAPTER 5

AT THE HOSPITAL

"I will make breath enter you, and you will come to life" *Ezekiel 37:5b (NIV)*.

THE AMBULANCE DOORS OPENED and my gurney was removed. The EMTs wheeled me into a brightly-lit area with rooms, a nurse's station, equipment, and curtains, everything to confirm I was inside the emergency area. I was surprised, as I had imagined I'd be taken to the reception area, given a number, and required to wait for my name to be called. I had never gone to the ER in an ambulance and didn't know the procedure, but I was relieved as I had been perturbed at the possibility of meeting someone I knew looking the way I did, as generally happens in a small city.

The gurney was placed in a hallway. The two EMTs chatted with a nurse and I thought of my health card. I looked around for Tim, but he had not yet arrived. Of course he couldn't have gotten there before us, because he had to pack the bag in case I needed to stay over, and packing took time.

"I - don't - want - to - wear - hosp-tal - gown," I had pleaded, enumerating the pieces I wanted: the pretty red silk PJs that matched the slippers I was wearing, the purple pair with the lacy top and thin straps, and the yellow negligee set. Tim knew where the PJs were kept, but as this was a new house and the closet was large, I had made doubly sure by saying, "The yellow set is near the door."

Then there was underwear, toothbrush, toiletries, and anything else I might need. To be fair, I had communicated all of that in sparse, terse language, but Tim understood my broken words and hand signals. He easily interpreted my needs, and knew that I liked my finery and all that went into presenting a decent appearance.

"Susan?" A voice broke into my reverie. I found myself looking at a nurse of medium height.

"Yes,"

"We'll be taking you to a room shortly."

"Thanks."

"You're getting the best doctor today," she added.

"What's his name?" My curiosity was piqued as this was the second unsolicited recommendation I had received about the doctor on call. I had not given thought to which doctor would be seeing me in the ER, but I was determined to tell of the blue castle to anyone, regardless of their credentials, age, or looks. She mentioned his name and I recognized it, although I had never met him.

Why was he esteemed so highly? Did the nurse mean the doctor was the best in his field, or that he was good-looking and had a great personality, or that he was a lovely person to work with? And if he happened to be all of the above, what were the odds that, on the day I had a vision of Heaven, this learned, handsome doctor would be on call? But then, wasn't everything pertaining to Heaven good, perfect, and the best?

While I mused, the nurse wheeled my gurney into a room. My first impression was that it looked like a storage room. She assisted me onto the bed. The door was partly open and each time someone passed by I checked to see if it was a male. Short of knowing the doctor's name, I had no idea what he looked like. The only clue might be a stethoscope around his neck and possibly a white coat. Not all the doctors wore a coat, however; the last one I saw had worn a three-piece suit.

The nurse asked me my name and date of birth. In her hand she held my health card. *Praise the Lord!*

"On a scale of 1 to 10, with 10 being the worst pain and 1 being the least, how would you rate your pain right now?"

"Between 4 and 5," I replied. "It was a 10 before I saw Heaven, but it came down after that." Uninvited, I recounted my story. She listened but did not ask questions, although she wrote about it in her notes. As I talked, I realized that my jaw pain was returning.

"What's the date today?"

"June 24th," I replied.

Next she explained that she had to ask me a question they asked all patients. "Do you have feelings of hopelessness, or is there anything worrying you?"

"No." I shook my head.

She gave me a form to sign. The title was Suicide Risk Screening Order Test.

The nurse left the room. When she returned, she fastened a computer-generated ID bracelet on my right wrist. This was my official admission into the outpatient emergency room.

"I'm going to check your blood pressure," she informed me as she pushed the loose sleeve of my robe up to expose my bare arm. While the cuff inflated, she took my temperature. Soon she was unwinding the sphygmomanometer from my arm.

"Is my pressure all right?" I couldn't see the numbers on the gauge, but I wanted to know everything.

"There's no need for concern," she assured me. But when I studied my health records later, my blood pressure had in fact been quite high. I put it down to the trauma I had undergone.

I didn't think I had a fever, and my temperature of 37.2 degrees Celsius confirmed this. No fever ruled out an infection, but the true results would be determined after my blood work was completed. The nurse placed the stethoscope under my robe to find my heart rate. It was 67 beats per minute. Then it was time to assess my lungs.

"Take a deep breath," she encouraged as she placed the instrument on various parts of my back. I inhaled deeply then blew out.

"One more time." I breathed in then let out my breath slowly.

Two hours ago I was exhaling earth and inhaling Eternity...

But now my oxygen level was 97%, and my respiratory rate was 16 breaths per minute. Both normal.

"*Thank You, Jesus,*" I whispered in my heart. "*Praise You, Lord.*" I was particularly interested in these results, because I had been gasping for air and losing consciousness. Now all had been restored.

The ambulance report had stated that my chief complaint was mouth pain, but Tim had told them I could not breathe. For us, the breathing, air expelling, was the crux of our concern. Then, in the observation room, I had a revelation:

Air expelling from my lungs in the natural correlates to water gushing in the supernatural.

It hooked in my spirit and I made a mental note to research the significance of being born of water and being born of the Spirit when I returned home. The nurse's voice broke into my thoughts. She had replaced the apparatus on the cart.

"Can you push against my hands?" She held out her arms with her palms facing me at shoulder level. The question seemed strange to me, but I pushed her hands. Then she asked me to squeeze her hand. I didn't ask why she wanted me to carry out these exercises nor did she volunteer any information on my performance.

"The doctor will be here in an hour, but someone from the lab will come and take your blood work and then we'll have a better idea of what is or is not happening."

"Thank you very much." I realized I was speaking much better than before. My words were coming more easily and I could enunciate more than one syllable at a time. I'm not sure why my fluency returned, because up to that point I had not been given any medication.

She adjusted the height of the bed and lifted the side rails so I wouldn't fall out. "Is your head comfortable on the pillow?"

"Yes," I replied.

"This is a call bell." She drew my attention to the cord with a button on the end. "Press this button if you need anything. We'll let you know when the doctor comes in."

"Thank you," I responded as she left the room. I was familiar with the call bell. In fact I was familiar with all of it—the entire routine of being in the ER and in the ward. The bevy of tests, blood work, X-rays, meeting doctors, swallowing medicine, my husband packing my bags ... Nineteen months ago I had been hospitalized.

It was there that I went on my second trip to Eternity.

I had no idea what time it was. Every device flashing the time in any and every direction at home—watch, phone, microwave, stove, clocks, TV, computer—were, of course, at home. My phone, thankfully, was on its way with Tim because I had gurgled my desire for the device to be brought with my other belongings. Two weeks later, when the ambulance bill arrived, it noted "Unit Clear:1300" which meant the ambulance was available to take another call as of 1:00 p.m. That helped me gauge time retrospectively.

The two EMTs who had brought me to the hospital came into the room to bid me goodbye. Their work was over.

"Thank you. Thank you very much for all you've done for me." I was genuine in my gratitude and especially happy that my health card was safe.

"You're welcome," they chorused. "Get better soon."

I settled back on the bed to wait for my husband.

The room was dominated by a large shelving unit, which had produced my first impression of a storage room converted into an examination room. In hospitals any space is coveted when the inevitable overflow occurred, but I hadn't seen any other patients and two rooms nearby were empty.

The shelving unit interested me as I recognized the labeling and organizing as a 5S exercise, the result of a kaizen, or improvement, in Lean training. CBC had reported that the province spent thirty-three million dollars on Lean training for health care workers,[1] and the figure is actually greater if indirect costs are considered. I myself had taken such training, and applied the practice to my home and business. Crutches of varying sizes hung on pegs on the wall to the left of the bed, while others had been propped in the corner. At the back of the room was a dispenser for sharps, and a picture hung to its left. The picture was partially obscured, but I caught a glimpse of blue sky and was reminded of my vision.

A movement at the door captured my attention. Tim had arrived, clutching a black bag. Was I ever glad to see him.

"How are you feeling?" he asked as he set the bag on a chair. He approached the bed and kissed me on my lips.

"Much better." I smiled. "Do you notice I'm speaking more clearly?"

"You sure sound better." He took my hand and gazed deeply into my eyes. This was our first moment alone since my near-death, and the most coherent exchange of the day. Our eyes spoke volumes.

"I haven't seen the doctor yet, but the nurse said he should be coming around two o'clock."

He nodded and lifted the bag. "I brought your purse with your makeup bag, too."

Oh, what a good husband! The handbag hadn't been enumerated, so I was thrilled. Now to beautify. I grabbed the red pick from the makeup bag first as neat hair is the beginning of a good impression. Tim held my powder compact up so I could see what I was doing in the small, round mirror. Next I dabbed Clean & Clear oil-absorbing sheets all over my face, hoping to freshen my unwashed visage. Powder would cake on oily skin so that was a no-no. I discovered how futile it is to try to fill in eyebrows with unsteady fingers—I simply didn't have the coordination for the light, precise strokes required for the delicate task and had to abandon my efforts. The final stage of this "makeover" was Grape Tutti lip gloss. It was not much, nor did it look great, but I felt a million times better about seeing the doctor.

With a quiet moment, a memory returned of the young man in the white T-shirt. I asked Tim if he remembered the man.

"That was the Fourth Responder," he remarked without skipping a beat. His characteristic humor was back now that the danger was over. "He arrived fourth on the scene."

I grinned at the moniker. The Fourth Responder was a pretty apt name, and I thought it was very clever of my husband to come up with the descriptor on the spot. The story in the Bible of the three Hebrew boys in the fire, along with the "fourth man" rose in my mind. By King Nebuchadnezzar's confession, the fourth man "is like the Son of God" (Daniel 3:25 KJV). I was relieved that this young man was flesh-and-blood, and not a visiting angel who had to be explained. I had explained a lot already and it was far from over. Nonetheless, the analogy and memory of Jesus showing up in the midst of crisis was not lost on me, and only served to underline the fact that I had been in the presence of things heavenly.

The Fourth Responder was in fact a first responder and the only person who didn't speak to me. Had he been roused from sleep when his cell phone jangled, informing him to get to our house? Had he been taken away from friends? What personal sacrifices did both responders make to rush to my assistance? These kind, noble volunteers are unpaid for their service to me and others.

And that day they may very well have saved my life.

CHAPTER 6

INTERROGATED

"... make a defense to everyone who asks you to give an account for the hope that is in you ..." 1 Peter 3:15b (NASB).

AT 2:00 P.M., THE doctor entered the room. If looks could have healed, I'd be well that instant! He was as striking as a Greek god in blue physician scrubs. Hallelujah. Blue seemed to be the theme of the day. The good doctor had no idea who was in the little room and appeared surprised when he saw my husband. Their paths often crossed at work.

He stood at the foot of my bed. "I apologize for this, Susan, but I must ask you, are there issues that might be causing you worry?" First the nurse, now the doctor—did they link my encounter with the afterlife to mental health issues?

"No," I replied truthfully. "Things are going well. We've just moved to a brand new house in the countryside and it's beautiful there. I love it." I paused for breath then added, "We did have some problems with tent caterpillars and that made me unhappy for a little while, but it's over now."

He smiled. "What's the date today?"

"June 24th," I replied. "I had my wisdom tooth extracted three days ago on Wednesday, June 21st."

He asked me to tell him what had happened to me that day, and I described the now familiar story, how while lying on the daybed, in pain from my wisdom tooth extraction, I began to weave in and out, from this life to the next, and had a vision of Heaven. I felt certain my stories of the castle had already reached him via both the EMT and the nurse's notes.

"What medication did you take?"

"I took 100 mg of Gabapentin at 5:00 a.m., and 200 mg at 9:00 a.m. as well as an extra-strength Tylenol at 9:00 a.m." I was speaking fast. Was I subconsciously trying to get the mundane details out of the way so I could get to the important part of my message, my vision of Heaven? "I had been taking Diclofenac left over from my daughter's prescription after her wisdom teeth surgery, but I finished them yesterday."

"You took Gabapentin?"

"Yes, I had leftover pills that I had taken for pinched nerve pain back in 2015. I figured there are nerves in my mouth so it would help." I hurried on before he could speak, because I had so much to say. "But I did not overdose. I knew from 2015 that I could not exceed 300 mg."

"So this was from a past prescription?"

"Yes."

The physician explained that Gabapentin would not treat the pain in my mouth because the pain is not caused by the nerves. I'd need pain-killers for trauma.

"What else happened?"

"My belly started to heave. I gasped for air and felt my breath coming out as if it were water. And I saw what in my opinion was Heaven, a castle in the sky. It was blue and had gold trim and the trim gleamed white in some places." My fingernails dug into my palms as I recounted my experience for the third time that day, four if I included my note to Tim.

The doctor opened his smart phone and began to type and scroll while he was talking to me. "Is this the first time you've had this experience?"

"No, it's happened three times now."

"When did it first happen?"

"On October 16th, 1998." My answer was matter-of-fact. He jerked his head and studied me, apparently surprised by the accuracy and quickness with which I had produced the date.

"I was pregnant and dehydrated and was in my OB's office in Toronto. I slumped forward on his desk, and the next thing I knew I was walking in a green meadow with someone besides me. When I came back and opened my eyes, the OB and my husband were leaning over me. I told them I had been in Heaven."

"When was the second time?" The medical practitioner's tone was professional.

"November 3rd, 2015," I replied. "I saw Eternity. I was a patient in the hospital at Melville, being treated for a pinched nerve, and I was in a lot of pain. In the dark hours of the night I went up a tunnel to what I believe is Eternity."

The doctor put away his phone. "Can you hold out your hands?"

I held out my hands. He then asked me to do a number of little things designed to test my coordination and strength. The tests reminded me of games we had played as children.

Can you touch your nose?

Can you squeeze my hand as tightly as possible?

Can you push against my palms but stop me from pushing your palms?

When he asked me to stand barefoot on the floor, I hesitated. I do not even walk barefoot in our house, and the thought of hospital germs made me cringe. Should I ask Tim to put some paper towels on the floor?

Just do it, Susan. You're in the right place if you pick up germs.

I gingerly placed my feet on the floor and stood up straight.

"Put your feet together and let your arms hang at your sides."

I stood like that for a short time with my eyes open.

"Now close your eyes," the doctor instructed.

When it was over I resumed my seat on the bed. He paused then gazed at me again.

"Do you ever feel as if things around you are getting really, really large and you are getting really small?"

"No."

"Did you feel like you were above looking down at yourself?"

"No."

"Did you see your life flash in front of you?"

"No."

"When you felt you were convulsing, did you urinate?"

"No."

"Did you go to the bathroom just before you lost consciousness?"

"No."

"Were you sweating?"

"No."

"Did you throw up?"

"No."

"Do you have a history of seizures?"

"No."

During the interrogation the MD had been watching me keenly. His gaze shifted now to Tim, before coming back to me.

"People who have experiences like yours are usually very, very ill and almost at the end of life. They cannot function. They have lost all their capabilities. You look very normal and healthy. In fact, I wouldn't know you had been sick at all by just looking at you and speaking to you."

He was right. I was coherent and articulate in my responses. I was not a candidate for hallucinations or delusions or seizures. The rapport he had witnessed between my husband and me attested to a strong marriage. I'm a responsible citizen. I'm a normal, stable, functional individual who had seen what God promised me in the Bible.

The doctor gestured to his phone and explained that he had been looking up the side effects of Gabapentin to see if seizures is one of them, but it is not. He was right again. I had no history of seizures, and I DID NOT have a seizure when I saw the blue mansion with the gold trim.

The physician stood up. "I'll have to look at your blood work. I'll check in with you again shortly." He turned and left the room.

I was thirsty after this long discourse, so I buzzed the nurse on my call bell. A dark-haired woman came in.

"May I have some water, please?" As she went to get it, I exclaimed to Tim, "I'm hungry!" It was after 2:00 p.m., and except for a few sips of water, I had nothing on my stomach.

"Me too," he chimed. Of course, with everything that had been going on, Tim had not stopped to make lunch.

The nurse returned with a jug and a glass.

"She's hungry." Tim rested a hand on my shoulder. "Can she have something to eat?"

The nurse set the jug down on the table tray. "We have sandwiches in the fridge."

I shook my head. Chewing was painful. Slurping was the best I could do.

"Maybe I can get something in the cafeteria," he suggested.

It was the nurse's turn to shake her head. "It's Saturday. The cafeteria is not open on Saturdays."

"Okay, thank you," Tim replied. The nurse left and he helped me sip the cool, refreshing water. Picking up his keys, he announced, "The fast food place it will be."

"Can you pass me my phone?" I held out my hand and he gave it to me. I was not able to surf the Net, but a couple of pictures would help me remember my unique experience.

While Tim was gone, the MD popped his head in and our eyes met. I was sitting up on the bed, leaning back against the pillow. He didn't speak to me—it was more of a check in, the kind nurses make to see if the patient is alert, alive, or in need of anything. He merely looked in and then was gone. Perhaps the nurses were busy and he was helping out. Or maybe it was his usual practice, which led to the reputation that had preceded him that he was "good". Of course, my story was not the one given by the typical ER patient. Maybe it was the intrigue of me being a one-off. Or maybe, just maybe … he believed.

A gentle knock on the door brought me out of my thoughts. I saw a cart before I saw the petite lab technician.

"I'm here to take your blood," she chirped. No doubt my face involuntarily screwed up as is usual when poking my skin with needles is involved. I always say that I could never be a drug addict because I cannot do needles.

I pulled up the sleeve of my robe to expose the inner part of my elbow. She dabbed at the spot with a damp cotton pad. "Clench your fist and relax," she instructed.

I'm often amused when I'm asked to relax. To relax is a verb and requires doing something, such as breathing deeply, or thinking of a favorite vacation spot. Unlike being told to sit, where the outcome can easily be achieved, asking me to relax does not result in relaxation.

"Is this going to hurt?" I grimaced. When hadn't it hurt?

"No," she consoled. "It's just a small poke."

"Is it one needle or more?" The colored tubes and vials were numerous.

"Only one." She picked up the offending needle. Locating veins on my brown skin always takes time and when she found one she injected the needle into my skin.

"Ouuuchhhhh! That hurt." My observation was a matter of fact, not a grumble. She placed a cotton ball and adhesive on the poke spot.

"We should have your results in about an hour." She arranged the items on the cart. I thanked her and she left the room.

Not long after, the door swung open and Tim came in, his arms laden with food. The logo on the bags—from one of my favorite restaurant chains—increased my anticipation. My husband had brought me chicken noodle soup and a bun I wished I could eat but could only look at wistfully, and a chicken sandwich for himself. He positioned the table over my bed and set the soup on it. On the first taste I almost spat it out. Boiled cardboard would have been more appetizing!

"This has got to be the worst soup I've ever had from there." I frowned. All the packets of salt and pepper could not remedy the poor cooking. But I hadn't eaten for hours, so I picked away at it for the sake of the gnawing in my stomach. Tim assured me his sandwich was more satisfying, and I was glad about that.

The door opened slightly, revealing the doctor. Again, he looked in without speaking then went on his way.

"That's his second visit to look in on me." I offered Tim a spoonful of soup as I brought him up to date. Judging from the way his mouth turned down, I knew I had not exaggerated the cardboard option.

"I haven't seen doctors do the checking up before, usually it's the nurses, but in less than two hours I've seen this doctor three times."

"No doubt he's earned his good reputation." Tim spoke through a mouthful of lettuce and cheese. I looked longingly at the chicken burger in the greasy paper.

Far from satisfied, I swung the table carefully in his direction. The bowl was still nearly full and it would not be wise to spill any on the floor—I could be asked to stand barefoot again.

"Toss this food out."

Tim had just about disposed of the food and cleared the table when the doctor came in with the results of my blood work. My heartbeat quickened. This was the telling moment.

"You don't have the symptoms people who see the things you told me you saw usually have," he began in his gentle manner. "Everything about you is fine. But we need to account for your loss of touch with reality." Still speaking aloud, but seemingly thinking to himself, as if questioning his medical training, he murmured, "Even if a seizure occurred this time, how do we explain the other two times …"

You can't, because it was supernatural. All three times.

He turned to Tim. "You saw this happen?"

"Yes," Tim replied firmly, his voice leaving no room for doubt.

My husband and my OB/GYN had both seen it happen in 1998.

The doctor contemplated me for a long moment. He shot a glance at Tim, then at me again, before walking out of the room. We had just undergone a clash of science versus the supernatural, and there was nothing more he could ask. In his professional capacity, he probably could not quantify a personal religious viewpoint of Heaven. If he believed in Heaven, he gave no indication through his questioning, except with the line, "How do we explain the other times?"

CHAPTER 7

OH WOW!

"He has also set eternity in the human heart …" Ecclesiastes 3:11b (NIV).

IT WASN'T UNTIL WE had returned home later that evening that I was able to begin to process what had transpired. It was astounding to say the least. Had it not happened to me, I might have wondered about the claimant, but doubt had no place now. Even so, the understanding was not immediate or downloaded at the same time. The unfolding came in pieces over the ensuing days and weeks, and yet more may come in years.

I thought back to the man's face that had flashed before me as I hovered between the two worlds. He wore glasses and had short, dark hair, and I recognized him as the computer magnate who had died a few years earlier. In my vision he was smiling at me. Then his face disappeared, and in the distance I saw the blue castle with the gold trim.

I have an iPhone and a MacBook Pro, but except for my warranty, I had zero interest in who made them. I did not care what kind of life they'd had, where they lived, what they ate, whether they were religious, or how much money they made. After all, one gets tired of keeping up with billions. What I did know was that the CEO and computer magnate had died. Could I surmise anything from that other than the fact that Steve Jobs is in Heaven?

I hadn't mention Steve Jobs to Tim until we came back from the ER, nor did I expand on the description of the castle in Heaven. But at home, in leisure, it was all I wanted to talk about. Sitting at the table with our wedding picture taken at the Trump International Hotel behind me, I described it all to Tim again. When I came to the castle he interjected, "I knew exactly when you saw the castle, although I didn't know it was a castle …"

He what?

I sucked in my breath and grabbed his hand.

"Wait!" I could hardly restrain myself. "How did you know when I saw it?"

"I was watching you while I was waiting for HealthLine to answer. Your face had been screwed up in pain and your eyes were closed. Then suddenly your eyes opened. They didn't just open, they widened. Your eyes were large and round and your face was devoid of pain …"

"Did that really happen?" My mouth felt dry. What were the odds of having a witness to my transitioning? Tim held up his hand as if the best was yet to come. I slid to the edge of my French script chair, my eyes boring holes into his as he sat in the orange and blue patterned one.

"In a blink your face was smooth and normal and you were looking over my shoulder as if you had seen the most amazing thing you could ever lay eyes on. You were enraptured." He chuckled, "And it was not me you were looking at."

I couldn't have interrupted if I wanted to. Words evaporated as the disclosure swirled in my head. Mindlessly I played with the damask tablecloth, rolling it around my fingers. Tim grew quiet as if sensing the turnings of my mind. I was having difficulty grasping it all. This was bigger than me. This kind of explanation could only be backed up by a God greater than me, in an Eternity so vast where I had stood bigger than my petite five feet two inches.

"Tell me again of my reaction," I whispered. The presence of God had filled the room so that we were now talking in subdued tones. Tim patiently described again the wonder on my countenance, the transformation from pain-filled to pain-free, the position of my body, and the opening of my eyes. As far as I remember I had been lying on my side with my face to the wall. My eyes had been closed, oblivious to the fact that I was being shown my home in the next life and was transfixed by it. I had no recollection of opening my eyes on earth, for I was in Eternity.

With Steve Jobs' features imprinted in my mind, we opened our laptops to search the Internet for pictures to verify his identity.

"Is this the man you saw?" Tim pointed to the most recent photo of Jobs. His face was thin and unshaven, with hair covering his cheeks and chin.

"No." I shook my head. "The person was younger and had a full, clean face. He was healthy, as if in his prime." I wished I had paid closer attention to the CEO whose products I'd been using for the past five years and which helped me understand the colors of Heaven. Tim continued scrolling, showing me more pictures, of both Gates and Jobs, but each time I shook my head. Then an idea struck and I typed in "younger Steve Jobs" in the bar to narrow the search. The pictures that came up were too youthful, and his hair was longer. I pressed the downward arrow on my MacBook Pro, scrolling for its creator. And then I stopped as goosebumps overtook my arms.

"That's him!" I shrieked. The ruddy face was as serene on the screen as it had been in the air. We had found our confirmation. Yes, the face I had seen was Jobs. In the picture he looked as if he may have been in his early forties. He was smiling and peaceful, just as I had seen him.

My next step was to find out if he had lived for Jesus. Why else would I have seen him in Heaven? And then came the mind-boggling, falling-off-my-chair moment when I read the eulogy written by his sister, a university professor and author. According to her, Steve's final monosyllabic words as he stared into the distance past their shoulders were, "OH WOW. OH WOW. OH WOW."[1]

I know what the computer magnate was so wowed at. And even now I can clearly picture Steve Jobs smiling at me, happy and healthy.

IN 2015, WHEN I had made the decision to purchase a MacBook Pro with Retina display, I could not have seen how it would play into Heaven. Not just the glimpse of its maker's face but in the tangible way it helped me analogize the colors of Eternity. It is frustrating trying to describe the details and incredible colors of Heaven, because language cannot impart the experience. Everything is a zillion times more beautiful than what you can see on this side of life. I've asked myself many times why the colors of Heaven are so unique. Why do we not see them on earth? For to describe something to another, there must be a point of reference, and such references for the colors in Heaven are limited by what we know on earth. What name do we create to explain what we see? And if we create new words, how will our hearers know what the vocabulary represents? The supernatural simply cannot be contained in natural words or imagination.

The Retina display overcame the obstacle somewhat. I compare the color experience to using another brand of computer versus a MacBook Pro with Retina display. Retina display is Apple's trademark for a high pixel-density display, which is a screen compressed with so many pixels one cannot see the individual cells with the naked eye. The resolution of the screen is of 2560x1600 or 4,096,000 pixels, or 226.983 pixels per inch (ppi). The images are ultra-sharp, clear, and crisp—as realistic as possible.[2]

I chose the Retina Display to reduce eyestrain, given the number of hours I spend on the computer. Having the best screen for my work is a no-brainer. I wear a contact lens only in my left eye as the vision is my right eye is fine, compensating for the deficiency in the left so well that I did not need reading glasses until much later in life. Interestingly, in my visits to Heaven, when my eyes are devoid of contact lenses or glasses, I have no flaws in vision. My sight is restored, enhanced, and complete.

Another comparison I can make to the details and colors of Heaven is to watching a movie in 3D or in High Definition Display where one sees amplification and precision that are not noticeable in regular streaming.

Because I knew for a fact that I was operating in two dimensions on June 24th—this life and the next—I felt emboldened to share my interpretations and viewpoints. I do not claim any of my interpretations throughout this book to be approved doctrine or infallible facts. On the contrary, I am merely putting them out for consideration in the hopes that they will provoke thinking and bring encouragement. So stay with me, will you?

One such view is being born of the Spirit and being born of water. I propose that the air I breathe in the natural life is akin to water in the supernatural life. I base this on my experience that, while I was aware of exhaling air in the natural, I was also aware of spilling out water in the spiritual world. This leads me to surmise that air in the physical could be living water in the spiritual. When God birthed Adam, He breathed His breath into him. He gave him air to function on earth. When we die and leave this earth, the air is no longer needed, naturally, and it leaves our body. But is it replaced by something else that's needed for the other life?

When Jesus was explaining the new birth to Nicodemus, He emphasized being born of water and of the Spirit. In John 3:5, Jesus answered him, "Verily, verily, I say unto thee, Except a man be born of water and of the Spirit, he cannot enter into the kingdom of God" (KJV). Being born in the Spirit is easy to interpret—it refers to salvation producing a new life through the forgiveness of sins, thus uniting us with Christ.

Being born of water is trickier to explain. Scholars and theologians of varying denominations espouse several views.[3] One view is a metaphorical representation of the new birth, the regeneration by the Spirit, where born of water and born of the Spirit are two ways of saying the same thing. References to washing with water are found in several passages in the New Testament (Titus 3:5; Ephesians 5:26; John 13:10; 1 Corinthians 6:11). A second view is that the phrase refers to water baptism by immersion. A third view suggests the water metaphor reflects the amniotic fluid or the sac of water in which a baby is encased in the womb. A fourth proponent is that water is used figuratively of spiritual cleansing as part of the New Covenant (Ezekiel 36:25-28).[4]

Sitting at the table after looking up the picture of Steve Jobs, Tim had another observation that arrested me, regarding the motions of my body. When I was departing this life, I had felt my abdomen doubling in a U-shape, fetal style, squeezing out the air of my life with startling intensity at the same time water was gushing out.

"Your body was NOT doubled up like a letter U." Tim was emphatic. "You were lying on your back and your body was straight on the daybed."

Stop. Time out.

Did Tim say he witnessed that my body was *not* doubled up?

"Are you sure, Tim?" My thoughts were swirling in my head. I had been heaving and had been doubled up. I was dead certain of it, if you'll pardon the pun.

"I am very sure." Tim's voice was clear and his gaze held mine. "You were taking deeper breaths than usual, but your body did not move."

That did not make sense. Had I had experienced something that could not be seen with earthly eyes? But then, I had thought my eyes were closed when I saw the castle, but they had actually opened, a fact Tim witnessed with *his* very eyes. Why were he, the observer, and me, the one it was happening to, perceiving things so differently?

You were seeing the spiritual side, while Tim was seeing the physical side.

Holy, holy, awesome God!

Could it be that water cleansed the child of God of the remnants of this human dust and impurities and washed her for entry into the presence of Jesus? Tiny prickles ran down my limbs as the revelation grabbed my spirit.

The ER interrogation began to make more sense. What I had explained to the doctor was not true of my human body as I was, in fact, describing my spiritual departing. Tim had not interrupted the interrogation with what he knew, because all of this had not sunk in yet. What I was talking about and what the doctor understood were two completely different and separate phenomena. Small wonder medical personnel are confused. Unless they have the near-death experience themselves, they cannot comprehend the distinction. Up to this time, I too had been unenlightened, but now I know. I have been awakened to the way in which death releases the spirit from the human body. I've always known from my religious upbringing that death is not the end of our existence as we go to Heaven when we die. But, like other Christians, I was clueless as to what exactly the process of giving up the ghost and arriving at the pearly gates entailed.

Not only are medical personnel confused, so are many established in Biblical doctrines. I say this respectfully based on the myriad of denominations that exist and the multitude of ways the Bible is interpreted. Each group is as difficult to convince; beliefs and education are nearly insurmountable hurdles to break through. Yet, the interpreters and scholars of the Bible interpreted from an in-human-body, in-body, on-earth perspective and not from an out-of-human-body, crossing-death perspective. One of my objectives of this book is to help Christians think more on these aspects, and I pray for wisdom to answer questions and break through established beliefs. I pray for gentleness to initiate conversations, for that soft word that turns away sneering, and as encouraged in 1 Peter 3:15b, that we will always be "ready to make a defense to everyone who asks you to give an account for the hope that is in you, yet with gentleness and reverence" (NASB).

Based on my near-death experience, I am persuaded that the squeezing out of air has a spiritual dimension of gushing water as if it's cleaning off the things of this world. In my state of transition, the verse had echoed in my spirit: "He that believeth on me, as the scripture hath said, out of his belly shall flow rivers of living water" (John 7:38 KJV). Could this be an aspect of living water that is only understood in death? My answer is: Why not? I'm convinced that my life as it had existed in my human body was being transferred into Eternity through the exhalation of air, and that air becomes water in death as a human takes on an eternal form. This is the fifth perspective I add to the theories of the scholars and theologians cited above.

This I believe: I was "born" of water as a baby, an experience common to all; I was "born" of the Spirit when I invited Jesus into my heart and received His living water (and was baptized by immersion in water too), an experience based on my decision. And my breath will give way to water when I die and transit to Heaven.

I have had three out-of-the body experiences (OBEs). Now stop. I want to make it crystal clear that when I speak of OBEs, I do not refer to an induced state as is practiced by eastern religions. No! My OBEs originated through the natural process of almost dying and are associated with death, as happened to Colton Burpo in *Heaven is for Real*[5] and Dr. Mary Neal[6] among others.

OBEs are not a new phenomenon to Bible-believing folk—they are recorded in Scripture. In 2 Corinthians 12:1-4, Paul speaks of his vision: "I must go on boasting. Although there is nothing to be gained, I will go on to visions and revelations from the Lord. I know a man in Christ who fourteen years ago was caught up to the third heaven. Whether it was in the body or out of the body I do not know—God knows. And I know that this man—whether in the body or apart from the body I do not know, but God knows— was caught up to paradise and heard inexpressible things, things that no one is permitted to tell" (NIV).

Paul was not allowed to share what he saw, but God has allowed me and many others to share what we saw. God chooses the time and the content of what He wants to impart, and He has shown me much in my lifetime. This corruptible human body of 60% water is made for earth and we must give it up to put on the incorruptible one. Just as we shower and dress carefully when going into the presence of a dignitary, so too removing the stench of this world must precede our entry into God's royal presence in Eternity.

When the doctor asked, "How do we explain the other times?" I had a ready answer: we can't. The natural cannot explain the supernatural. Medicine operates in the natural and God operates in the supernatural.

This was my third glimpse of Eternity and I testified before a learned man of medicine. The reality of the eternal is this: when we depart the earth in the process called death, when a heart stops beating, when brain activity fails, and the body slows down, growing colder by the second, what in fact happens is that the spirit transitions to the afterlife. The spirit is independent of the brain. Consciousness and soul and spirit are not dependent on the brain. They are independent and alive, created in the image of God. Adam's human body of dirt with its organs, including the brain, was inert and lifeless until God breathed His Spirit into him, and only then did Adam become conscious and alive. The brain does not control the spirit, it's the other way around.

But when one comes in for a medical emergency, the nature of the clinical process is to collect data, provide therapeutic or diagnostic evaluations, give prescriptions, and point to more of this natural world. Fortunately, I had undergone an MRI of my brain in March of 2016, and everything had looked good.

Seeing the afterlife is not new. It has been witnessed by millions around the world. Why, in the US alone, one in every 25 Americans has had a near-death experience, seeing both Heaven and Hell.[7] It is a widespread phenomenon. The night I came home from the ER, I prayed for the physician to feel the nudge of the Spirit through a stirring in his own spirit, for him to think and rethink about what had transpired, that he would not dismiss our conversation.

"Let my experience not be lost on this learned man, Lord. If he does not have it already, help him gain eternal life."

I prayed that, as I carried Heaven's message, the anointing on me in seeing Eternity would touch the doctor and he would be led to salvation. Like the sick woman who touched Jesus and was healed through His virtue, I hoped the doctor would sense that, through a sick woman, he had been in contact with God.

Save him because of the virtue I carried from being in Your presence just hours earlier, Lord.

When I decided to include my visit to the ER on June 24th, 2017 in this book, I wrote to the doctor as a courtesy. In his reply he saluted me as "Dearest Susan" and indicated that he is a rather private individual, so I did not use his name. I smile when I think of a line in his letter, "I am humbled by your testimony." Would a person be humbled by something that lacks merit? No! This makes me jubilant. I know he had to ask me the professional questions as is expected of his practice, but I feel that personally he believed my story and my experiences with Eternity. My primary care physician also confirmed to me his knowledge of numerous stories like mine, and has read the research on the afterlife. I praise God that many in the medical field, and a lot of nurses in particular, who attend to end-of-life patients, attest daily to the supernatural intervention of God and Heaven in the lives of dying patients.

After June 24th, my desire to research and read about experiences like mine exploded. While growing up, I had given in to the superstitions associated with death, and this carried into my adult life. I hated attending funerals, and when I went, I refused to view the person's face in the coffin. Driving past cemeteries was terrifying. On June 24th those fears vanished. I hardly recognize myself in the 180 degree turn I have adopted concerning death. I have become a different person. I have always been vocal about my faith, having preached and taught the Word of God for three decades, but now my passion for the things of Eternity is unmatched. My priorities and desires have changed. My post on social media a few days before our wedding anniversary in July attests to this:

> I did not remember our wedding anniversary coming up this weekend because I'm engrossed in writing and researching and reading. When my husband broaches the subject, "Think of what you'd like for a gift," I haven't the foggiest idea what he is talking about.
>
> "Gift for what?" My mind is blank and I wrinkle my forehead.

"Our wedding anniversary." He is surprised at my consternation.

"When is it?" He's probably wondering if I have a fever.

He tells me the date and I give my answer. "Amazon Gift Cards."

To buy more books about heaven. It's crazy. In past years it's been airplanes, trips, jewelry, restaurants, hotels, shopping, sight-seeing— earthly joys. But when Heaven grabs a hold of you, the things of earth become dim. I want to be near the dying, the fearful and the ones with questions, for many do not know how to deal with death. But I do. I know with absolute certainty that death is not an end to life. People are afraid. Even many who believe in Heaven distance themselves from it. The unknown is too spooky. They don't discuss these topics; when the subject arises, they … run from it.

I want to normalize the conversation about eternal life, just as I've normalized my trips to Paris or Hawaii or the Caribbean. Preparation and planning are keys to a great trip, and it is no different with de-parting this life. This is now the direction of my life, for I have seen, and I know, and this I would like to impart. Such experiences, if they happen at all, come once in a lifetime—I have had three. Could it be that my education, training, and connections were lining me up for this moment? How else could my life count for Eternity except it be a head count of men and women, boys and girls, saved through the stewardship entrusted to me?

One of the books I bought with my anniversary gift dollars is entitled *Life After Life*, by Raymond A. Moody, Jr., M.D.[8] In it he shares near-death experiences of individuals who, like myself, have died or been on the brink of death and returned to tell their tales. (NDE is a term he coined in 1975.) I've concluded that NDEs are not for the religious only or for those in-terested in the paranormal, as can be easily assumed. An NDE is about mortality, and all humanity is mortal. Any concerns I may have had about theories that dismiss life after death such as the dying brain, hallucinations, neurological illnesses, etc., vanished as I read his work.

In addition to the testimonies of Dr. Moody's subjects, Dr. Mary Neal, an orthopaedic surgeon, died in a kayaking accident and penned *To Heaven and Back*.[9] Don Piper, the Baptist pastor who died when a semi crushed his car, describes his trip in the book *90 Minutes in Heaven*.[10]

Likewise, Todd Burpo, a Wesleyan pastor and author of *Heaven is for Real*[11] recounts events in Heaven as experienced by his three-year-old son Colton, when the child left his body during surgery. My experience is closest to Colton's in that neither of us was pronounced clinically dead. Rev. Howard Storm, former professor and chairman of the art department at Northern Kentucky University, had horrors in the darkness when he died—and was rescued by Jesus— and relates them in his book *My Descent into Death*.[12]

Like these authors, I am of Christian beliefs, and the interpretation of my experiences is done through a Biblical framework. Surely we can indeed see Christ as we transit to Heaven—ask Stephen. Acts 7:55 records of his stoning: "But he, being full of the Holy Ghost, looked up stedfastly into heaven, and saw the glory of God, and Jesus standing on the right hand of God" (KJV).

What is the glory of God? One of the meanings is His manifest presence.[13] In the Old Testament, God repeatedly showed His presence in the cloud that hovered over the tabernacle, and the cloud that covered the top of Mt. Sinai, issuing fire and lightning and thunder. The root word of lightning is light, and fire is light. When Moses came down from the mountains, carrying the tablets, his face shone because he had been with God. The people could not look at him, so he had to place a veil over his face. God's glory is His radiance, a brilliant shining light. Light so pure and clear that it appears white. That's the Light I saw, the One that so many across the globe have seen, the One Stephen saw as his spirit transitioned heavenwards.

The most compelling change in people who visit Heaven is the mission with which they come back. The paradox of my life, my purpose, is expressed in another post on social media in July 2017:

> The question rises from my inside, the way the Holy Spirit communicates in wordless language: *Do you prefer to be weak and see Heaven OR healthy and not see it?*
>
> Oh, the paradoxes of the kingdom of God. *Paradoxos* in the Greek means "contrary to expectation, belief, or perceived opinion."[14] The Bible is supernatural and we, humans, are natural. This in itself is paradoxical. Only when we are reborn by the Spirit do we embrace the supernatural and the paradoxes begin to make sense.

Give to get ... the simple confounds the wise ... to live we must die ... be humble to be exalted ... the last will be first ... looking at things unseen ... having nothing, possessing all things ... when I am weak, I am strong.

Was that how Peter felt when he had a choice to deny Christ and remain alive—healthy—or confess him and be killed? What will I do with my health? Use it to create and store wealth in banks to buy material things I don't need? Didn't Judas Iscariot sell our Lord for the contents of banks, the silver of material things? A clip of the movie, *Heaven's Gates, Hell's Flames,* flashes before me. A never-ending circling of coins in Judas's palms, each burning his flesh as it rotates. He's haunted, tormented, and cannot be redeemed.

The answer I know and have always known ... I cannot be like that. I must lead any and all to Christ."

I give great credence to the books written by followers of Christ in the field of medicine, for they know both science and faith and are in a position to discredit dismissive theories of medical knowledge. One month after my interrogation in the ER, I read Dr. Moody's *Life After Life,* and my eyes grew larger as understanding sank into my mind. He writes:

"Finally, there is an additional factor in the case of physicians which may help to account for why so many of them seem unaware of near-death phenomena, even though one would suspect that doctors, of all people, should have encountered them. In the course of their training, it is constantly pounded into M.D.'s-to-be that they must beware of what the patient says about the way he feels. A doctor is taught to pay close attention to the objective "signs" of disease processes, but to take these objective reports ("symptoms") of the patient with a grain of salt. It is very reasonable to do it this way, because one can deal more readily with what is objective. However, this attitude also has the effect of hiding near-death experiences, since very few physicians make it a practice to ask about the feelings and perceptions of patients whom they resuscitate from clinical death. Because of this attitude, I would guess that doctors—who should be the group most likely to uncover near-death experiences—are in fact not much more likely to hear of near-death experiences than are other persons."[15]

Oh, the relief of this enlightenment for the millions who have had NDEs. I empathize. Many of their details match what I experienced, while many transcend what I experienced, and none experienced all of what I did. Our reports are often similar, but our interpretations are different.

My health records show I had been screened for drugs after reporting my NDE in the ER on June 24th. Methamphetamine. Cocaine. Marijuana. MDMA. Methadone. Morphine. Benzodiazepine. TCA. Barbiturate. Amphetamine. Oxycodone. All were negative.

Drugs did not alter my mind, Jesus did. He took hold of me in childhood and He renewed my mind.

I am indebted to the medical practitioner for covering every angle of my NDE when I presented at the ER. I can only guess that a minuscule fraction of those people are treated respectfully when they speak about their NDE. The doctor's diligence and attention made me feel valued as a person, and his thorough examination and the corresponding records add substance and validity to one of the claims of this book—that our souls survive physical death by transiting to Eternity.

CHAPTER 8

ABOUT THE HEART

"My flesh and my heart fail; But God is the strength of my heart ..." Psalm 73:26 (NKJV).

I WAS THE SENSITIVE one in the family, and this sensitivity led to God showing me pictures, speaking to me, and speaking through me. This was not because I was good but because *He* is good, and He looks at the heart.

My parents were old-fashioned Pentecostals, the kind who forbade wearing makeup, pants, jewelry, and piercing ears. Their word was law, so I did not wear makeup, and did not pierce my ears until I was in my twenties. Thanks to cold Canada, I did begin to wear pants after I immigrated. But my parents were well-intentioned. They were committed to prayer and believed the book of Acts is as relevant today as it was in New Testament days. Back in the 70s, revival meetings were popular, and speakers were often invited to our church—Siparia Pentecostal—for these special services. One such week focused on the Holy Spirit and speaking in "tongues", a description given to a language one speaks to God but which is not learned as it is a gift given by the Holy Spirit. This practice is called charismatic.

I was eleven years old when a revival took place. The meetings were directed to the adults, but my parents took us children along as usual. They even decided to go a step further—lay hands on us at home for the gift of tongues.

The following Saturday afternoon, I returned home after taking lessons at school in preparation for what was then called Common Entrance, an exam which determined secondary school placement in the tiered education system in Trinidad. I had just gone to hang out at a neighbor's house when my brother hollered that our mother wanted me to come home immediately. A review of my recent behavior raced through my mind, and no misdemeanors stood out, but that didn't lessen my apprehension at being summoned so unexpectedly.

I came home dutifully, but was not prepared for what came next.

"Kneel down!" she commanded. I kneeled, knowing she had been immersed in prayer for some time.

"Close your eyes. Pray. Praise the Lord." Her commands were terse, leaving no room for argument.

Meekly I obeyed. My prayers always started with asking Jesus for forgiveness, for Him to remain in my heart, and to make me a good girl. I likely brought up the spoon of powdered milk I had eaten quickly while preparing a bottle for my toddler sister. An ongoing request was to pass for Iere High School (which I did pass) which I figured Jesus wouldn't mind me asking in the session meant for speaking in tongues. I thanked Him for my blessings and said a lot of "Hallelujah" and "Praise the Lord" which, in spite of its repetition, was a sweet sound to Him from my eleven-year-old lips.

This continued for a long time, or so it seemed. Of course, everything is magnified when one is small. Anyone who knows my mother knows she is identified by prayer and could easily spend hours on her knees. My knees, on the other hand, were bony, and kneeling hurt a lot. I had no idea why my knees hurt so much, but the pain did not let me off the hook.

Then something happened that day as I praised God. My English words ceased and strange words began to flow from my mouth in a foreign language I had not learned. It was a full-bodied, fluent sound that spouted at first then gushed like a stream from a rainforest mountaintop. This went on for about ten minutes until, satisfied, my mother gave me permission to stop. I had been filled with the Holy Spirit, baptized by fire as it's called in Pentecostal circles. *I was touched by Eternity.* My brother later described how all my siblings had crowded around to witness it.

I officially invited Jesus into my heart at age thirteen during a week of Kids Crusade at church. I say officially because I had repeated the prayer for salvation each time it was led, and with my own daily prayer that He remain in my heart, that amounted to thousands of times. The prayer was something like this: *Dear Jesus, I have sinned and I need your forgiveness. I invite you to be my Savior and Lord. Help me to be the kind of person You want me to be. Thank You for dying on the cross for my sin and for giving me eternal life. Amen.* (Friend, if you pray this prayer and mean it, you will make it to Heaven.)

I had not yet been baptized by water, but when I turned thirteen I was baptized by immersion in the ocean at Beach Camp in Palo Seco.

I had no knowledge of how my baptism in the Holy Spirit and gift of tongues would change me, but every so often I'd mumble the strange words. This continued until my mid-teen years, after which I forgot about spiritual gifts as I focused on education.

I went off to university and started another chapter of my life. I'd come home most weekends and head straight to church for youth meeting. One Friday in 1985, the youth leader gave an on-the-spot announcement that we would be heading to a neighboring church that was culminating a week of revival meetings. I was wearing a little white T-shirt, not the way I typically dressed when visiting another church, but off we went to Siparia Open Bible Church. The message was about the power of the believer who speaks in tongues, and how this person speaks mysteries unto God. I squirmed under the conviction that I had ceased to speak mysteries to God.

Services in Trinidad usually end with a call for prayer, be it for healing, needs, salvation, or other. This night the invitation was, "If anyone would like to receive the baptism of the Holy Spirit, come up to the front." I was not a candidate for the altar call, as I had received the Holy Spirit at age eleven, but I did come face to face with the dryness of my teen years when I did not speak in the spiritual language the Holy Spirit had so graciously given to me.

Susan, you are not the demographic they are referring to.

"God wants to fill you tonight." The pastor's voice broke into the conviction that intertwined me like ivy on tree. This was not going as I expected.

Should I go or should I remain seated? I was mortified about my apparel. It was appropriate for school but felt sacrilegious in God's house. To walk up in full view of the crowded church was inviting well-earned criticism. I had cut my T-shirt short, leaving strips hanging from the midriff and sleeves. It was a popular style on campus, but I was not on campus at nine o'clock that Friday night. I was in a church, and not even my own church. It was a shame to dress like a heathen in my own church, but to have gone in this manner to another denomination was an even bigger disgrace. I regretted succumbing to our youth leader's request.

But I was being drawn by something powerful, something deeply convicting and convincing that overlooked my fashion faux pas. Rising from my bare midriff was the desire to speak mysteries to God again. It was so compelling, so overwhelming, that it drowned out my concerns, and I surged down the aisle to the altar to meet the Holy Ghost who had rushed like a wind so mightily in Acts 2.

A lady not much older than me laid her hand on my shoulder and began to pray quietly. Whether she prayed in English or in another tongue, I don't remember. What I remember is that shortly after I commenced praying words began to gush from my lips in the language I had not learned, in a full-bodied and fluent fashion. The forgotten language had returned, and I'm thrilled to say it has never left. Tears streamed down my face and the volume of my voice increased. I tried to keep quiet, but it was as if I could not contain the torrent of the rainforest mountain stream bursting from the core of my abdomen. It was beautiful and exciting, and I wanted to continue even as I wanted to restrain it. I became aware that everyone in the church was now quiet, listening to me belting out foreign words and speaking mysteries to God.

And then, on this night for strange things, another strange thing happened. I switched again into English. I wish I knew if what I said was a prayer or a translation of the foreign words, but I don't remember. Gradually my tone grew quieter to merge into the silence of the congregation. Then the pastor of the host church said, "The Lord has visited us and spoken."

His announcement took a while to register. The Lord had spoken? Where? How?

This was confusing for I was not dressed in a manner for the Lord to speak through me. Why, I was wearing a short T-shirt cut at the waist. Raising my arm exposed my belly. I had raised both hands at the altar, and I chuckle to think how, instead of the Lord striking me dead, from my belly had flowed living water, and He had entrusted His spiritual gifts to me. Once I digested the implication of "the Lord had spoken through me," the realization came that it's not about the external appearance, but it is about the heart. God sees the heart, and judges or rewards accordingly (1 Samuel 16:7).

I had been touched by Eternity again.

Then the pastor said something that made my large eyes grow even larger and set the course of ministry for me. "You have both the gift of Tongues and Interpretation of Tongues."

That assurance, confirmed by 1 Corinthians 12:8-10, gave me much confidence, and I set out to do my own research on the gifts of the Spirit. I found I was able to interpret other people's tongue language in English, which is the gift of Interpretation of Tongues. That was exciting because, although the gift of Tongues can stand by itself in an individual, for the body to be edified, there must be an interpretation. As promised in Ephesians 3:20, the Holy Spirit had given me exceedingly abundantly above what I could ask or think. I also found if I laid hands on people who desired to speak in tongues, an impartation would occur and they would become filled with the Holy Spirit.

As I grew in my walk with God, the gifts expanded to include the Word of Knowledge and a prophetic anointing that is part of the gift of Prophecy. I'd "know" what was happening in the lives of people I had never encountered. I would begin to pray for people in prayer lines and the Lord would show me through pictures or through words entering my mind what was happening, what had happened, or what might happen in the future to a person or someone close to them. Many confirmed the details with amazement, shaking their heads at how on the mark what I said or saw was. David alludes to God's omniscience, the state of knowing all things, in Psalm 139. I believe I peek into the omniscience of God through the power of the Holy Spirit with these gifts. Faith activates the gifts, and I fervently believe that what happened in Bible days can happen today. For a period, the gift of healing was evident in my ministry. I say this all for the glory of God, and I point each and any to Him, the Giver of the Gifts.

The avenues for speaking opened dramatically after my marriage to my first husband, the Rev. Thomas Harris. My first time as the "preacher" came in October 1988, at the annual Thanksgiving service of the Women's Missionary Council (WMC), as the ladies ministry was called in the Pentecostal Assemblies of the West Indies (PAWI) denomination. With responsibility comes accountability, and in order to accurately interpret the Word, the next year I enrolled in the Certificate in Biblical Theology course through the South Trinidad arm of the West Indies School of Theology. In 1991, gowned in red, I delivered the valedictory address at graduation.

The fire of God burned in me brightly, bringing invitations to speak at mainstream services throughout Trinidad as men also wanted to hear the "little lady preacher". I was the feature speaker at crusades, evangelistic meetings, and churches, and partnered with other traveling ministers to share the gospel. The scope broadened to youth groups and children's ministry. I served on the board of Women's Aglow International in Trinidad and was sought out by Aglow when I immigrated to Canada. My first book, *Golden Apples in Silver Settings*, is a compilation of some of the talks I did in the Caribbean and Canada. (And while updating this manuscript in 2018, a notable organization added me to their national speakers list.)

I've noticed that most of the gifts to which I've been entrusted involve words and talking, in keeping with my love for writing and speaking. Teaching is another gift the Holy Spirit has blessed me with, and it led me to a career. During my teen years I had tutored pupils, and at nineteen, I was hired by the Ministry of Education as an assistant teacher to middle school students. After university, where I specialized in Management of Business, I taught high school for a dozen years, as well as adult school at night. I am grateful for my formal training in teaching and preaching, for it allows me to research, prepare, and share the Word of God in context.

Alongside the working of the Holy Spirit in my heart, unbeknownst to me, other shiftings were taking place in the organ that beat in my chest. I was fourteen years old when, unexpectedly, my wrists, knees, and finger joints became so swollen and painful I had to be taken to the ER at the San Fernando General Hospital in Trinidad. My diagnosis was rheumatic fever, and I was admitted as an inpatient. I was the only child among the adult females in Ward 9. In Trinidad, patients bring their own bedding, toiletries, and clothes to the hospital, and I preferred to wear my dresses instead of night clothes. The other patients often commented that I looked too well to be in the hospital. I stayed there for about ten days, and then was transferred to a convalescent home for children for another two weeks at Paradise Pasture in the suburb of San Fernando.

Rheumatic fever is an inflammatory disease that can develop as a complication of inadequately-treated strep throat or scarlet fever.[1] I never had problems with my tonsils and no one remembers me having either strep throat or scarlet fever, so it is surprising that I became a victim of rheumatic fever. There's no history of the sickness on my father's or mother's side. No one in our circles—not in the town, at church, or at school—knew anyone who had contracted it. How I came to suffer from rheumatic fever remains a mystery. Even four decades later the illness has never surfaced in another family member or relative.

The doctors agreed I'd have to take a penicillin injection once a month until I was nineteen, but my mother prayed for me constantly and believed God for healing so I would not be dependent on injections. After two years I ceased the injections. I hate needles with a passion and the injections stung and burned, so I was ecstatic when my mother decided to call them off. But there was no relief for my bony knees, and kneeling had become nearly impossible. To this day I don't kneel when I pray. Another condition that affected my body was thoracic scoliosis. The spine in my upper back was slightly curved, but this did not produce pain or affect my daily functioning until I moved into my adult years.

At age twenty-seven, I attempted to take out my first life insurance policy. The agent was an older woman who had once been the choir director at our church, and a school teacher, so I trusted her as a Christian and a professional.

"The insurance will not cover what you are asking," she disclosed. "Your medical report shows you have a heart murmur."

Joy, oh joy. Rheumatic fever had left me with a heart murmur.

"Then I'll go to another company," was my swift rejoinder.

"Another company will not be different. The insurance companies all operate under the same rules." She was correct, and I compromised and took what was offered, although I would change companies before cashing in my policy when I left Trinidad.

I had learned that rheumatic fever can cause permanent harm to the heart, including damaged heart valves and heart failure. Since my teenage years I have been mindful of the need to protect my heart. I must take antibiotics as a precaution against contaminated blood entering my heart during dental work, surgeries, or any procedures involving blood. Being otherwise healthy, I took antibiotics only for dental cleanings, and had no reason to be concerned about my heart.

The scoliosis, however, had worsened to the point where I experienced intense pain in my lower back on a daily basis. Since the curvature of my spine was slight, a brace to provide lumbar support would suffice. The brace was about 15 inches long and looked like a wide belt that reached from my ribcage down to my hip. It was made of a breathable but firm material with Velcro straps to hold it in place around my body. It added bulk to my mid section and I had difficulty fitting it under my existing clothes. Normally, I'd be excited for any reason to add to my wardrobe, but not this time. New unshapely clothes were a visual I abhorred, the reminder of my imperfect body dominating my life. *Why me, Lord?* My self-esteem plummeted the year I was prescribed the brace.

One day my husband urged me to accompany him to a meeting where the film of a well-known televangelist was being shown.

"Come with me, you'll enjoy it," he urged.

Enjoy it? That was as sure a lie if there ever was a lie.

"I'm not going." What could I enjoy in my miserable condition?

"We'll go for pizza when it's done."

The meeting was at the Gulf City mall where I could shop afterwards. Admittedly, the worldly, material pull was stronger than the spiritual one, or, as I can theologize it, looking back, "God moves in mysterious ways". One of those ways, for me at least, is shopping.

The meeting room was dark and uninviting. The air conditioner was set at arctic frigidity, the volume deafening. My back hurt and I fidgeted, casting baleful glances at Thomas who was absorbed in what was playing across the screen. God was present all over him. I couldn't read the time on the tiny face of my watch, but it didn't look as if the shopping hour was close. I shifted in my seat.

Somewhere between the shifting and squirming, the preacher's voice penetrated my cloud of pain and cold. What was he saying about the power of God moving in someone's body? This was a taped replay, but still, something came alive in me. I gazed transfixed at the bespectacled evangelist's face filling the huge screen; he was describing someone in pain and how God wanted to bring healing to that person. At the same time, a warm sensation crept across my lower back. Miraculously, the pain receded. Oh, how I wanted to remove the brace. Just as my self-esteem had plummeted, my excitement now rose in inverse proportion as it dawned on me that I was probably being healed. I glanced at Thomas again, but his focus was still on the screen. Good.

Sneaking to the bathroom, I pulled the elasticized skirt to my knees, not caring that the hem was touching the floor. Skritiiiiiiich, skriiiiiiitch. Crackling filled the cubicle as I peeled off the Velcro and freed my body from the constricting layer. I rolled it and slipped it into my bag. I was especially careful not to let Thomas know what I had done—yet. I sat through the rest of the service pain free and was able to enjoy both it and the shopping afterwards. The next day was Sunday and I sat on the hard wooden church pew without the brace. Ding, ding, ding. But the real test of healing was the ability to stand for hours without the brace, a feat that had otherwise been impossible.

Two weeks later, the South District of the PAWI held its annual Sports Day. I had volunteered on the field in the past, noting the places of participants as they raced across the finish line, but had not been sure I could be involved this year. When I spent the entire day walking and standing without the brace, I knew that I had truly experienced my first miraculous healing. *I had been touched by Eternity for my first healing.* And when I told Thomas what had transpired, he simply nodded, not surprised at all, as if he was privy to inside information.

I stepped up my jogging in the park in my hometown of Siparia, and life continued happily there. In 1997, I took a one-year leave of absence from my teaching job and immigrated with my husband to Canada. If I did not like it there, I'd return home.

CHAPTER 9

PREGNANCY WOES

"The LORD sustains them on their sickbed and restores them from their bed of illness" *Psalm 41:3 (NIV).*

IN 1998 I FLEW back to Trinidad to finish my teaching contract. At the end of the term I resigned the job and returned to Canada. One day in August I was lying in bed in my cool, dim bedroom when I saw it, a quick flash and then it was gone. Since we couldn't paint the walls of the rented condominium, I had picked blue and white bedding to create a cheery nest. The warm brown of the oak closets contrasted against the pristine white walls, and tiles winked in assorted hues of aqua through the door of the master bathroom. A brass-trimmed frame enclosed the bed, its golden arms encircling as if to embrace me. A crystal chandelier hung from the ceiling, its faceted points sparkling indigo, red, and silver when the switch was activated.

But this morning there was no prismatic effect. No lights. No music. Nothing. I lay on my bed, groaning and restless, trying to find a position to relieve the nausea. I wanted to feel normal, but I didn't know why I felt unwell.

Could I be pregnant? The thought crept in unbidden. I had never been pregnant before, so I had no reference point for it.

That's when I saw a ray of sunshine on the white wall, and the word radiance dancing in uppercase letters. I rubbed my eyes. Was it my imagination? The drapes were drawn, so the sun could not have peeped in. Besides, it was mid-morning and the sun was still casting its glow on the eastern balconies of the seventeen-story edifice. Our apartment faced west.

Where did the ray come from? What did the word radiance have to do with me? What did the message mean? In hindsight, it might have been more appropriate to wonder who was sending me this message.

As quickly as it had appeared, the beam disappeared.

A few weeks later, my pregnancy was confirmed, the day after we buried my brother Ronald in Trinidad. I had been active in the preparations, even stacking and unstacking the iron chairs we had rented for the wake.

"The Lord takes one and He gives one," the people around had commented. Everyone was joyful.

My husband made known his wish for a boy right away, and with equal immediacy he turned to the Bible for names. I'm sure he didn't do a lot of research, for in a wink he had picked a name—one beginning with the letter S. I should have been thankful for the sentiment, as my own name began with an S and his did not. Sentiment hadn't played a part in the choice, however—the unimpeachable character of the prophet Samuel had magnetized him. The name Samuel epitomized what a son should be. Samuel had also established schools to train prophets, mirroring both our teaching and preaching careers.

A baby boy would have been fine, and the name may have been okay ... had my aunt not taken me to her in-laws, had not a certain young man been their neighbor, had I not been his sister's teacher, had he not wanted to date me, and had his name not been Samuel.

While covering a maternity leave contract at age nineteen, teaching English to middle-grade students, one of my pupils had shown me off to her brother from afar. He had been smitten; I had been clueless.

A few Sundays later, while visiting with my aunt on her husband's side of the family, one of her husband's nieces brought me a message.

"My neighbor next door wants to know if you are an English teacher from Ste. Madeleine Junior Secondary," the curious young woman said, giggling.

"Yes," I replied.

She disappeared from the room, and the next thing I knew a young man came over and introduced himself as Samuel. We chatted.

He was educated. Check. He was a Christian. Check. My plans were to pursue university the next year, meaning that I was not ready to date a businessman, smart though he was, and even if he and his family liked me. No check. On Samuel's next business trip, he brought me a bottle of perfume called Toujours, a French word translated as "always". I had determined it would be "Never". Triple no-checks. So no, Samuel was not an option as a name for our son.

As news of my pregnancy spread, many joined in the naming game. The new dad-to-be had announced that he wanted a boy, and that appeared to be signet-sealed by those who heard it. I had asked for the results of the ultrasound so I could shop wisely for a specific gender. Green for a boy and purple for a girl.

"I'm sick most days, so shopping is going to be difficult," I said to the ultrasound technician. "If I know whether it's a boy or a girl, it will help my preparation."

When the technician's face softened, I dared to hope that she would impart the information I needed to help me shop and decorate with purpose and do all the wonderful but oh-so-tiring work demanded by my baby's impending arrival.

Then her lips pressed together in a thin line. "I don't know."

The baby continued to be a boy in our imaginations, and the hunt for boys' names escalated. Samuel hovered invisibly, but my husband was wise and kept silent, perhaps fearful that mention of the name might induce another bout of vomiting. Lance was at the top of my list, a name I had first heard from a television personality. Dimitri was another choice, born from a romantic connection with Greek literature. Klein was also a favorite.

While my husband was discreet, a friend was more forthright.

"Klein!" she shrieked. "Don't name your baby Klein. That's the name of a premier out west and he's not well-liked."

I had not heard of Ralph Klein in Alberta, as I was still new to Canada and lived far from him in Ontario. I didn't mind being associated with someone deemed unpopular, because I know no person will ever win the favor of everyone. I had owned a perfume called "Anne Klein" and loved the sound of the unusual monosyllabic name. I tried to stifle the unpopular-politician versus the good-prophet connections, but I couldn't come around to Samuel. And if I let my friend who didn't like Klein have her way as well, I'd have no name for the baby.

October holds special significance for me. It's my birth month and there's the anticipation of surprises: presents, parties, and trips. October 1998, however, would be memorable for another reason—and not a fun one. Weight loss, nausea, and vomiting marked the day, as they had marked the entire first trimester of my pregnancy. Later I would learn the name of this debilitating morning sickness is hyperemesis gravidarum, or HG,[1] now made prominent by Catherine, Duchess of Cambridge. But I was sick day and night, and not just mornings.

Smell was my worst enemy. I could have joined the K-9 unit in sniffing out scents were it not for the nausea that washed over me from food, cologne, toothpaste, and everyday household products. It reminded me of swash carrying seaweed and depositing it in a limp heap when the backwash recedes; I was the seaweed, helpless and immobile until the next wave slammed.

Taste conspired with smell to whirl my head in dizzy circles, so the morsels of toast and milk I attempted were rejected before I could swallow them. The calcium needed for my baby's bones lay in a putrid mess in the little pail next to the bed. When did clear, refreshing water morph to this pungency that spewed from my mouth as soon as the glass was set to my lips? I longed for drink, but my thirst was mocked. The popsicles my obstetrician-gynecologist suggested I try relieved me for an hour before the biliousness would rise again. I couldn't take the supplements that pregnant women usually take because of my inability to keep anything down. Over and over my stomach heaved—at times nothing came because there was nothing in there, yet I wanted to throw up.

My other senses joined the rebellion. The television had been the only reprieve for getting my attention off my miserable plight, but sight signed the partnership with smell and taste so that the mere viewing of food advertisements stirred queasiness, and the loathing would rise from my stomach. Since there was no telling when a food ad could appear, the television remained a dark screen.

At least my hearing was okay, or so I consoled myself. The disillusion would come all too soon. A kind friend across the street used to prepare meals for my husband since cooking and microwaving were strictly banned at our house. At the required hour the phone would ring, indicating the food was ready for pick up. Then a strange thing happened. As Pavlov's dogs would salivate at the ring of a bell, I began to nauseate at the sound of the telephone's ring.

Noise added to my distresses. Sounds were so greatly amplified I could not listen to music, not even the Bible on tape. Reading was out of the question as the words spun before my eyes.

"Oh God, help me. Jesus." I whispered, resting my hand on my still-flat belly. The name of Jesus is a complete prayer and it was ever uttered in my soul. Jesus became my constant, my go-to.

Friends from church took up vigil during the day while my husband worked. They wanted to talk to cheer me, but I was too exhausted to converse. With mouse-like quiet they'd tiptoe in to check in on me. They sacrificed their comfort for a boring, silent sick-house. Those dear ladies needed to eat, but as the noon hour approached another "Pavlovian" instinct kicked in. The time on the clock began to induce the nausea. I'd smother my face in the comforter when I smelled the sandwiches to keep the retching at bay, gagging and groaning under the covers. Associations were made too quickly and soon the rustle of foil-wrapped food or a plate clinking as it was taken down from a cupboard set off the nausea. I could not hurt the feelings of those compassionate mothers who cared for me with such tenderness, who nursed me for weeks, but I couldn't go on like this.

"I can't have anyone in the house. I have to be alone," I implored my husband. I could be transparent with him only. He was the other constant in addition to Jesus. He understood my agony, having lived with it for weeks. Selflessly and gently he attended to my needs, denying himself the conveniences of normal living to make the apartment scent-free, noise-free, food-free, everything-free. His toiletries found a temporary home at his workplace.

"Tell them I am well. Tell them I'm not sick anymore." It was an expression of faith. "I'll phone you if I need anything. You can come home for lunch." I was desperate and my pleading increased.

Reluctantly, he agreed to my urging. The ladies no longer came and I remained in my bed a recluse, a prisoner in our condominium apartment on Ridelle Avenue in Toronto. My own blood family was over four thousand kilometers south in the Caribbean. The Atlantic Ocean beating upon the shores of Canada and Trinidad symbolized the waves of sickness copiously beating my tiny body.

But Thomas did not have control over the wafts from the kitchens of the other residents in the building. The delicious aromas I had once savored sent me into revulsion, and no amount of sealing of the windows could prevent the abhorrence from seeping in. Daily I threw up—five times, fifteen times, twenty times. So violent was the retching that I expected to see the baby spew in the pail. How I lived during the first trimester of my pregnancy finds no explanation other than through grace.

Supernatural power from on high kept me alive.

October 16th dawned a crisp Friday in autumn with the sun yellow in the sky. The coolness of fall revived my overheated body as I dressed for my second appointment with my OB/GYN. A friend would drive Thomas and me to the office on Queen Street. I was thirteen weeks pregnant and the vomiting and lack of appetite had reduced me to a sorry ninety-five pounds.

"You are dehydrated. You are not well," Dr. Im exclaimed as soon as he looked at me. Eyeliner and mascara could not hide illness from his expert gaze, filled with concern. He peered at my sunken, yellowish eyes, grave, even worried about my round-the-clock condition of HG.

Tears filled my big brown eyes at his empathy. Finally, *someone* understood I was not doing well. When I was dressed for church few could tell that I was struggling. My hair was a luxurious mane and my skin had taken on the glow of new motherhood, thanks to progesterone and estrogen. Powder and lipstick took the look up a notch, and I still wore high heels. My appearance did not indicate my suffering. But it was the eyes, those windows of the soul as Shakespeare astutely coined, that were overlooked by everyone except the professional in front of me. In halting statements I described how odors, real food or pictures of food, everything and anything, made me retch. The popsicles helped a bit, but I could not keep them down for long. I threw up anything I attempted to eat or drink.

"Everyone says I look good, which makes it seem as if I'm making up stories." I sounded pathetic, but it was the truth, and my voice cracked. "They keep telling me pregnancy is a normal condition, not a sickness." I whimpered and sniffled.

I had worn a lilac dress with an empire cut sewn by my seamstress in Trinidad. The fabric was a soft rayon chiffon with boxed pleats that fell gracefully to my ankles. The high-waisted dress provided enough room for my slowly expanding tummy. The bodice was decorated with iridescent sequins that sparkled green and purple.

"You are like the women in my country," the kind doctor consoled me. "Many throw up and are very sick in pregnancy."

Another balm to my soul. I had resented the barbs of a few caustic observers who cited in loud tones so I could hear how *they* were not sick when *they* were pregnant. I had bitten my tongue as a lot of pastors' wives do. The comparison was mean, but I was too polite to dish back sarcasm and too exhausted to even try.

"You need home care." Dr. Im's tone was urgent and he picked up the phone to arrange for a nurse to come to our address. He explained the reason for his call to the person who answered and was placed on hold. Suddenly the call was disconnected. He redialed, outlining the immediacy of the situation. One more time the call was dropped, perhaps in an attempt to transfer it. I felt valued by his empathy and determination to get a nurse to attend to me at home. A third time this wonderful doctor dialed the number, but I never knew if he got a hold of the department. For at that moment, I slumped forward on his desk.

CHAPTER 10

IN HEAVEN'S MEADOW

"Whoever dwells in the shelter of the Most High will rest in the shadow of the Almighty" *Psalm 91:1 (NIV)*.

SIMULTANEOUS WITH MY MEMORY of slumping on the doctor's desk is one where I am walking uphill on soft green grass. The place is bright as if the sun is full out and it is daytime. On my right a huge person strides, and I walk in His shadow. The shadow encompasses me in a circle, similar to the way the midday sun casts a shadow around a person, as opposed to the evening when shadows are long. I feel as if I know Him. I know where I am. I am in Heaven in the Shadow of the Almighty, as spoken of in Psalm 91.

I do not see Him, but I know He is there. It's as if knowledge enters my mind at the particular time I need to know something. We do not speak, but we seem to know each other's thoughts. Our communication is a wordless language through this transfer of thoughts, similar to when I operate in the gift of the Word of Knowledge on earth. As it says in Isaiah 65:24, I know His and He knows mine.

We walk unhurriedly. There is no haste and no strain of climbing uphill—it is as effortless as walking on level ground. There is no path, yet we walk in the same direction, purposeful of where we are going on the wide-open, grassy space. The green is a shade I've not seen before and, as such, is indescribable. The words do not exist in my vocabulary. The hue has more yellow than I've seen on earth.

I walk at my usual pace, taking small steps, and He keeps up with me. One would expect that a person as large as He would have a big stride, but although He is much bigger than I am, and towers at my side, our paces never fall out of sync, nor does it appear that He is slowed down.

We are in a large meadow and the expanse before me is vast. Far ahead of us are trees, vibrant, healthy, green trees, but not deep, dark forest green as on earth. The colors in Heaven do not exist on earth and hence I cannot assign them a name. The colors are brighter and happier and rapturous to my eyes. Above us it's cloudless. Clear. It reminds me of a tropical day in the Caribbean, except there is no heat to drain my energy. There is no wind either. The temperature is ideal. Everything in this unimaginable, indescribable place is perfect.

The person walking with me leads to me to the top of the hill and I sit down. His shadow still hovers over me, as if shading me even though there is no heat to burn my skin. A most incredible sense of peace permeates this heaven-o-sphere, as I call the atmosphere of Heaven. Words may yet have to be created to describe Heaven. My words cannot do justice as they fall short of what Heaven is. Parts of speech fail to deliver the emotions of being in Heaven because Heaven is an experiential concept rather than a theoretical one. A picture might convey details, but I have no pictures to show as the pictures are embedded in my consciousness.

Peace fills me and pulsates through my being, settling in every hidden part of my insides, into my cells, bones, nerves, and fibers. The entire meadow is laden with peace. Such astounding peace can only be felt, not described. Even if one thinks of his or her most relaxed and refreshing moment on earth, it would be but an imitation of Heaven's peace.

Where I am, there is no sense of time. Time as we know it on earth is linear and irreversible. Not in Heaven. There is no dimension to time. All is still. I inhale deeply. I am contented and satisfied in ways I could have never imagined as I absorb this quietude. I have no pain. I have no worries. I do not remember any sorrow. There is no hint of things negative.

I gaze around. Down the hill the meadow tapers out to flat land. A lone tree with a giant trunk stands in the middle of the even ground. The tree is huge, with branches at the very top that spread out like a gigantic, living umbrella. I recall pictures of similar ones I've seen in the African savannah, or the real ones at Busch Gardens in Florida.

Under the tree a group of children are playing a game. They are far from me, yet I can see the details. I have perfect vision in Heaven, and there's no need for the one contact lens I wear in my left eye. Interestingly, I do not squint in the light as I do on earth with the astigmatism in my eye. I am able to see things close up as well as I can see them far away.

There are about a dozen children ranging in age from perhaps two years old to eight, and three teens are interspersed among them. The scene reminds me of a babysitting one, where the older children take the younger ones out to play. The children are dressed like children in Trinidad, with short-sleeved clothing, and they all wear socks and shoes. The little boys wear shorts into which their shirts are neatly tucked, and the girls are in dresses of white or soft pastel shades of blue, yellow, pink, or green. The children are holding hands and moving in a circle in a counter-clockwise direction. Again, they have no sense of rush, no push, only calm and gentleness.

From my spot on the hill I am drawn to a little girl wearing a pale green dress with puffed sleeves, white socks, and black shoes. She may be a taller two year old or a smaller four year old. I cannot see her face as her back is to me. On her right side is a little blond boy with a white shirt tucked into his khaki pants who also looks about four years old. On her left is a little girl in pink about the same age. To the left of the girl in pink is a young teen dressed in a blue skirt that falls below her knee in midi-style, paired with a white blouse. She wears flat shoes but no socks. On the opposite side of the circle is a little girl in buttery yellow. The sight is precious and I let out a sigh of contentment. It is beautiful and perfect. No one shouts, there is no noise, only quiet. No one pushes or is impatient. Unlike the typical scenes at playgrounds on earth, the children are in sync with each other.

Suddenly the little girl in the green dress stumbles and falls. Her hand is still held by the blond boy and the girl in pink on either side of her. Everyone pauses, the circle stops. No one speaks, but each knows what to do. The teen extricates her hands from the ones she had been holding and joins their hands together so the circle is still unbroken. She goes over to the fallen child and ever so gently picks her up. It's played out as in slow motion. There is no sense of hurry in this wonderful place, but time seems to slow even more as she picks up the child. I am spellbound by all the little ones, fascinated at how mature they are, but my interest in the little girl who fell is more acute than for the rest. I feel I know this child.

The little girl is upright again and stable on her feet. The teen goes back to her spot and the children continue to move counter-clockwise in the circle.

I keep drawing in deep breaths and exhaling them with sighs of satisfaction, as if I can't get enough of this peaceful stillness. This beauty, these colors, the children. I, who had been alone, imprisoned on a sick bed with unquenchable thirst, find my release in the tranquillity and calm. Here I am with children and Almighty God in this perfect, flawless meadow, my mind relaxed, my body at rest. Unfettered, with no cares, no pain, no worries, only goodness and perfection and health. This is all I desire. This is where I belong. This is what I had believed and lived for, and this is where I want to be.

The thought comes that it is natural for Heaven to be filled with peace, because Jesus is Peace and He is there. Peace as we know it on earth is a noun, but Peace in Heaven is a Person and, according to Isaiah 9:6, has a name—Prince of Peace. Here He envelops me so I am inundated, filled and overflowing with Him. It's the difference between what is felt on earth and in Heaven. If Jesus brings snatches of His peace to me on earth, they are but a taste of what I'll have in Heaven.

Up to now there has been no verbal communication in the meadow, no human voice, but without warning I become aware that I am talking.

"I don't want to go back," I protest aloud. "I want to stay here."

I am being pulled away. But this unbelievable peacefulness my ninety-five-pound body ached for and finally found is mine, and no one is going to take it away.

"I don't want to go back," I beg again. But it is too late.

"YOU MUST COME BACK."

The voice is soft, but carries a finality I cannot argue with. The words hold complete authority. I have no choice.

Faster than any speed I could imagine, I find myself receding from Heaven, sucked back to somewhere. Someone is at my side, but not as close as when we walked in the meadow. The way back looks like a dark road spiraling as in a drawing—widest at the Heaven top, but fish-tailing to thin nothingness at the other end. I feel as if I am flying backwards, my face towards Heaven, my feet pointing in the direction I am traveling. I am in a horizontal position, whizzing through the air at this speed that I cannot measure but which feels like the twinkling of an eye as described in 1 Corinthians 15:52.

Still mumbling that I wanted to stay, I opened my eyes to see Dr. Im's and Thomas's faces hovering over mine. I was lying on a narrow bed in an examination room in the clinic, whereas when I left earth I had been sitting on a chair in Dr. Im's office.

Which one of them had requested that I come back?

I remember asking Thomas about the incident the same day, but did not record the details. I've regretted that I didn't pay better attention to this unusual occurrence. Many times over the years I thought about it and asked him again. He says I was out, unconscious for maybe three minutes. When I collapsed on the desk, he lifted me and took me to an examination room as directed by Dr. Im. He placed me on the bed and the doctor adjusted it so my head was down and my feet were up. Thomas described how the doctor kept me this way for about a minute, and then adjusted the bed to bring my head up again.

Dr. Im gave me something to drink, which could have been either plain water or a drink with electrolytes, Thomas wasn't sure. He recalls their communication, how the doctor said more than once, "We are losing her," because he couldn't find my pulse and heartbeat. Thomas explained that when I regained consciousness I appeared to be in a daze and said to them, "I was in Heaven."

I remember murmuring those words too. He said they both had listened but neither asked me any questions. They were relieved my life had been spared, Thomas more so as it absolved him from the grim undertaking of breaking the news of my death to my family. Far away in the Caribbean they were unaware of my tenuous condition. Thomas said he had been praying from the moment I collapsed and all the time I was in Heaven. I know his faith, and I know his prayer is the reason I was brought back to earth. Such is the power of prayer—God hears and answers.

I had not been pronounced clinically dead—what happened to me was what I would learn nineteen years later is termed a near-death experience (NDE) as described in the earlier in the book, a visit to the afterlife. My first out-of-the-body experience (OBE).

I never get weary of thinking about it, nor of asking about it, or speaking about it. After my third NDE on June 24th, 2017, I was consumed afresh with the details of my first visit to Heaven. I wanted to tell my story accurately and in August decided to phone Thomas to find out which of the men had called me back. I could feel the thrumming of my heart through my cotton dress when he answered.

Briefing him on the reason for my call, I rushed on breathlessly, "Which one of you said 'You must come back?'. Was it the doctor or you?"

"I can't remember all the details, it was so long ago," he answered. Whereas nineteen years had elapsed and his memory had dimmed, my memory of Heaven's meadow remains stark and fresh. Throughout the years, I had simply assumed it was Thomas who had spoken. He was my husband, so it seemed natural that he would ask me to come back. Thus it had never occurred to me to ask for confirmation or clarification. But it was necessary for writing this chapter.

"Was it you?" I prodded.

"I really can't remember all the details," he repeated.

"Thomas," I begged. "Try to remember. You must remember. I have to know who spoke, so I can put it in the book."

The line was silent before he replied. "I was praying and the doctor was doing the medical procedures." His slow response was indicative of pondering as he traveled back in time in his mind. "I don't think we talked to you because you were out. We talked to each other, but not to you."

Then he added, sounding suddenly sure. "We did not talk to you."

Who then had spoken to me?

The hairs on my entire body rise as if doing the wave at a sporting event as I write this sentence. After nineteen years I still cannot write or speak about this without becoming emotional.

I know who spoke!

And if He told me to "come back" it means He was present in the place I was coming back to.

Could that be the reason I have had so many supernatural experiences since? Did God plan all along to partner with me and show me things for a greater cause?

I thanked Thomas for the confirmation and let my body sag on the loveseat. Until that day, I had lived in a state of relative oblivion to the implications of being in Heaven and hearing God speak directly to me in Eternity. Hearing Him there is different than the Holy Spirit speaking to me on earth. I heard the voice that said "Let there be" and stars fixed themselves in the galaxy. Waters flooded the oceans, and the animals appeared. Though the tone of the injunction given to me to come back was low, I had the impression it echoed throughout Eternity.

As I wrote this chapter in August 2017, I felt the Holy Spirit impressing on me: *You have been in the Shadow of the Almighty. You have been in the Secret Place. You have been with the Prince of Peace. Peace surrounded you. He filled you inside and it settled within you. You are a Carrier of Peace. Go now and carry Peace.*

I broke down. I have fallen short, too short, of carrying peace. "Father, forgive me," I whispered brokenly through tears. "Forgive me."

My cry was one of repentance at my shortcomings in burying the responsibilities entrusted through visits, visions, and encounters with angels. I had been schooled by God Himself and I had remained silent.

"I'll be silent no more, Lord," I vowed. I meant it, and He knew I meant it too. I had already begun to proclaim my supernatural realities publicly on social media one month earlier in July.

It wasn't until nineteen years after it happened that I began to comprehend the magnitude of my visit to Heaven. In writing this book, I turned to the Childbirth Diary I had purchased from the Women's Health Care Centre of St. Michael's Hospital. It is more than a pregnancy record or a keepsake of my only childbearing experience—it is evidence of the facts I write.

On the cover is a hand-drawn illustration of a newborn nestled in his mother's arms, head tucked on her chest. The word MYSELF is printed above the word CHILDBIRTH, and MY BABY is printed under the word DIARY, all in dark burgundy letters. The burgundy complements the pale pink soft cover with its white comb binding, making it a pleasing, feminine possession.

The page entitled, My Weight Gain Week by Week, has columns headed Weight, Date, and Advice/Treatment. To this I added a fourth column for numbering the weeks. The notes leading up to October 16th indicated my nausea, and that I was losing weight. The stark facts of my condition are succinct on the page:

13 weeks
95 lb.
Oct 16/98
Dr. Im & hospital. Fainting spell & IV.

It was easier to write fainting spell, as I had not yet processed Heaven.

After my visit to Heaven, the next entry reads:

15 weeks
98 lb.
Nov 4/98
Dr. Im says I'm ok. Baby's heartbeat heard. Blood pressure normal.

Like an invisible note, the truth gripped me as I studied the pages. *I had been healed of hyperemesis gravidarum and started to eat and gain weight after visiting Heaven.*

Holy, Holy God!

Nineteen years later I'm weak as I assimilate that I had been taken to Heaven to receive a personal healing. *To be touched by Eternity.* My second miraculous healing. I am in awe of my miracle, and I believe my baby—now an adult—will have a life beyond anything I could imagine. God had intervened for both of us.

I grew more inquisitive about this wordless communication with the Almighty and the process whereby thoughts entered my mind. People have the ability to talk and sing in Heaven, according to Revelation 14, so non-verbal communication could sound suspicious to the person who has not experienced it. And I too might have been suspicious had it not happened to me.

I sought the Bible regarding communication by thoughts in Heaven. Genesis 6:5 contains one of many references to the fact that the Lord knows the thoughts of people. "Then the LORD saw that the wickedness of man was great on the earth, and that every intent of the thoughts of his heart was only evil continually" (NASB). In Matthew 9:4, Jesus knew the thoughts of the Pharisees. "And Jesus knowing their thoughts said, 'Why are you thinking evil in your hearts?'"

But only the Trinity is all-knowing. Humans cannot know another person's thoughts, as Paul confirms in 1 Corinthians 2:11, "For who among men knows the thoughts of a man except the spirit of the man which is in him? Even so the thoughts of God no one knows except the Spirit of God".

You may be asking: If only Father, Son and Holy Spirit knows thoughts, how then did I get to share in those thoughts? The answer is simple—I believe that when I was in Heaven, the Spirit of God filled me and enabled me to partake in this divine knowing-of-thoughts process. It's His doing for when He wills.

I've read accounts of others who have not experienced NDEs, but who also attest to their ability to leave their physical bodies and communicate through thoughts.

Stop!

This practice is not biblical and we need discernment. One should pay close attention to the source of the out-of-the-body experience (OBE). The acid test in Scripture that determines whether an OBE is God-driven is if the experience acknowledges Jesus is God. The warning is given in 1 John 4:1-3, "Dear friends, do not believe every spirit, but test the spirits to see whether they are from God, because many false prophets have gone out into the world. *This is how you can recognize the Spirit of God: Every spirit that acknowledges that Jesus Christ has come in the flesh is from God, but every spirit that does not acknowledge Jesus is not from God*" (NIV, italics added for emphasis).

The good thing about an NDE is that it can happen to whomever God chooses to bring back from death or near-death. There is nothing unique about those of us to whom it has happened. Some people can scuba dive, some can be elected president, and some get taken up to the afterlife. I happened to experience the latter. But the price for it is dear, and I would never wish for it. Such things generally happen to people, at best, once in a lifetime. It has happened to me three times. Two of those times I felt I was escorted by an angel. He was a guide, like a tour guide as when I'm in a new place. We did not speak, but I knew he was a protector, just as when I am traveling to new places on earth and I enlist the services of a guide who knows the way and can keep me safe as I travel along it.

CHAPTER 11

OUR CHILD IS BORN

"For unto us a child is born ..." Isaiah 9:6a (KJV).

INSTEAD OF HOME CARE coming to me, I was sent to the ER at St. Michael's Hospital, the same hospital where I would have my baby. There they treated me intravenously with bags of fluid hanging from a silver pole that fed life into my veins. After the IV was given, I remained under observation for another hour or two. I remember a social worker named John visiting me and engaging in conversation. He spoke gently and altogether was kind and compassionate. He asked about my background and I told him I was awaiting my teaching acceptance by the Ontario Teachers College. He asked other questions and remarked that I appeared to enjoy the profession.

I told him we were fairly new to Canada and my husband was a pastor. Tears blurred my vision and rolled down my cheeks as I described how my oldest brother had passed away and we had buried him a few weeks ago. Ronald had been struck by a vehicle when a driver drove through a red light while he was crossing the highway, and he died within minutes of being hit.

John held my hand and in his soft voice commented how this memory was no doubt very taxing to my health and the fragile condition of carrying a baby. He nodded as I described my "fainting spell" in Dr. Im's office. I don't know if the doctor's notes that would have been sent along with my referral to the ER mentioned Heaven. I had not processed what had happened, nor did I know about NDEs then. John talked about the effects worrying and grieving could have on my unborn child and encouraged me to think positively and to draw on my faith. I cannot forget the kindness of this stranger to me.

When I was healthy, I never gave thought to Medicare, Canada's publicly-funded health care system where, instead of a single national plan, the thirteen provinces and territories offer health care insurance plans under which residents can access hospital and physician services without paying out of pocket. Under Medicare, all medically necessary services are insured. I had no idea how grateful I would be for our health care system until more than a dozen years later.

On January 20th, 1999, I had an echocardiogram (ECG) done, and the note I made of the cardiologist's comments in my Childbirth Diary is, "She predicts a boy." At last we knew we were having a son! I was determined that the stereotypical colors of blue or pink would not be perpetuated at our house, and so the crib bedding was the unisex color of green.

The day came in April when I went to the hospital to have my son, whose name was not yet decided. Twenty-two hours after labor set in, the OB/GYN (not Dr. Im) held up the baby. I stared in wonder. I had never seen a newborn, and the back view of a head full of hair did not tell me much. I knew we were having a boy, but I had to ask all the same.

"Is it a boy or a girl?" I sank back against the pillows, relieved the ordeal was finally over.

"It's a girl!" He smiled and staff cheered.

I froze.

A GIRL? Not a boy?

If Thomas was surprised I couldn't tell, but I knew he was happy that the baby was here. My mind was a whirl. No wonder we could not agree on a boy's name because *we did not need a boy's name.*

The doctor placed my little daughter on my chest.

A nurse murmured, "She's going to be a look-er all right."

"Do you have a name?" someone in the room wanted to know.

We had never discussed girls' names!

I was glad they couldn't see the buzzing in my brain. My mind was not on looks or the nurse's prediction. A memory popped up and I time-traveled back to the day in August, nine months earlier, when the yellow ray appeared on the wall of my dim bedroom with the word RADIANCE dancing on it.

A proclamation from Eternity of the name she should be called.

"Radiance," I whispered.

In unison, the team exclaimed comments we'd hear in the future whenever someone encountered her name.

"What a beautiful name. What an unusual name."

"How did you come up with that?"

"I've never heard it before."

Then someone said, "Her Apgar score is a perfect 10."

I made a mental note to find out what an Apgar score² was.

I must have radiated when I said *Radiance,* because Thomas asked me later if I'd known the ultrasound results showed a girl and had not told him. The confidence and the ease with which the name rolled off my tongue made it appear as if I had planned this all along.

Someone had planned it, but it wasn't me.

"No," I replied honestly, "I did not."

I reminded him of the cardiologist's prediction of a boy earlier in January. I myself had forgotten about the ray in August. Too much had happened in the following months that buried the memory. Why, I didn't even have a doll or a dress for her. I had nothing except white and green unisex sleepers. A few days after she was born I told Thomas the story of "Radiance on a ray" on the wall. I had not mentioned it to him, because I had no real context for its interpretation, and also because I had forgotten about it in the first trimester when I was so ill with HG.

It was not my knowing. *It was a intervention from Eternity that brought the memory and the name into the maternity ward at 1:37 a.m. that April morning. And it was a supernatural ray that had appeared nine months earlier.*

I didn't know I was having a girl, but I didn't need to know because God knew and had chosen her name Himself and sent it on a ray. Her name had appeared on the wall, from Heaven, a brand for life for this child. She had visited Heaven while in my belly. God knew her before she was in my womb. She is a unique brand.

As the months passed, my desire for pink blossomed, and on her first birthday I redecorated the nursery in pink. I was not giving in to convention or stereotypes. Rather, I genuinely liked pink, and pink and purple are staple colors in both her and my wardrobes to this day.

The revelation of our daughter's name was not the only epiphany I had.

Years later, another one would give me pause. When she was born, Radiance was showered with countless gifts from friends and family, including a little pastel-green dress with short puffed sleeves and a white collar embroidered with the same green. As related in chapter 10, on October 16th, 1998, I had fled earth and walked in the Shadow of the Almighty where I had been healed.

Even now I can look at the sky and relive my time in Heaven. The dozen little ones playing under the tree and moving in a circle in a counter-clockwise fashion. A little girl in a pastel-green dress had stumbled and fallen, and was picked up and re-established in the game. I was fascinated by her, more acutely interested in her than the rest. I had felt as if I knew this child, that we had a connection. I had been framing photos when suddenly a holy awe ran up my body and chills swept over me. As if someone had brushed cobwebs from my face, I knew who the child was.

The little girl was my child, the one I carried in my womb when I collapsed in the OB/GYN's office. The dress the little girl in Heaven had been wearing is the same design and color as the gift Radiance received and was wearing in the photo I was framing!

God had allowed me to see her as He saw her. Her "falling down" was symbolic of the precarious position she was in, given my condition. But she did not remain fallen. Her being "picked up" was symbolic of restoration and healing.

Father God took me Home and showed me how this infant child, whose life depended on mine, would make it. I would become well and she would live.

As the Scriptural phrase goes, "It had come to pass." She lives because of Him. I lived because of Him. I lived so that she could be born and live on earth. I'm here for her sake.

All the time we had thought I was having a son. We'd shortlisted names and couldn't come up with one but hadn't thought of any for a baby girl. But Omniscient God knew. He had already ordained her name. Radiance belongs to Jesus. Her face will shine, be radiant like Moses' after he spoke with the Lord and came down from Mount Sinai with the two tablets of the covenant law in his hands. The words of the tablets, the commandments of God, will be Radiance's standards to live by. Radiance belongs to Jesus. I belong to Jesus, and one day we will live forever in Eternity face-to-face with Him.

This revelation has been one of the most overwhelming ones to grasp. How is it I was able to witness something that had not happened on earth yet? As I pondered, the concept that everything is created twice came to mind. Take writing a book, for example. The first creation is an idea, the intangible creation. Creativity resides in God—He is spirit, intangible. The second creation of a book is the physical manifestation of preparing a manuscript and unfolding the publishing process.

Similarly, I learned of the afterlife, heaven and hell, in theory (intangible) through the Bible, and that was followed by the (tangible) reality of experiencing it. This concept is even more evident in the spiritual. That's why I was able to see Radiance in person before she was born. "Before I formed you in the womb I knew you" Jeremiah 1:5 (NASB). God knew her (intangible) before He formed her (tangible).

I also reflected on Jesus' way of teaching. Through parables, He used tangible earthly stories to impart intangible heavenly meanings, a reverse of the process mentioned above. This was apparent in my NDEs and visions. Traveling and visiting places on earth prepared me for trips to the other world. Holding the position of Tourism Manager with the City of Melville in Saskatchewan helped me assimilate later that I was a tourist in Eternity. My earthly frame of reference served as the tangible prerequisite for the intangible. In both scenarios, I moved from the practical or the tangible on earth, to the intangible or abstract in the spiritual world.

Glimpses of Heaven widen our appreciation of the Word. When I sat in the meadow, there was a sense of timelessness such as cannot be found on earth. This may be difficult to comprehend, but it can be followed logically. Hebrews 13:8 asserts that God is the same yesterday, today, and forever. That is, past, present, and future. He encompasses all the time frames. In other words, He—and the place where He dwells—is timeless. God is not confined by time or defined by it. He simply exists outside of time. Heaven does not mark times the way we do on earth.

On October 16, 1998, when I saw Radiance before she was born, I was assessing her through the earthly concept of "future" time. In the concept of Heaven, she had always been there, planned by God and kept in Heaven, waiting to be sent to earth in April the next year. The same is true when I saw my sisters—adults currently living on earth—in Heaven as children in 2007 (chapter 14). This aspect of Heaven is affirmed by the fact that I experienced an NDE and a vision nine years apart, but what I saw during each aligned with the other. Knowing that God has confirmed the same message through different methods assures me that I am tuned in to Him, abiding in the vine. And I want to live this way forever.

The dear senior lady who gave Radiance the gift is now in Heaven. She could not have known the significance of the outfit or what I saw in the meadow, because I had not told the details to anyone except Thomas. I interpret the receiving of the dress as God's way of telling me that God has a plan for Radiance that I cannot imagine, and He will watch over her on this temporary earth until she, too, goes Home.

CHAPTER 12

CLASS OF 2017

"Train up a child in the way he should go …" *Proverbs 22:6a (KJV).*

As Hannah vowed to train Samuel in the ways of God, so we vowed to raise our daughter. Radiance was dedicated to the Lord, and from an early age we taught her to memorize Scripture and pray. She invited Jesus into her heart when she was only four, and also received the baptism of the Holy Spirit and spoke in another language at that age. I took her to churches and meetings when I was invited to speak, so her tender spirit could begin to shape for ministry. God began to show her things unseen. I could write a book just on her experiences, but I'll highlight one spiritual event that took place also at age four.

I had been longing for the manifest presence of God and thought continually about the tribe of Israel led by God in the desert with a pillar of cloud. I devoured books about the revivalist Jonathan Edwards. I was even more inspired by the ministry of Kathryn Kuhlman and desperately wanted to see God's power in my life as it had been manifested in hers.

In November 2002, I was reading one of her titles, *I Believe in Miracles.*[1] In short time a warm, relaxed feeling stole over my body. I put the book down so I could savor the peaceful moment. Within seconds, Radiance shifted to look at the door.

"Mom, there's water around the door."

"There can't be water around the door, because there was no rain and we have no holes in the roof. Did you dream of water?" I spoke slowly so she could follow the logic.

"No, I was not sleeping." She was alert and staring. "Mom, there's water around the door and it is getting higher."

"If there was water, we would get wet and the bed would be soaked."

"I don't know why the bed is not wet, but there is water in the whole room now." She has always been an articulate one, an early talker with a good grasp of language.

I was convinced that the manifest presence of God was in our house. The Bible uses seven symbols for the Holy Spirit: cloud, fire, seal, dove, wind, oil, and WATER. I had felt the warm, calming presence of God (reminiscent of fire), and Radiance had seen a vision of God as water (Isaiah 44:3; Joel 2:28-29). That was the only time on earth I experienced a fraction of the peace I had experienced in Heaven in 1998. I craved carrying God's presence, and He had already filled me with Heaven's peace—Jesus—but I had failed to carry out the commission. That night I realized revival has a face. It's in the sick, the broken, and the lonely. But it wasn't until I became sick and broken myself that I'd really understand it.

In the summer of 2011 Radiance was baptized, and in fall she entered high school. Fast forward to June 2017 and she was about to graduate. One week before the graduation exercises my first tooth had been extracted. On June 24th I had my third NDE and glimpse of Heaven. In the ER I was prescribed Tramadol, but the pain persisted, so three days later, the day before graduation and on the traveling day, my dentist added Oxycodone to my meds. My speech was slurred and I swayed on my feet like a drunken sailor, but at least the pain was subsiding.

Packing the suitcase was daunting—all I wanted to do was to lie down. I moved at a tortoise's pace and wished I didn't have to go to Saskatoon. Over three hours I assembled shoes, purses, dresses, jewelry, cosmetics, and gifts. I hoped I had not forgotten anything significant for the most auspicious event in my daughter's life.

At 5:00 p.m., Tim and I set off for Saskatoon.

"Please drive slowly," I implored, nausea clamping on me as he swung a corner. He wanted to arrive at the hotel by twilight and we had 370 km to cover. I needed to take my medication with food, so we stopped for a quick supper at the 24/7 Travel Centre restaurant in Dafoe.

Thanks to the long summer days, it was still light when Tim pulled into the parking lot of the Hilton Garden Inn at 9:30 p.m.

Sweet relief. After a quick shower, I collapsed into bed, grateful that TCU Place, the location for the function, was located opposite the hotel's parking lot. That would allow time to polish my nails the next morning.

Wednesday, June 28th dawned sunny and bright, the perfect day to graduate. At nine o'clock my phone rang. It was Radiance.

Earlier that morning she had written on Facebook, "Mom, it's not going to be the same without you, but I understand if you can't make it. Get better soon."

Her excitement was sky high as she assimilated the news that I was actually in Saskatoon. She gave a rundown of the day's schedule, ending with, "Be sure to get to the church for 12:30 if you want pictures. I have to go in promptly at 1:00."

"Church? Which church?" My drugged-up brain was confused.

"Cathedral of the Holy Family on Nelson Road." She sounded astonished at my incomprehension, given that the school had sent several emails.

"Isn't it happening at TCU Place?" This was not good.

"No." Radiance's tone took on the tolerance one used with children. "The banquet and dance are at TCU place tonight, but the mass and ceremony are midday at the church."

My brain clicked. Mass usually occurs in churches. This new information lent urgency to the day. The church was across town and we had to factor in driving time—with a buffer in case we got lost—so we could arrive at 12:30 p.m. for photographs. Our hotel was downtown and there might be detours and construction.

I had wanted a French manicure, but the wisdom tooth drama had kissed that goodbye a week ago. This morning it had taken me an eternity to shower, put on makeup, and style my hair, so one coat of red Miracle Gel would have to do. Every movement made me tired, but in between nibbling breakfast and resting, I managed to get my nails polished and change into my Ivanka Trump dress. Tim and I drove to the Cathedral on Nelson Road, only to find the parking lot was full. Eventually we found overflow parking at a nearby business place. Leaning on Tim, I walked across the lengthy lots and into the church.

My daughter looked gorgeous in her loosely-curled tresses and blue gown. Her face glowed. Radiance has always lived up to her name, but more so today. It was her day, her achievement, with her friends of the Class of 2017. We posed for quick pictures before taking our seats in a pew. Radiance had agreed to be a torchbearer, another symbolism of her name, and she was first behind the bearer of the cross in the opening ritual of the mass, her silver sandals peeking under the gown. While shoe-shopping, I had remarked that the sandals looked like the style Jesus wore.

"Jesus didn't wear sparkly sandals." She had grinned, nonetheless pleased at a fashion statement linked to Him. Today she radiated and shone from head to toe carrying the torch. The silver necklace with its cubic zirconium pendant fit perfectly into the V-neck of the royal-blue gown, and round stones sparkled on her ears. Real diamonds glittered on her pinkie finger.

Click. Click. Click. My camera captured every move she made, every angle from which I could see her as I snapped photos of peoples' heads and the background beyond. Still pictures were not enough. I had to capture this sacred moment on video. But as I filmed, I was conscious of my hands slowing down, my body sagging, and the throbbing ache in my head. I slumped against Tim.

"Could you get me some water, please?" I whispered. He went out and came back bearing a mug. I sipped it, grateful for the refreshing coolness. Minutes later I gulped down the rest with an Oxycodone pill.

The prayers and hymns were peaceful and the speakers interesting. I was soothed by the Catholic service, so different from my Pentecostal style. The graduates' song, "Go Light Your World,"[2] held deeper significance for me, as I had seen Heaven and a Light only four days earlier. The call to seek out the broken and bring hope to the hopeless, to go in the darkness and spread the light, had become my renewed mission on June 24th.

The commission to the graduates was mine.

But instead of seeking a mark on earth, I am driven for eternity. Unbidden, the memory of my time in Heaven's meadow crept into my mind, and tears welled up in my eyes. I had been deathlike then, and I was deathlike now. And the same reminder came, as it had when she was a baby: *Radiance belongs to Jesus. I belong to Jesus, and one day we will live forever in Eternity, face-to-face with Him.*

The mass came to a close and the graduation exercises commenced. Honors, awards, and certificates were handed out, and I snapped the golden cord being placed around my daughter's neck, the distinguishing mark of the Principal's honor roll. Then more of her receiving her diploma in a green folder, which matched the green V-insert of her gown. This was the crux, the culmination of fourteen years of schooling, seventeen if I considered the fact that I started educating her when she was just a year old.

I relaxed while the other students received their diplomas then resumed taking pictures at the recessional. I was lightheaded and wished I could lie down on the pew. Then the ceremony ended with the reminder that the banquet would begin at 7:00 p.m.

We got back to the hotel at 4:00 p.m. and I quickly changed into a soft yellow silk robe and flopped onto the bed. Radiance was getting her makeup done and would arrive at any moment for me to do her hair. She had worn her hair down to accommodate the blue graduation cap, but was sweeping it up for the banquet to best show off her stunning evening gown. She had not been able to get an appointment at her hairdresser's, so I had been drafted to help.

It started to rain. That was not good for the walk to TCU Place. With his usual foresight, Tim stepped into solution mode. He dashed across the street to Cornwall Mall to buy an umbrella for Radiance and me to use. What a blessing this husband of mine is. In six years of marriage he had witnessed major declines in my health, not once but twice, and an NDE the weekend before, and in the tenderest manner had cared for me.

Everything seemed to be running late as tends to happen on days like these. Well after 5:00 p.m. Radiance made her appearance in flawless makeup, jeans, and shirt. I struggled to stand in the bathroom, congested with the chair we had brought in for the hairdressing. Worse, I felt incapable of pulling off a style to match the face and dress. Somehow I managed an up-do with wispy curls falling around her face. I fastened sparkly stones in an arc in the front and finished the look with silver glitter hairspray. Leaving her to get into her white Tony Bowls dress, I stumbled back to the bed.

When she emerged from the bathroom, Tim and I sucked in our breaths. She was radiant. The dress was everything the website described and more: "Up your attitude in an edgy gown from Tony Bowls TB117139. This strappy style is crafted with a cut out neckline and cutaway sides. Streaming sparkle flashes down the length in a curling design. The mermaid skirt is snug to your hips and flares to the floor with excellent ruching for a statement-making appeal."[3] We had purchased this red-carpet dress at NWL Contemporary Dresses in Regina.

My husband and daughter looked at me hunched on the bed. I was sapped of energy, and had no time to redo my own hair or to apply fresh makeup. I took my Ralph Lauren sheath dress into the bathroom and exchanged the yellow robe with the red gown. Then I slipped into red pumps, and with my eight-hour-old makeup, was ready for the night.

"My purse, Mom. Where's my silver purse?" Radiance asked.

A cold feeling oozed into my stomach. I had been through my suitcase many times since we arrived and had not spotted the silver clutch. It was too late. The clutch with its sparkle to match the Tony Bowls dress, the diamond bracelet, and hanging earrings, lay at home … somewhere. I had taken it out along with three other bags, a red, a black, and an off-white one, but sadly, the red one to match my red dress and the silver one for her dress were a five-hour drive away.

"I'm sorry. I'm so sorry, Radiance. I thought I had packed it after you texted."

I was angry with myself. Radiance had sent a text on Tuesday afternoon reminding me to bring the silver clutch and I had taken it down from the closet. Tears filled my eyes. The gems on her sandals matched the silver on the stones on her dress; the purse would have topped it off perfectly, and I had ruined it. Thanks, Oxycodone! It was her last day as a child and my imperfection was at its best. I berated myself, the emotional pain of the forgotten purse more acute than the physical one pounding in my body.

Will I ever get it right, Lord?

"It's okay, Mom, don't worry," Radiance consoled me.

But I continued to castigate myself. This was too important an event, and it had been too long in the planning, for this error to have been made. I hated myself for forgetting and I hated this pain that caused me to be so incompetent.

"You can use this one—it goes well with the dress too."

I held out the glossy off-white purse with dainty gold and silver bars on the front. It was true that it complemented the dress. That left the black one I had tossed in for good measure for me. Huddled under the umbrella, we inched our way to TCU Place. Radiance's teeth chattered in the cold air.

The excitement was palpable in the banquet hall. The graduates looked their finest, garbed in bedazzling colors, princess gowns, and stately suits. The young people were every bit the promising citizens of Canada's tomorrow.

I picked at my meal, taking photos and uploading them to social media in real-time. I had done the same at the ceremony, but the Internet reception in the church had not been as good and only two or three photos had uploaded. Nonetheless, our wonderful friends shared our joy, beaming their love and congratulations as the pictures appeared in their feeds.

The day had been too long for me, and it was now after 8:00 p.m. I couldn't hold out much longer, but there was still the grand march, the speeches and PowerPoint slides, and the dance. Not that I was dancing, but I wanted to take pictures to the very end. I recalled how I had stammered to Tim while we waited for the ambulance that if I died, he was not to tell Radiance yet. Let her graduate first. Let her wear her cap and gown. Let her wear her dress and be happy.

And here I was witnessing it all in a hall pulsing with joy and happiness, beauty and pageantry. I was not in the morgue waiting to be buried. I wanted to stretch out every second, to let a day be like a thousand years so that this most auspicious day of her life would never end. But Oxycodone does not give heed to function or fashion. The floor looked inviting and it took every ounce of self-control to fight the urge to flop down and go to sleep. Instead, I sat glued to my chair while Tim went back to the hotel to gather Radiance's belongings. He had hoped to stay a little longer when he got back, but shortly after 10:00 p.m. I informed him that I needed to lie down. Leaving Radiance and her dad to enjoy the celebration, Tim and I left.

The next morning my head was heavy and I was even more lethargic than the day before. We had to check out by noon, so I roused myself to get up and get dressed. I did not make conversation and later Tim told me it was obvious that I was terribly unwell that morning. I took another dose of Oxycodone and a Tylenol.

As we stepped into the fresh air in the parking lot, I inquired, "Does your skin feel clammy?"

"No," he replied. "I feel fine."

In the car I positioned the vents to my face and the coolness of the air conditioner revived me. Tim handed the cashier our parking ticket and we headed out of Saskatoon. Neither of us had any idea what would happen within the hour.

CHAPTER 13

CRISIS ON HIGHWAY 16

"The LORD keeps watch over you as you come and go ..."
Psalm 121:8a (NLT).

As we got on to Highway 16 en route to Yorkton, the clammy feeling gave way to queasiness, and reflux started to rise in my chest. I pressed my hand to my mouth while I tugged at the plastic bag we keep for trash and spat into it. My head hurt, and the motion of the car and side effects of the Oxycodone were a losing combination. We had just passed the sign for the town of Allan when my mouth filled with saliva and my breakfast rose in my throat.

I motioned for Tim to stop. Yanking the door open, I threw up my insides on the parched brown grass. I paused, then started the process again, ejecting yogurt and coffee as cars whizzed by. After a while my stomach settled and Tim resumed driving. I could still feel the dizziness, but it was manageable. I was not paying attention to time—it could have been fifteen minutes, or more, when the motion of the car proved unbearable again. Once again I buried my face in the bag.

"Stop!"

Tim veered the car on to the shoulder of the road and with lightning speed came to the passenger side. He opened the door and I huddled on the edge of the seat and spewed whatever was left of what I had consumed that morning. Each time I thought I had nothing left to bring up, another heave would grip my stomach and liquid would come up. It reminded me of my hyperemesis gravidarum condition during pregnancy. Three times I started and stopped, started and stopped, started and stopped, until I half expected to see my liver on the grass. The smell was putrid, and my throat burned from the harsh gastric acids.

"Water," I panted.

We had none in the car.

"I'll get some at the next town," Tim said as he dove behind the wheel. That would be in Colonsay. I continued to fill another plastic bag with vile-smelling retching while he stepped on the gas.

I gazed outside through dim eyes. The sky was overcast, but a circle of bright blue peeped through the dull gray. I thought of the blue mansion I had seen a week ago, and the next words I spoke were involuntary. Totally unplanned.

"You must say you'd let me go. You must always say that I can go. You have to release me, so I can go."

I choked on the words and tears spilled from my eyes.

Tim placed his hand on my knee as the car picked up speed. His voice was shaky when he replied, "I will do what is best for you to keep you out of pain, just as I would want you to do the best for me."

In that moment we had an understanding that if either of us was going through the kind of agony I was experiencing, we would not hold on to each other on earth for the sake of keeping the other alive. We would not be selfish. We would surrender each other to God.

This expectation of Heaven is not morbid; on the contrary, it is filled with excitement like when one anticipates Christmas. Having seen Heaven, I could no longer be content on earth. I've grumbled to God about teasing me with perfection and peace and then bringing me back … here. Why? Oh why, Father, have you done this to me THREE times? It seemed like a mean and cruel joke, but then I'd beg for forgiveness, knowing that I had blasphemed the Lord. It's not that I don't love my family and friends, it's just that I've seen and experienced Eternity and there is nothing, not one thing, on earth that compares to Heaven. I want the beauty, the bliss, and the peace again.

In uttering the words to my husband that he must release me, I gained a new understanding of life departing.

People must give the dying one permission to die.

Permission to leave this body, this shell of dust, so the person could take on the eternal. When the brain shuts down the body dies, but the spirit cannot die so it goes on to eternity. When people pray for the departing one, God hears those prayers, and because He answers prayers, the person who wishes to go remains torn between the two worlds.

This does not mean one shouldn't pray for loved ones. Pray on if that is the wish of the dying one. But it's always best to pray for the will of God to be done rather than imposing human demands on God. The will of God brings strength, comfort, healing, and peace. Though those remaining behind sorrow, the joy of the reunion is our hope. I want unselfish prayers when next I am dying. I want to be told, "I release you to God," so I can whiz unfettered to my Lord and King, and not feel as if I have to hang on to earth because someone needs me or wishes me here. I want to be free of pain. And because this revelation had never hit me before, but now it had, I want to enlighten others.

The town of Colonsay came into view. A newly-built Co-op store greeted us, but it had not yet opened for business, so Tim drove into town to the old store. He brought me the water and I swallowed it so greedily it dribbled down my chin. My thirst met relief, but my nausea had not found a counterpart.

"Could you buy me Gravol?" As he went back in the store, I quickly opened my iPhone and posted on social media: "Nauseous and throwing up on the highway 6 times. Prayers appreciated." That would be my last post for a while.

Tim returned and his glum expression told the outcome before his words. "They don't sell Gravol here. We have to go to Lanigan."

He was already in the driver's seat, backing the car down the street and onto the highway. Lanigan was the next town with a pharmacy, about sixty kilometers east on the highway. The drive was long and I kept groaning and regurgitating into the bag. Something was dreadfully wrong. Water was not helping me; in fact, each sip I took came back out as it had done in my first trimester. I would not keep a Gravol pill from the pharmacy down. I needed Gravol injected directly into my blood stream. I needed acute care.

"I need to go to a hospital."

Once again the car sped up. One does not pay attention to signs for the nearest hospital unless one is in a predicament and needs to go to one. The road signs I searched for now indicated that the nearest hospital was also at Lanigan. Later that night I read that my friends that been admonishing on social media that I GET TO A HOSPITAL RIGHT AWAY in uppercase letters.

Tim pulled into the hospital's parking lot. Leaning on him, I half-dragged, half-walked to the reception desk. The hospital records show my registration at 13:35 on June 29th, 2017. The receptionist led me to an observation room where Tim helped me changed into a gown. A nurse came in and he related my wisdom tooth saga to her. She directed questions at me and I looked to him to be my spokesperson.

"She took Oxycodone and Tylenol for pain this morning. She's been vomiting on the highway for over two hours. We think she could be experiencing side effects from the Oxycodone."

The nurse wanted to know my pain level so I held up three fingers.

"How are you feeling?"

Her eyes bore into mine. She wanted to hear from me, but I looked at Tim again and he took my cue and responded. That did not appear to please her, but I simply could not formulate sentences. I could hear and understand, shake or nod my head, but I could not articulate words.

"Is she usually this unresponsive?" the nurse asked Tim.

"No," he replied. Why wasn't the nurse getting it that an ill person who had been vomiting over the last two hours would have difficulty responding? I was far from normal. The constant pain, weakness, exhaustion, dehydration, dizziness, and nausea had taken a cumulative toll on me.

"We were going to buy Gravol but came here instead as she was getting worse," Tim added.

"You could have gotten Gravol at the pharmacy in the mall," was her response. We already knew that. Then she acknowledged, "But if she is vomiting, the Gravol would not have stayed down." We had figured that out too. So why her attitude?

"What did she eat for breakfast?"

"Yogurt, egg, coffee—"

"Nothing unusual?" the nurse interrupted.

"No."

I shook my head in an attempt to participate. We both had eaten from the same plate and Tim was fine, so I thought I could rule out food poisoning and allergic reactions, but maybe not. The nurse took my vital signs and informed us that she would be in touch with the doctor on call who was attending to patients in his office.

It felt good to lie down. Soon the nurse returned and informed us that a blood test was needed to be done. I was still nauseated and hadn't received any Gravol, nor was there mention of a hydration IV, which is routinely administered in cases of extreme vomiting like mine.

The nurse studied me and asked more questions, and I made eye contact with her as a way of communicating.

"Is she usually this unresponsive?" she asked Tim for the second time.

"No," he replied patiently. I thought of the words Author and Speaker on my social media pages and business cards. No, I am not usually this unresponsive. I am articulate and clear. At the moment, however, I was incapable of being either.

Within minutes, a lab technician came in to draw my blood and I winced at the sight of the needle. The technician was sympathetic and gentle and punctuated her blood-drawing exercise with reassurances such as, "This won't take long," and "You're doing just fine," and "It will soon be done." I appreciated her sensitivity—she was well suited to her position.

After the technician left, the nurse came in with an update.

"The doctor isn't able to come to see you yet, but it sounds as if your vomiting was a result of your medications interacting." I had taken Oxycodone and Tylenol, and we had considered that an interaction was possible, but the pharmacist had advised that they could be taken together.

"How are you feeling?" she asked me again.

I shook my head.

"Is she always this unresponsive?" the nurse asked Tim impatiently for the third time.

"Grrrr ... vlll," I slurred, making every effort to please her by talking. My dry lips were stuck together and I could not get those vowels out.

The nurse was bigger than me and I was beginning to feel afraid of her. Why wasn't I given any Gravol? I knew from past experience that after vomiting so much I would need fluids intravenously to combat dehydration, but there was no mention of IV. It wasn't until 14:25, according to my record—fifty minutes later—that the long-awaited Gravol was finally offered through a shot in my arm.

Shortly after the injection, the nurse came in with another update. I was not in danger, but the doctor would still like to see me at the end of his work day, which would probably be at 4:00 or 5:00 p.m.

"How are you feeling?" she asked me again.

"Sleepy." My voice was weak, and she didn't hear the answer.

"Speak up, will you?" she commanded roughly.

For the second time that day I felt afraid of this woman who held power over me in my vulnerable condition. My only consolation was that Tim was with me all the time and I was safe.

Perhaps she sensed my fear, because she seemed to mellow. "Yeah, Gravol does make you sleepy."

The head of the bed had been elevated for my comfort, but gravity had taken advantage of my plight and I had been slowly sliding down. I gestured to Tim and he communicated to the nurse that I wanted to be repositioned.

"Pull yourself up on the bed!" she demanded.

"Can't," I mumbled and shook my head.

Without warning, she grasped the sheet near the pillow and yanked at it, pulling me up in the process. The movement was totally unexpected and I felt nauseated again. It would have been so much nicer if she had told me what she was about to do.

A urine sample was needed, so Tim helped me to the bathroom. The nurse reported that nothing of concern showed up in the sample.

I felt as though I was not wanted there, as if I was a burden. I was certainly not treated with respect. I'm sure the hospital in general was good, but our patience was tried by a nurse who, for whatever reason, seemed completely lacking in empathy and bedside manner. There was little evidence of the Patient First culture that is encouraged in Saskatchewan hospitals.

The Gravol shot was doing its magic, making it even more difficult to communicate. In stuttering sentences, I had a conversation with Tim. "Why are they keeping me here?"

"The doctor has to see you."

"What will he do when he comes?"

Tim was unsure. Maybe they would officially discharge me. There was nothing to wait for, no reason to remain there. The nurse had informed us that nothing had shown up on the tests and that they suspected my situation was due to medication interaction. All they could give me was the Gravol. She wanted me to talk, and I couldn't talk. I wanted to sleep but couldn't sleep there. The doctor was not coming to the hospital anytime soon, because my case wasn't urgent.

"Let's go home," I urged Tim. "I need to sleep, and if something happens on our way, we will go to another hospital."

Tim sought the nurse and expressed my desire to leave. Interestingly, a gentleness I had not encountered before came over her.

"You're welcome to stay," she said. "We can't do very much here. We're a small hospital, but you are welcome to stay."

"Thank you for what you did for me," I stammered.

"*You* will have to sign a release form if you want to leave." She directed her gaze at me. "*You* have to sign it, not him."

I signed the document in spidery writing, changed my clothes, and hobbled out on Tim's arm. Neither of us noted the time we left. As I wanted to include the time I signed out in this chapter, I requested my personal health record from the hospital.

I was stunned to read that the time the nurse had written for departure was 14:15. Why, my blood test had been taken at 14:15 and my urine sample had been handed over at 15:40! The lab reports were computer-generated, and I believed those, which meant that the nurse had recorded my signing-out time incorrectly. I thought back on the unprofessional treatment I had received at her hands. As I studied the record further, I realized that this employee had also bypassed critical observations in her overall assessment of me. That was unacceptable. In order to correct the record, I had to contact the health authority and make a formal request for an Amendment to Personal Health Information, which I did.

CHAPTER 14

ON TOUR

"… I will pour out my Spirit on all people … your young men will see visions"
Joel 2:28 (NIV).

I OFTEN REFLECTED ON my uphill walk in Heaven's meadow in the huge shadow of my guide in the years following the experience, and pondered it in my heart. Other than to Thomas, I had only mentioned it briefly in 2004 when I spoke at an Aglow conference in Regina.

Joel 2:28-29 states, "I will pour out my Spirit on all people. Your sons and daughters will prophesy, your old men will dream dreams, your young men will see visions. Even on my servants, both men and women, I will pour out my Spirit in those days. I will show wonders in the heavens and on the earth …" I believe these promises apply to me through the work of the Holy Spirit.

In 2007 I had two visions. They happened concurrently during the dark hours of the night, so at first I thought they were dreams. However, unlike my dreams, which I can't recall, the details remain clear, leading me to conclude that they were something bigger. The clarity and conciseness have not faded over time, and that is consistent with my other supernatural experiences. In retrospect, it is possible I may have been caught up to Eternity, similar to what happened during my NDE in 2015. I wish I had paid closer attention to the date and details of my life that day, but I could not have known of their significance.

For this writing, I will consider my experiences of 2007 as visions. In the first vision, I am in Heaven. The scene, however, is not the meadow. I am in what I will call the suburbs of Heaven. There are streets, but they are not visible to me, as a mist or cloud fills the entire area. I don't know if the streets are of gold or some other material. It appears to be early morning. The Bible states that there will be no night in Heaven, for Jesus is the light (Revelation 22:5), but perhaps there is less light at some times. I don't say this as theology or doctrine, rather, I express this as a personal interpretation of the dimmer light in the scene I found myself. I also contrast this to my visit in 1998 when the meadow was as bright as in the midday sun.

There are small houses in rows as in a subdivision, separate and identical in design, hence my description of suburbs. The architecture is perfect and winsome and it appears as though a home is provided for each person. The cloud-mist hovers at the base of each house and in between the structures. I think of the mountain where God used to come to speak to the Israelites in the form of a cloud. I also think of fog as seen on the prairies.

I have knowledge of people and things while I am here, just as I had in other visits. Of interest is that those people are actually alive on earth today. They are not people who have died. I have general knowledge that a number of people are in Heaven, and it is highlighted to me that my missionary sister is there, although I do not see her. The only people I see are my three younger sisters (who are adults on earth at the time of this writing). In Heaven they are a teen and children, playing and giggling in a carefree manner just as they had when they were a teen and children riding in the backseat of my car. They are running and romping along the streets, having fun in the morning haze. I distinctly remember my youngest sister wearing a dress she wore when she was small—a sleeveless white dress with random red shapes cut in hipster style. I am in my late 20s, wearing a denim skirt and white crop top, with brown leather sandals on my feet. I do not talk to them, and all three giggle and run off after meeting me.

Taking into account our families on both sides, I know for sure one person was not there, but everyone else who is close to me was in Heaven. I can only infer what age people will be in Heaven, as the Bible is not clear on this subject. Time as we know it on earth does not exist in Heaven, because God marks time differently. 1 Peter 2:8 talks about a day being as a thousand years, and a thousand years a day. This paradox is incomprehensible to our natural minds, almost nonsensical. But the reference to days and years are measures of time, and morning, midday, and evening are elements of time. The Bible states that there is no night in Heaven as the Lamb is the light, and I infer from this that there are no periods of darkness. Varying shades of light, perhaps, but not blackness.

When I was in Heaven's meadow, it appeared to be as midday. In this vision, I feel it is early morning (as when the sun is not fully yet up on earth). Time in Heaven is different and I believe it is not linear as we know it on earth. I believe that our bodies in Heaven will reflect our prime when we were on earth, when we were our best and happiest, and this prime age will vary with each person.

A parallel of this vision to my first trip in Heaven's meadow is that I know and see people who are alive, or who soon would be. In 1998, God had shown me my daughter in a green dress before she was born. In 2007 I saw family who were alive. I believe God showed me my daughter to reveal to me how he saw her—alive. I wish I could explain why I saw my sisters alive when other writers see deceased relatives, but I can only relate what I saw. In fact, when I was taken to Eternity as a tourist in 2015, I saw details that I've not read in the writings of others. God chooses to show each person what He wills. I'm also aware that some details may have been hidden from me once I returned to earth, or may be revealed futuristically, but I report what I remember.

I walk beyond the suburbs in Heaven towards the edge. There are no houses here. Instead, a big, tall double wall with a narrow gap in between falls to a sheer drop way down .below. The walls seem to be made of cement and they are the gray color of unpainted concrete. I am reminded of the double walls that guard cities. I look down, beyond the wall, and know instinctively that it is Hell, although I cannot see the details from where I stand. I know that it is mammoth, that it is far more spread out than the city of Paris had appeared when I viewed it from the top of the Eiffel Tower.

As I survey this place of gloom from afar, my second vision begins. I become aware of someone walking beside me and that I am walking downwards. His is a large presence, and I see his shadow. It is similar to the shadow I had encountered in 1998 in the meadow, but I knew that shadow to be the Shadow of the Almighty, as in Psalm 91:1; this time I sense it is an angel. I cannot see him, but I know it through the communication process where thoughts enter my mind that he is dressed in black and is a warrior.

Whereas the large person had walked on my right as we went up-hill in the meadow, this person is on my left as we go downwards. Interestingly, the right side is heavenwards, so the warrior is on the left where the danger lurks, to protect me from it. He keeps about half a pace ahead as we descend long, winding steps hewn out of rock. It feels as if we are inside a deep mountain, walking down dozens and dozens of steps in a dark stairway with thick rock walls on either side. The stairway is narrow, able to accommodate two people at most, and it follows the contours of the mountain.

I do not fear tripping because somehow I can see through the darkness, as my sight is also heightened and clear. Like a nocturnal animal I have perfect vision and agility. This is both amazing and interesting, because in the natural I am very cautious of going down steps and always look for a handrail or a person to hold on to. Yet here I am without a handrail in the dark and I am treading down confidently and surely.

The angel of the Lord leads me to a deep abyss. Former atheist, Rev. Howard Storm, describes horrors at different levels of his journey in his book *My Descent into Death*,[1] but thankfully I am not shown those. The knowledge is transmitted to me that I am a visitor on tour. This is a place that I cannot come to alone, because I am a foreigner and do not belong here. I have not asked to see this place, but the tour is being offered to me and the angel is my tour guide. This parallel is easy to understand, because in my travels to foreign countries, and even my native Trinidad, I've accessed the services of guides for both security and informational purposes.

As we grow closer to where the angel is taking me, a dark orange glow becomes apparent. It reminds me of Halloween colors and sights I have seen on television. I shrink back, my steps slowing. I hear faint shrieks in the distance that grow to louder wails, as if people are being tortured. The anguish is undeniable. The dark orange glows and glowers. It is spooky and terrifying, and I move closer to the angel as we continue down.

We turn a corner to the left. And I see it.

Hell.

A place of fire just as the Bible describes.

The fire comes in waves, as water rolls in the ocean. Waves of fire. The fire "ocean" looks like an endless, flat surface. The fire waves are gigantic from far off and become smaller as they crash onto the burnt rocky shore with its blackened sand. The fire recedes and surges, surges and recedes, like swash and backwash on beaches. And in it are people, as if they are bathing in the ocean, tossed to and fro by the waves in the fire. They are screaming and many have their arms upraised.

I am extremely familiar with waves and oceans. My native Trinidad is a Caribbean island bounded by four bodies of water: the Atlantic Ocean to the east, the Caribbean Sea to the north, the Gulf of Paria to the west, and Columbus Channel to the south. Churning waters rolling blue and crashing waves with white frothy tips are the norm. They are cool and inviting, awesome and powerful. But Hell is the opposite–tormented and cursed, where the burnt-orange rolling fires are tipped with black.

I stand with the angel on the corner and watch Hell, witnessing the very real suffering of those who mocked the Christian gospel, who rejected the invitation that would have kept them out of the inferno. We do not talk, but there is an understanding that I am not permitted to go any closer. Nor do I wish to go closer.

I don't know how long we spent watching Hell, because in Eternity a lot seems to happen in a short space of time. I can only extrapolate from my 1998 experience when I was unconscious for three minutes on earth, but saw, knew, and felt so much of Heaven. I also did not know how much time I spent in Heaven this time.

Our time is over. We walk up the stairs to Heaven and I go first with the angel behind me. At that point I came back to reality on earth, full of the dread and horror I had seen of the place prepared for the Devil and his angels. I do not know why I had been chosen for an unsolicited tour, but this would not be my last view of Eternity.

I was so occupied and pre-occupied with living that the whispered secrets of the Living God were drowned out by the noise of the busyness of my days. The things He showed me zig-zagged around the roles I assumed and their accompanying tasks. Career, motherhood, wife, church leader, friend—these were the music to the dance of my hustled life. Not that they were bad things, far from it. I was a popular itinerant speaker and constantly sought the Lord for direction. I was particularly excited to become involved with the Women's Ministry of the Pentecostal Assemblies of Canada (PAOC) Saskatchewan District and to serve on the executive team as co-ordinator for the south-east zone. My passion for prayer led me to become the provincial representative for the Canada-wide Esther's Army.

Except for the one reference to my visit to Heaven's meadow at the conference in 2004, and later to my sisters, I stifled the details until 2017. In hindsight, I believe I was being prepared for more, and it may not have been the time for me to disclose the happenings until now.

Another factor that prevented me from sharing it was my divorce in 2009. Mount Everest with its 29,029 feet above sea level is termed the highest mountain.[2] The Grand Canyon is at minimum 6,000 feet deep.[3] Upon my divorce, I went from Everest to Canyon. Few people in the church wanted anything to do with me. But God is a restorer, and by the end of 2011 the invitations had begun to come in again. The truth that surged in my heart was that the deepest depths of despair and sin cannot outdo the height of God's mercy and grace. And His restoration sets one higher than the highest mountain.

More recently, my experiences in Eternity caught the attention of many, and several who judged me have eaten their words. I've noticed that once people go through their own sorrows or that of their children, their hearts become more accepting to the plight of others. It is my fervent wish that this book will liberate and reaffirm individuals who feel ostracized because of their life decisions. I will weep with those who weep because I feel compassion.

I sincerely hope that if you are reading this book and have felt rejected by people who once supported because you made a different choice than they would have, that you will hold on to the fact that God cares for you. He loves you and He will restore you if you continue to trust in Him. Flee iniquity if iniquity there is. Seek His face for the truth. Measure it against the Word. Don't give up. Walk through the loneliness, for there are roads on which to walk and a staff to comfort you. Flowers grow in the valleys too, ones that are not found on the higher ground, and you can enjoy them. Plants can be found in the desert. Yes, beauty and peace can be experienced in the synclines of life.

The second time I mustered the courage to talk about my trip to Heaven was in 2010. I was single and didn't want to spend Christmas alone, so I flew to Trinidad. One night my sisters and I were on our way out when I recounted the experience. The car was quiet as I told my story about walking in the Shadow and sitting on the hill watching the children at play, but I sensed the uneasiness as they listened.

Suddenly one of them shouted, "There's Rudolph on the roof!"

We were at Oropouche Junction and the lights ahead were spectacular. Sure enough, Rudolph and the rest of the reindeer, along with Santa and the sleigh, gaily lit up the roof of a house. This was a sight my sisters saw annually, but the ensuing babble that filled the car over Rudolph communicated to me how much validity they were willing to give to my experience. The plastic toy provided the much-needed diversion from my kind of story. Mine is associated with mysticism and that is something many Christians avoid. Thankfully, books and films are making steady headway into toppling these barriers.

CHAPTER 15

A WEDDING AND A SURPRISE

"Two are better than one ..." Ecclesiastes 4:9a (KJV).

I DIDN'T REMAIN SINGLE for long. My fiancé Tim was a white-collar professional in one job and grain farmer in the other. Much time couldn't be taken for a summer wedding due to the busyness of the short farming season, so we had held a private marriage ceremony in Las Vegas, and a larger reception for relatives and friends in Saskatchewan in November, after harvest was over. Not only did I get to wear my gorgeous dress twice, but we also celebrate two anniversaries each year.

We wanted to go to a place we had not visited previously for our honeymoon, but one that was fairly close since we had only taken one week off work for our wedding. Las Vegas met the requirements.

Then Tim suggested, "Why don't we get married in Las Vegas too?"

Why not? It was a great idea, so obvious, yet I hadn't thought of it. Las Vegas is known as one of the most famous places to get married, and in this hot destination the wedding industry is a professional one with personnel available around the clock. After an Internet search, I settled on the beautiful Las Vegas Wedding Chapel for a romantic, candle-lit ceremony. I'd seen the chapel on television, so to say our vows in that historic location was thrilling. It came decorated with flowers and offered traditional wedding music, and I love both the traditional music and vows, so it was perfect. The Las Vegas Chapel delivered a personal and romantic wedding in a quiet location, and on July 22, 2011, Tim and I exchanged our vows.

We had chosen Trump International Hotel for our honeymoon, because it was smoke free and game free. There aren't many smoke-free hotels near the Strip, and since smoke bothers me and gaming hotels are congested, the choice was a no-brainer. The pictures on the website were beautiful and immaculate, and our familiarity with the Trump standard increased the anticipation.

Even though I knew Trump Hotel would be impressive, I was not prepared for the magnificence and stateliness of the slim-line sixty-four-story tower of golden glass. The building was incomparable to any I had set foot in. It is a glittering monolith set high above the Strip on top of a hill on Fashion Show Drive, a gold nugget against the blue Nevadan skies.

The exquisiteness took my breath away. The foyer, halls, lounges, and common areas were spotless and pristine. The elegance, polished floors, and lofty bouquets with heady scents instantly set this hotel apart from the others at which I'd stayed. The location is an oasis away from the bustle and noise of the Strip, yet easily accessible via walking or shuttle services. Across the street from the hotel is an entrance to Fashion Show Mall. From there one can get to the Strip by walking through the mall, as it opens directly on to the Boulevard.

Our reception was warm, friendly, and professional. I was starry-eyed at the Superior Room we had booked, which was larger than I had visualized. Everything was larger than life, more splendid than I could have imagined, dazzling and glamorous, which I interpreted as a symbol to characterize our upcoming marriage. The private entryway to the room was laid with marble. Inside, the decor was sleek and modern, the furnishings lavish. At the end of the room, the floor-to-ceiling windows gave a blanket view of the Strip.

The bathroom was a girl's dream. The pink Italian marble on the countertops, floors, jetted spa tub, and double sinks oozed romance and class. The shower and toilet were in separate glass stalls opposite the tub. An unexpected delight was the television inlaid in the mirror, a luxury I had not experienced before, and I styled my hair without missing the news.

Over and over I thought how this kind of pampering in such a stunning hotel for our special celebration could be indicative of our new life together. The experience catered to all our senses, dazzling and holding us spellbound, filling us with wonder and joy, qualities we hoped our marriage would emulate.

After the ceremony at the Wedding Chapel, we went up to our room to freshen up. But the best was yet to come. Upon learning that we were there for our honeymoon, the manager went beyond the call of duty and gave us a surprise gift that humbles us to this day.

The phone rang and I picked it up. "Hello?"

"This is the front desk," a cheery voice announced. "We would like to offer you a complimentary stay for your honeymoon in one of our one-bedroom corner suites."

I paused. Had I had heard her correctly?

"You're doing what?" My voice rose by a couple of octaves.

Although Tim and I were gainfully employed and earning substantive salaries, we didn't think we could afford the high-end suites for a week at Trump Hotel. The room we had booked had already exceeded our expectations, down to the basket of fruit, chocolate, and handwritten note that welcomed us to the hotel.

"We would like to offer you a complimentary stay for your honeymoon on the 55th floor," she repeated.

"A complimentary stay in the honeymoon suite on the 55th floor?" I parroted.

I was on auto pilot. Did such things happen?

"That's right," she confirmed.

"Do we have to pay a discount price for the honeymoon suite?"

I wanted no mistakes or surprise billing when we checked out. After all, the booking had been made on *my* credit card.

"No," she replied in that sprightly tone typical of employees in the Trump organization. "You do not have to pay *anything*. This is complimentary. It is free."

Still astonished, I stuttered, "Thank you. Thank you so very much."

Then practicality reeled in. We were in our wedding finery going down for dinner.

"Can we move tonight?"

"You sure can," she replied. "Just come down to the front desk when you are ready."

We made our way to the circular booth we had reserved in the DJ T restaurant. The large booth set into the wall was secluded enough and had sufficient room for our small wedding party that we didn't need to book a private room. The evening before, we had eaten supper there as a dry run to gauge what to eat attired in our wedding splendor. We could not risk gravy splashing on my satin or on Tim's white tuxedo. I didn't think I could eat anything on my wedding day, as I was filled with so much joy and excitement.

When the restaurant manager realized there was a wedding party, she went into energizer mode and the buzz began. Additional servers were assigned to our table. She personally brought our party complimentary champagne. I do not drink alcohol, but Tim and another guest enjoyed this lavish gift. To this day Tim jokes that, "President Trump paid for the booze at our wedding." Such kindness and generosity, thoughtfulness and service, blew our minds. I could barely absorb the over-the-top graciousness. I am grateful to President Trump for the bar he has set, for it is the same one his employees live up to, and we are testimonies to his excellence and goodwill as first-hand recipients of his panache.

The manager requested that the staff prepare a special dessert for us. She came in bearing more gifts and keepsakes with the Trump logo—water, pens, notepads, lotions, and vodka. I had planned to keep a vodka bottle as a souvenir, but unfortunately, when we returned home, the bottles were missing from our suitcases. The entire staff in the kitchen and restaurant took turns coming out to congratulate us and wish us well.

A classier, more beautiful, serene wedding festivity I could not have imagined. Being in a hotel plated with twenty-four karat gold loomed as a symbol of the future we envisioned for our life together. This was a perfect start to our marriage and we could not have been happier.

After dinner we went back to our suite. Tim layered our belongings in our suitcases and I sat on a chair in my princess dress with its ball-gown skirt and cathedral lace-and-ruffle train emblazoned with sparkling beads. The elegant bodice with its soft pleats tapered in an empire cut to encircle my waist in lace and glittering beads. I supervised the packing process, appreciative of Tim's good husbandry and anticipating the gift of the honeymoon suite.

The luxurious one-bedroom corner suite on the 55th floor cannot be beat for a honeymoon. The floor-to-ceiling views from every room—living room, bedroom, and bathroom—offered a panorama of the surrounding Las Vegas mountains. The hotel was already an oasis away from the Strip, but the abundance of glass found in the corner rooms, through which I could see the rolling mountains, was the zenith of perfection. In the mornings, the mountains were covered by a slight haze that looked like gossamer, misty and mysterious.

Upon entering the suite, we discovered a round dining table with French chairs set up in the middle of the room. To the left was the kitchen, equipped with full-sized refrigerator, stove, dishwasher, garburator, and wine rack. Delicate white china crockery and heavy gleaming silverware filled the cupboards and drawers. To the right of the dining table sat the living area with black leather pull-out sofas, beige chairs, and a coffee table in the middle. A 50-inch plasma television graced one wall and pictures were hung on the opposite wall. Golden glass made up the other side. Off the dining room was a marbled bathroom with a shower.

A door led to the bedroom, dominated by a king-size bed with soft white comforters and downy pillows. Tables with golden lamps stood guard on either side of the bed, and his and hers closets and easy chairs finished the decor. Yellow walls and shimmery ochre drapes mimicked the sunshine they kept out.

The master bathroom was a stunning depiction of high-end design and flawless detail, the hugest I had ever seen in a home or hotel. A whirlpool tub ran the length of the glassed wall. Even now I can close my eyes and relive gazing at the sky and mountains while immersed in warm bubbling water, experiencing the ultimate relaxation.

A shower and toilet were enclosed in frosted glass, and a wide counter with double sinks was set between the frosted stalls. The entire wall was mirrored, with the signature television inlaid for viewing while in the tub or getting dressed. The smooth, pink Italian marble floors were a dream, an unparalleled luxury.

We reflected on the blessings of God to us through Mr. Trump.

"Thank You, Lord," I whispered. "This foretaste of luxury and posh is but a shadow of how we will live in Heaven."

I couldn't have known then that a few years later I would see the blue castle that would trump any building I'd ever laid eyes on, including Trump Hotel.

CHAPTER 16

NIGHT OUT ON THE STRIP

*"... He will command his angels concerning
you to guard you carefully" Luke 4:10b (NIV).*

FOLLOWING OUR WEDDING, WE decided to immerse ourselves in the
Las Vegas reality. Tim and I wanted the experience of spending an
entire night on the iconic Strip. Las Vegas is known for its night life, and
the four-mile-long Strip is the hub for tourists. Not being "night-people",
on Saturday afternoon we took a nap so we'd be fresh for the expedition.
Casinos, bars, dancing, gambling, and alcohol are not elements of my life,
but I was a tourist and I wanted to see what went on in Vegas. For if, as the
saying goes, "What happens in Vegas stays in Vegas," was true, I'd never
know what happened there if I didn't see it for myself. Thus, I was going to
be a star in my own night out on the Vegas Strip.

It's hot in July in Las Vegas, so I chose to wear a tank top and tights
for the adventure. The white eyelash cha cha tank with soft little pleats
edged in black and matching black tights was a flirty and feminine outfit
apt for the occasion. I chose comfortable footwear for the long walk,
leather thongs I had bought at a Naturalizer store in Orlando for walking at Disney World. I loved the cushioned gel pads on the heels.

My husband wore a white golf shirt and black walking shorts, with
runners on his feet.

At 10:00 p.m. on Saturday we set off down Fashion Show Drive.
At the lights we turned right on to Las Vegas Boulevard, as the Strip is
officially named. To say it is scenic or picturesque is an understatement.
The Strip at night is dazzling. It is glittering, a frenzy of color and lights.
The sidewalks were crowded with people dressed in their best. I was par-
ticularly mesmerized by the high stilt heels the young ladies wore. I like

fashion and back then owned over one hundred and twenty-five pairs of footwear, but none boasted the five-inch stilettos these damsels sported.

In the bathroom at one of the hotels I met a group of beautiful and beautifully-dressed young ladies. The one closest to me wore a gorgeous form-fitting dress in blue. If anyone possessed a perfect figure for a sheath dress, it was that woman.

"You look amazing," I complimented her. "All of you are a sight for sore eyes."

I included the entire bevy in my gaze.

She smiled. "Thank you."

Her face was flawless, the makeup intact, and not a strand strayed from the coif.

"I love your shoes, although I could never wear something that high. I don't know how you walk in those, but kudos to you."

Her black pumps were platform-style to the front with thin, long pointed heels.

"I'm already regretting it," she replied with a wry grin.

"Do your feet hurt?"

"They're okay now, but later I'll have to take them off."

She looked down at my thongs with their gold buckles and eyelets.

"I wish I had something like what you are wearing." I felt the sincerity of her words.

"Do you have flats in your bag?" My question was a silly one, because her tiny clutch purse looked like it could hold a lipstick and a credit card, and possibly a phone.

"No." She laughed good-naturedly. "I'll walk barefoot when I take them off."

She was nonchalant, as if it was the most natural thing in the world to walk around Vegas in bare feet. I was scandalized. Bare feet in a casino? Bare feet on the street? Why, I didn't even walk barefoot in my own house! But I kept my opinion to myself.

To cover the awkward moment I added, "It's my first time in Las Vegas and my husband and I plan to walk the entire Strip—that's the reason for the flats."

"We're going to the casino for the night," she offered in turn.

"Have fun." I meant it.

"You too." The beauty smiled again and we parted ways.

From the intersection of Fashion Show Drive and the Strip where the Wynn hotel stands, we walked all the way to Mandalay Bay. Several hotels led from one to the other and we took those paths as well as going over the crosswalks and on to the pavement of the Boulevard. At Caesar's Palace we stopped for a rest, and I sank into a plush armchair for a foot rub from Tim. The thick smoke made me cough, however, and we had to leave all too soon.

We took photos with other tourists and paused to enjoy the dancing fountains of Bellagio with its magical lights. It was a balmy, idyllic night and I ogled at the glitter, my mind and body energized by the excitement.

As we progressed along our walk, the area started to look less attractive. By that time it was well past midnight and the scene had started to change. Police cars were parked at every intersection. Horns blared when jay walkers tried to cross the street. I had never seen so many cops and cars in one place or heard sirens go off so frequently. We had started off holding hands, but Tim had since placed his arm around my shoulders. I pressed closer to him as the crowd thickened and intoxicated people swayed on the pavement.

"I'm thirsty," I said.

He was too. We had passed Walgreens where we could have purchased water, and the casinos were full of smoke so I couldn't go there.

"Let's go to McDonald's," he suggested.

Weaving our way toward the iconic golden arches, we entered what seemed a dark building after the bright lights of the outside. I don't remember the name of the building, for I was only focused on the sign.

"What's this?" It didn't look like a burger and fries joint.

"It's a bar," Tim replied, increasing the pressure on my arm as if suspicious I might dart outside. "McDonald's is at the back."

Unbeknownst to me, the building was a casino and hotel—to prove it, the tell-tale smoke I had tried to avoid hung thick in the air.

Placing a hand over my nose, I took in the scene as we maneuvered past slot machines and people. Then and there I had my most telling moment in Las Vegas, a tableau that may never be erased from my mind. Sprawled across the countertop of the bar were men and women. The mouth of a middle-aged man hung open, his gray blazer falling off one arm, his yellow tie flung across his shoulder. A white shirt gaped open at the neck and his snores filled the air. A woman lolled against him, her pink sequined mini dress riding high up her thighs. Silver high-heeled sandals lay in a heap under the barstool. Several more people had flopped their heads down on the dark countertop—a young lady in a short black dress, a man in a dark suit, too many to recount.

Around the tables drunken slurs amputated conversations, and high-pitched laughter erupted as if the funniest jokes were being told. At another table, a woman's hair was tangled, hiding her sleeping face from my curious gaze. As far as my eye could see, those awake looked limp and dull, puffing cigars or sitting dejectedly with faces propped on their hands. Waitresses dressed in skimpy suits with fluffy bunny tails attached to their backsides scurried across the floor.

I shrank closer to Tim, my eyes huge with horror in the stifling atmosphere. I had never seen anything like this. Not that I hadn't seen drunk people, I'd just never seen as large a number as this closeted in one space. Witnessing the degeneration in such a huge number of people in such a short space of time bewildered me. If hopelessness had a face, it would be this.

This is human depravity at its worst.

Only a few hours earlier, the men we'd seen were dignified with their cigars and drinks in hands. They were properly attired in suits and ties. Their conversations were not unusual, neither was their laughter. Their behavior was what one would expect from people who were enjoying themselves. The ladies could have been models on runways, poised and fresh.

How did they become this?

I wondered about the young woman I had chatted with in the bathroom. Was her blue dress falling off? Was the up-do still in place? Was the entire group passed out unconscious with drink, or possibly drugs? Would the shoes make it home with her?

In a daze, we purchased our water. The lines were long and we waited more than half an hour to be served.

Back on the streets the cool air revived me, but the stench prevailed. Sweat and drugs mingled in a rancid odor. Men lumbering down the sidewalk drunkenly reached out to grab at females as they passed by. More than once Tim pulled me away from oncoming pedestrians whose glazed eyes seemed incapable of perceiving direction. More than once he changed course so we would not be trampled on. We had walked the entire length of the Strip before we saw the *Welcome to Fabulous Las Vegas* sign.

"We've got to get out of here." He was authoritative and I was only too happy to acquiesce.

We crossed at an overpass so we could experience the other side as we walked back, but sightseeing and photographs were not a luxury anymore. Peddlers waved their wares and little "business" cards in our faces. Tim strengthened his arm across my shoulders and I quickened my pace to match his. There was an unspoken urgency to our movements now. The presence of the cops at every intersection relieved me, and I felt safe as long as we stayed on the Boulevard itself instead of taking the meandering walkways through the hotels.

As the Mirage and Treasure Island came into view, I breathed easier. Our first room had overlooked Treasure Island, so we were getting closer to our haven of safety. We caught glimpses of Trump Hotel from the Strip but needed to walk down to the Wynn in order to get there. The mall was closed, so we could not take that route, which was unfortunate as that would have been the safest.

We made it back to the Wynn and crossed the pedestrian walkway to Fashion Show Drive. At the top of the hill Trump Hotel loomed against the sky, gleaming richly in the dark night. Relief surged through my body as I beheld "home".

The uphill walk was gentle, but uphill nonetheless. The only time an uphill walk has been effortless has been in Heaven's meadow. The hotel was on the right side, so we walked on that side of the street. The mall loomed large on our left, its brand name stores silent.

Suddenly we heard loud swearing. It wasn't unusual to hear swearing on the Strip; as a matter of fact we had heard a lot of it that night, but until that moment had not felt concerned by it. But Tim and I were the only ones on this street, and an alarm pinged in my head. Someone was swearing at *us*. Involuntarily, my eyes flicked in the direction of the voice, and I saw a youth of African-American descent walking parallel to us on the left side of the road. I don't remember what he was wearing, but he was keeping pace with us. We sensed danger and Tim once again tightened his hold on my arm as we changed our pace to one between walking and running.

The youth gave a shrill whistle, which Tim told me later he had interpreted as a call, perhaps a gang signal. Then the young man began to comment on our appearance. We don't remember what he said, but I am brown-skinned and Tim is Caucasian and that difference was the subject of his insults. Fear pressed its hand on me. I looked up at the hotel, willing it to move from its golden foundation and come to us. Perspiration broke out on my body and my palms were sweaty. My thongs started to slip from my feet as we made haste and I figured if they fell off I would have to leave them and run barefoot to the hotel, just like the lady in the blue dress had said in the bathroom. The irony was not lost ... when in Vegas do as the Las Vegans do. But there was no time to laugh or think about germs or needles on the streets.

Another bird whistle sounded, which we could only assume was a response to the call the youth had made. Upon hearing it, the young man started towards us. By now we were halfway up Fashion Show Drive and still had quite a bit of road to cover. Not that it was a long walk, but with danger looming, time seemed to slow and distance increased exponentially. I grabbed Tim's arm with my free hand, digging my French nails into his skin.

Suddenly I spotted a person ahead of us. Oh sweet relief! I hadn't seen him before, but Tim informed me afterwards that he had. The man was big, over six feet tall. He was dark-skinned, possibly of Mexican descent, and he sported a crew cut, a black T-shirt, and black shorts that came down to his knees. On his feet he wore dark sandals, not runners like Tim was wearing. He stood with arms folded, watching us.

I squeezed my purse tighter under my arm as we pumped our legs. Surely this stranger would come to our rescue if the youth decided to attack us. He would be a witness that we had not initiated a fight with anyone.

The young man had crossed to the middle of the road. At the same time I saw the big man, the youth stopped, as if he had bumped into something. He turned around and started to go back to his side of the street. His boisterous swearing and threats gave way to muted angry mutterings.

My heart drummed in my rib cage and the pulsing of blood echoed in my ear drums. Had the hotel moved? It felt that way. Tim and I raced past the man, who still stood quietly on the edge of the pavement. As we sprinted up the hill, I was aware of him following us. I couldn't hear his footsteps, nor did I turn around, but I knew he was walking behind us. Tim verified later that he didn't hear footsteps either but saw the man walking behind us when he glanced back. I didn't know who he was or what was on his agenda—I only knew that his presence had deterred the youth from possibly harming us.

We leapt onto the empty driveway and dashed through the revolving doors into the golden refuge of Trump Hotel. Only then did I become aware of how loudly I was panting. It didn't matter—we were safe. The lobby was quiet and I didn't pay attention to who was at the desk. It didn't occur to us to speak to the staff about our experience. Tim merely showed our room key card to the security guard as is customary procedure, and we darted towards the elevators.

Being on the 55th floor required us to use the more private elevators and not the general set closer to the gift shop. Inside the lift I sagged against the mirrored walls, my breaths still heaving my chest. For the first time I was oblivious to the grandeur of the surroundings, which otherwise never ceased to evoke my admiration. A night out on the Strip would not be one I'd repeat. Henceforth, midnight would be my curfew.

We had not yet pressed the button of our floor when another passenger entered the elevator. It was the big Mexican guy.

What is he doing here?

He pressed a number. It was higher than ours, perhaps the penthouse. I made no eye contact with him. Our gaze was fixed on the numbers above us, and when our floor lit up and the door opened, we rushed out. I was still shaken from the ordeal of fleeing the youth when we unlocked the door to our condominium and turned on the Do Not Disturb light.

It was about 5:00 a.m. and still dark. Exhausted, I headed for the shower, the refreshing water cleansing me of the muck of the Boulevard and the terror we had just encountered. Why, we could have been ... I shook the thought from my mind and the water washed it down the drainpipe. Then Tim showered, but we couldn't go to sleep yet as our night out was supposed to finish at 6:00 a.m.

Around 5:45 the sun rose over the mountains in glorious brilliance. I snapped a few pictures while admiring the handiwork of our Father. As soon as the luminous digits of the clock declared 6:00 we tumbled into bed and slept the entire morning. For the rest of our stay we came back to the hotel during daylight hours. The unpleasant occurrence was forgotten, as was the large man who had escorted us to the elevator.

CHAPTER 17

AN ANNIVERSARY AND AN ELECTION

"We love because he first loved us" *1 John 4:19 (NIV)*.

BEFORE WE KNEW IT, we had reached our first big milestone of five years. However, as it is the second marriage for both of us, we recognize each day as a milestone and try to live as though it is indeed one. In June 2016, out of the blue—a color that has taken on literal meaning to represent things of Heaven for me—Tim surprised me with the glorious suggestion: *Let's go back to the Trump Hotel in Las Vegas in November for our fifth anniversary.*

I needed no persuasion. We had held our reception in Saskatchewan in November the year we got married, following the end of harvest, and had maintained a tradition of celebrating in both July and November. But in 2016 it was doubly exciting, for the United States was gearing up for its 45th presidential election, also scheduled for November. More intoxicating was the fact that Donald Trump was the Republican candidate.

Since the early 2000s, I had faithfully followed episodes of *The Apprentice*, which was later changed to *Celebrity Apprentice*, the star of which was Mr. Trump. Until he ran for the presidency and left the show, it was my favorite one on television. Both Tim and I felt giddy at the thought of being in his hotel and a part of the election, possibly witnessing him become the 45th president of the United States of America.

We booked our tickets and arrived in Las Vegas on November 7th.

"Is this your first time here?" the cheerful clerk at the registration desk inquired as she checked us into the Superior Room I had reserved.

"No," I gushed. "We had our wedding and honeymoon here and are back for our fifth anniversary."

"Congratulations, and thank you for coming back." It was her turn to gush. "Loyal customers deserve a reward. I'm going to upgrade your room to a Deluxe King room with a view of the Strip."

I was breathless and flabbergasted at the kindness. This emphasis on loyalty, a trait Donald Trump underscored repeatedly in *Celebrity Apprentice*, prevails as his company's culture. Widely-acknowledged marks of Mr. Trump's success are that he surrounds himself with loyal people, and he rewards loyalty. Here was the culture of loyalty in action, and we were the recipients.

This time our upgraded room was on the 36th floor overlooking the Strip, a spectacular picture of hotels and casinos, landscape in the distance, and lights everywhere. From the bed or the plush loveseat of suite 3605 we took in the sweeping view of Treasure Island, the Palazzo, and a host of other hotels. Their signs were a hypnotic show of flashing lights and changing colors. Beyond and below Nevada sprawled far and wide.

The meals we ate were consistently superb. My well-done steak that night was more tender than I ever imagined beef could be. Tim also rated his medium-rare as better than any medium-rare he had eaten elsewhere in the world, and he grew up on a cattle ranch. A quick peek at the Las Vegas website had named fried chicken and waffles a must-to-taste when visiting. Fried chicken I love, so there was no contest for our first breakfast on November 8th, election Tuesday.

Election fever had gripped us as much as it had the Americans, and we were privileged to be first-hand observers at a polling station in a school three miles from the hotel in Clark County, Nevada, on that historic day. We signed the observer forms and took seats in the designated section. The voting was done electronically, and I was intrigued at the sophisticated method, compared to the manual system in Canada for voting and counting ballots. I had worked with provincial and municipal elections in both Canada and Trinidad, and my strong interest in this area had escalated my fascination with the American electoral process.

The Assistant Edge Officer directed voters to the voting terminals while announcing, "Yellow goes to yellow," a reference for the yellow part of the card to be placed in the yellow slot of the terminal. I was impressed at how educational and transparent the explanations of the issues on the ballot were, and how individuals voted for major decisions such as climate change. I consider it an honor, an unrivaled experience, to have been an observer of the U.S. 2016 presidential election.

Upon our return, we passed a dozen or so protesters on Fashion Show Drive, standing a discreet distance from the hotel. They held placards and were saying things that were not discernible to us, but they did not disturb the peace nor did they enter the Trump premises. The city police had taken up posts outside the hotel alongside security. My excitement heightened at the implication of their increased presence.

I smiled at an officer and remarked, "We are standing on the premises of the future president."

He smiled and made a gesture. I knew that in his capacity he could not concede or deny the success of candidates.

"As tourists, we are blown away to be in a historic place at such a historic time."

I was eager to share my joy. We made a bit more small talk before going inside. In our room, we showered hastily and got dressed, then headed back down for the party.

The atmosphere was electrifying, pulsating, and galvanizing at Trump Hotel that evening. The energy in the bar/lounge was palpable as we gathered around the large screens. We had taken red Canada T-shirts and flags to use at the election party, but I wore a chic red dress instead. Tim wore his T-shirt. Our red hats from the gift shop splayed TRUMP in white letters on our heads.

The crowd was a mixed one of diverse ethnicities, and we were welcomed with warm smiles and greetings. "In one accord" was a theme as cheers and chants for Donald Trump alternated with boos and thumbs down for Hillary Clinton. As the results began coming in, the crowd swelled, and even standing room became difficult to find. We couldn't hear the television because of the noise in that packed crowd, so we had to read what we could and cheer in unison with the rest.

An avalanche of results came in and then, unexpectedly, a lull in the coverage was filled in with interviews. The tension was mounting. Something had happened and the interviews were a way of stalling time. I guessed at it then the caption flashed "Ryan calls to congratulate Mr. Trump" and I inferred that Donald Trump was the new president.

By now it was nearly midnight, and we decided to leave the party and go up to our room so we could actually hear President Trump deliver his address. That was personal to us on many levels: we had received much kindness at Trump Hotel, a direct result of the culture of the Trump organization that came from the head himself. We admire Mr. Trump's children and his ability to integrate them into his current marriage and into one harmonious family. We did not jump on a Trump-train because of the election. I had liked him since I saw him on *The Apprentice* more than a dozen years earlier, and Tim and I had supported the President-Elect when his title was only "Mr.". And here we were standing on his property as he was declared the 45th President of the United States of America.

That historic experience is unmatched and the memory indelible. We stayed up until around 2:30 a.m., reveling in the news and reruns of the unprecedented victory, until at last we turned off the television and sleep overtook us.

CHAPTER 18

ANGEL AT TRUMP HOTEL

"... the Father of glory, may give to you a spirit of wisdom and of revelation ..." Ephesians 1:17 (NASB)

I AWOKE AT 8:30 a.m. to a feeling that might be described as hung-over. I've never drunk alcohol, but perhaps that was what it felt like the next day. I was not used to partying—my head throbbed and my throat ached from the cheering and staying up late. It was not unbearable, so we decided to go out for a stroll. But it had to be cut short as I quickly grew tired. Back at the hotel, I sought DayQuil™ from the gift shop then gratefully fell into bed.

"Help me to get better, Jesus," I prayed several times during the day. "I want to be well for the show."

We had bought tickets the day before for the Donny & Marie show scheduled for that evening. I hoped the prayer, medicine, and rest would pep me up as my anticipation at seeing the famous duo for the first time was high.

The day passed and night arrived. The show was enjoyable, but I couldn't help dreaming of my bed and of DayQuil™. That was not re-assuring, because we had also purchased tickets for the Grand Canyon tour, scheduled for the next morning, Thursday, and those cost a hundred and twenty-five dollars American apiece. Regrettably, the tickets were non-refundable.

But Thursday morning found me worse. When the alarm sounded at 4:30 a.m., my head was pounding and my nostrils were plugged. I felt dizzy at the thought of the bus ride.

"I can't go to the Canyon," I moaned to Tim. "But you must go. Give my ticket to someone."

He shook his head. "I can't leave you alone."

"I won't be alone," I assured him. "I'll order room service, and the maid will bring me more water."

Water was actually the only thing I wanted. My throat was sore and the thought of food, repulsive. Tim shook his head again.

"Go and enjoy it," I pleaded. "You will see a wonder I've not seen."

If there's one thing I love as much as reading it is visiting new places, and I'd done a fair bit of traveling and sightseeing over the years. To be so close to the Grand Canyon and not see it, and having purchased a ticket and being too ill to use it, was pitiful. But we could mitigate the losses if one of us went. Besides, it simply was not fair for Tim to be hotel-bound just because I was.

At 5:15 a.m., he reluctantly left with both tickets for Treasure Island where he would board the tour bus. I snuggled back into the piles of luxurious sheets and down comforter and pillows, certain I had breathed in a virus during the election party. A cold and flu smack dab in the middle of my week-long holiday was simply dreadful.

"Settle my stomach and help me to feel better, Lord," I prayed, groaning and moaning from the dizziness. "Strengthen me, please."

I didn't want a full breakfast, so I did not order room service. On the main floor opposite the gift shop is a "To Go" kiosk that opened for a couple of hours each morning at 9:00 a.m. I could get fruit there to take with the DayQuil™ since taking meds on an empty stomach does not usually go well.

The news channels naturally carried fevered coverage of the election of President Trump, and my unusually warm body indicated my own fever. I tuned in to Fox, a channel I did not get at home. It was a pleasant diversion and helped to pass the hours. At 9:00 a.m. my head was still throbbing, but by now my nose was runny. I slipped on my robe, grabbed some tissue, and shuffled to the elevator, happy for the relative privacy of the kiosk's location. There I purchased a banana and a croissant. The female security guard near the elevator encouraged me to feel better soon.

Back in the room I nibbled on the croissant. It melted in my mouth, reminding me of the ones I'd had in Paris earlier in February, but I could only manage a morsel. The banana was easier to get down. I took another dose of DayQuil™ then turned down the volume on the television. I must have dozed, for the next thing I heard was a knock on the door.

It was the maid. I didn't have the energy to reply, and she, clearly assuming the quietness meant no one was in, entered.

She started when she saw me. "I'm sorry, I'm sorry." The petite housekeeper was clearly flustered at her intrusion.

"It's no problem," I wheezed. "I wanted you to come in."

"Are you feeling well?" Her voice was filled with concern.

"No," I replied, "I'm feeling very sick. Don't make my bed, just change the towels and give me some more water, please."

"Oh, let me make your bed," the enthusiastic employee beseeched. "You will feel better if the bed is made up."

"I really can't get up," I replied. "But you could give me more water."

Still begging to make my bed, she whipped out a little notebook. Part of their responsibility in housekeeping was to know what was happening in each room and with each guest. She tugged at the sheets to achieve some semblance of order and fluffed the pillows Tim had slept on. I had to admit it was cheering to see the bed neat. She replaced the towels and tidied my cosmetics in the bathroom, replenishing the fragrant toiletries in their svelte square bottles with gold lettering and lids. Next she emptied the trash, lined up seven bottles of water in the kitchenette, and placed an extra box of tissue on the night table. Then she pulled a waste basket close to the bed. My purse was on the bed so I fished out a tip.

"Thank you very much," I croaked. "You're very kind."

"I hope you feel better soon," she replied, accepting the tip. Then she turned her cart and exited the room.

Help me, Lord. Help me to feel better.

I blew my nose on the soft tissue. My head hurt at the motion. The water felt good on my parched tongue, although my throat burned when I tried to swallow it. I thought of Tim on the bus trip and me shut up in the hotel and felt a little sorry for myself. Why weren't good things happening to me?

That's when I prayed, "Let something good happen to me today, Lord. Anything."

I closed my eyes and was soon asleep. Half an hour later I awoke to quietness. The television was still on with no volume. I sipped more water, wide awake now, and that's when the revelation came. The "remembers" as I like to refer to them.

Remember that morning when you were coming back to this hotel from the night out on the Strip? Remember the African-American youth coming at you and the danger? Remember the tall, big guy in dark clothing on the hill who looked like a Mexican? Remember how he waited and was watching you? Remember how the young man turned back when he saw him? Remember how the man followed you to the elevator?

That was no ordinary man. He was an Angel!

The hairs on every pore on my limbs rose at right angles to my body. I had been shivering and turning with a fever and the flu, but this response was not due to my illness. This was the voice of God. Not a loud, external voice, as the words were not audible. Instead, they came from somewhere inside me. My mind went back to the pre-dawn hours of Sunday, July 24th, 2011. I could close my eyes and relive it—the fear that had gripped me as the incensed youth strode towards us swearing, hurling insults, and whistling calls to gang members.

The big man was dressed in informal street clothes, not the typical attire of a guest of the Trump Hotel, a high-end luxury hotel that attracts a certain clientele. The Angel could easily have been a street-tough bodyguard.

A bodyguard from Eternity.

I believed it. I believed it was an angel with every fiber of my being. God sends angels on missions, and one of their missions is to protect us from physical danger. The Bible described the angel of the Lord shutting the mouths of the lions so they could not harm Daniel (Daniel 6:22). He sent one in Las Vegas to protect us. Angels are invisible unless God opens our eyes and gives us the ability to see them. When that happens, they take on the appearance of real men, as in Abraham's case (Genesis 18:2-15). In Acts 12, Peter's eyes were opened to see the angel who came to rescue him.

As my mind absorbed this revelation, I wondered why, in the five years since that night, I had never thought of that. Why here, back in

Las Vegas, while lying sick in Trump Hotel, had the truth finally been revealed?

As I typed this chapter, I paused, overwhelmed by another revelation dropped in my spirit:

I'm always sick or vulnerable when I experience my biggest spiritual moments, because that is when my attention is on the Lord. Nowhere else. I turn only to Him in those times.

Even though I was immersed in an opulent hotel, I was oblivious to my surroundings as I called on *Him* to make me well. God showed me He was in this place. Yes, God is everywhere, ever-present. Some refer to Las Vegas as "Sin City", but it is no more sinful than anywhere else. Wherever there are people, there will be sin because people are the ones who commit sin, and people abound everywhere in the world and not just in Las Vegas. The Scriptures say, "Where there is sin, greater grace abounds. But where sin abounded, grace did much more abound" Romans 5:20 (KJV).

If sin is bigger in Las Vegas than elsewhere, it stands to reason that God's bigger grace exists there. Should it be called Grace City instead?

God and His angels are present everywhere on this earth. God sent His angel to protect us in Las Vegas. God gave me the revelations right there on the soil of Las Vegas. It is in those times that I am sick that God speaks and shows me things that remained unrevealed until then.

I had lots of time to ponder as I lay in bed, and I did. Fashion Show Drive is a quiet street off the busy Strip. The mall was closed and there were no people around. It was not a spot where friends hung out. No buses ran there. Why was a big, tall man standing there at that hour of the morning? Who was he waiting for? Who was he with? Why did the African-American youth stop suddenly in the middle of the road as if he had run into a barrier? Did he in fact see a barrier?

The Bible story of Balaam's donkey and the angel popped in my mind, along with a memory of one of my childhood books by author Susan Coolidge. In *What Katy Did* a rhyme about Balaam went like this:

Balaam's donkey saw the angel
And stopped short in fear.
Balaam did not see the angel
Which was very queer.[1]

Did the young man see the angel the same time as I did? Once I had seen the man, I had felt relieved, happy, not at all fearful, as if I knew, somehow, that he was on our side. Did the youth turn around because of fear of who—or what—he saw? The Mexican-looking man appeared as though he'd be right at home in the roughest situation. He was dressed the part, and his brawn and size backed that up. Had the youth met his match?

Although Tim had seen the man walking behind us towards the hotel, I had not. But I *knew* he was there through the thoughts entering my mind. That was consistent with my other supernatural experiences. The man's shoes had made no sound. I have no recollection of him entering the revolving doors or walking across the immaculate floors. But angels have the ability to appear visible or invisible as needed. Was he invisible to the "good" people and visible to the "bad" guy? Did the front desk staff see him? I'm sure they were good people, so maybe not. How about the security guard? He was good too. Employee loyalty was evident at Trump Hotel, so it is far-fetched that any rough and tumble-looking visitor would proceed beyond the elevators unnoticed. Security was high as well. We had to show our card every single time we went to the elevators. We had even seen a well-dressed young lady denied entry to the elevators—she had to notify her party to come down and escort her.

I could hardly wait to share the news with Tim, but I knew I'd have to hold off until the next day, for he'd be getting home late. Around 10:00 p.m. he came in exhausted from his trip with a 3D postcard of the Grand Canyon for me. I took another dose of DayQuil™ and we drifted off to sleep.

The next day was Friday, our last full day in Las Vegas. I felt better, so we ventured out to buy souvenirs. We kept the shopping trip short, as I was far from able to walk the Strip. We ate a late lunch at the Food Court in Fashion Show Mall then decided to go to the pool.

The 110-foot heated outdoor pool is located on the 7th floor of Trump Hotel. We settled on lounge chairs, drinking in the beauty of the green palms waving against a blue sky. More palms were arranged attractively around the pool. Families swam lazily in the water. The sun blazed hot at four o'clock, burning my bare arms, but the heat didn't bother me. Without preliminaries, I rushed to the heart of the matter.

"Tim, do you remember that morning when we were returning from the Strip?"

"Yes," he replied. "It's hardly something I can forget."

"Tell me what you remember."

He contemplated me, scrunching his forehead. My urgent tone was a giveaway that I wanted details. He looked at the pool then back at me, as if knowing he could not go in until the conversation was finished.

Tim proceeded to describe how the African-American youth had hurled swear words at us, then whistled and had a whistle call returned. He talked about us hurrying up the hill, and the young man starting to walk towards us.

"Do you remember who was ahead of us?"

"A tall, big man who looked like a Mexican."

"What was he wearing?"

"A black T-shirt and black shorts that came down to his knees."

"What was his hair like?'

"Short and cut close to his head."

My questions kept tumbling out. "What was he doing?"

"He was standing near the top of the hill and was looking in our direction."

"What was his posture?"

"He was standing straight."

"Do you think the youth turned back when he saw him?" I asked.

"I'm not sure when the youth saw him, or if that was the reason he turned back, but it seemed to coincide." Tim jumped into his usual analytical mode. "All I know is that when he got halfway across the road, he stopped as if a chain had tugged him back."

"I felt the same." I grabbed Tim's hand. "It was as if he bumped into a wall and could not move forward so he turned back. Were you afraid when you saw the Mexican man?"

"At first I wondered if he was in cahoots with the younger man, but the youth turned back and the man didn't do anything to us," he replied.

"I wasn't afraid." I shifted in my chair. "I felt that this man could be a witness that we did not provoke a fight with the other man."

I exhaled loudly. "Do you think he was dressed like the average guest at a hotel like Trump's?"

"No." Tim's response was swift.

"But he got in the elevator, and only guests who show a card are allowed there."

I hadn't looked to see if the man had a card. I didn't make eye contact. I had been rattled by the incident and only wanted to be alone with my husband. I couldn't shake the thought, though, that angels can be visible and invisible as needed.

Above, the sky was cornflower. High mountains surrounded us. I recalled the psalm of King David: "I will lift up mine eyes unto the hills from whence cometh my help. My help cometh from the Lord which made heaven and earth" Psalm 121:1-2 (KJV).

I breathed in the beauty, my soul full as I pondered on my Lord.

"I was wondering why the man started to follow us. I figured if he was up to no good he could have snatched my purse or done something bad. But he didn't do anything like that."

"It's a mystery what he was doing at that spot at that hour. It's not a usual hanging-out spot. It's not impossible that's what he was there for, but it's very coincidental." Tim was thoughtful too.

Unless someone wanted to protect a hotel guest.

"Do you remember what floor the man punched?" I gripped the arms of my chair. Would Tim remember? I hadn't paid attention to the details, but how was I to know we were experiencing something miraculous?

He shook his head.

"Tim." I grabbed his hand and he stared into my face. "The thought came to me yesterday that the Mexican man was an angel sent to protect us. I prayed and asked God to let something nice happen because I was feeling so down, and that memory came. I believe God revealed it to me."

Tim appeared to digest that information. "If ever we needed an angel to show up, it was then."

I nodded. "Do you remember what the African-American man was wearing?"

"No."

Neither did I.

"But here we are five years later, and we both remember the description of the Mexican man and our accounts match up. That is supernatural. Can you remember another person as conspicuously as that from our other travels?"

Tim couldn't remember anyone of significance from our travels with such details, nor could I. Neither of us could recall what any of the guests wore to our wedding five years ago. Yet here we were calling up memories, clear descriptions of a mundane fellow in street garb walking behind us and getting into the elevator with us. That kind of remembering is consistent with my visions of and visits to Heaven—the details of the supernatural remain stark and vivid.

"Do you believe, Tim?" I had to know. This was too important. The revelation had been like an electric current running through my body, but he had to feel it too.

"I believe." His simple reply was sincere. Then, with his usual humor, he added, "Using Las Vegas terms, it might be better to say, 'I bet that's what it was'."

Abruptly I got up from my chair and, hand in hand, we walked the length of the pool and beyond, scrutinizing the private air-conditioned cabanas with their wet bars and plasma TVs. Nursery-sized palms grew in pots set near the bars. Through the glass doors leading back into the building, we could see the 11,000-square foot Spa at Trump®. Tim changed his mind about taking a dip, so after our exploration, we headed back to our room.

As we got into the elevator, we looked at each other. Was he thinking the same thing I was? We had been blessed materially twice at this hotel, and he had encountered his first angel here.

The implications were bigger than I could wrap my mind around. Why would an angel protect us while another person went unprotected? We had not walked wilfully into danger, nor had we gone to indulge in fleshly desires. Ours was a tourist stroll for taking photos and seeing how "iconic" the iconic Strip really was. Even so, if our lives had been extinguished we knew our spirits would live on in the afterlife. Was God preserving me for a greater cause? This year was 2016 and I'd already had two visits to Eternity, so the revelation of a supernatural experience with an angel that had happened in 2011 was not far off the radar.

But whereas it was Tim's first encounter with an angel, it was not mine. Our conversation had reached deep inside and awakened a sleeping memory. By the time he pressed the button marked 36 in the elevator, I was back in Trinidad and it was 1995.

CHAPTER 19

ANGEL AT PARK STREET

"For he shall give his angels charge over thee …" Psalm 91:11a (KJV).

I HAD COMPLETELY FORGOTTEN about July 1995 when my then-husband Thomas made a solo vacation trip to Canada. I had been in the early stages of signing up for a Masters Degree program at the University of the West Indies, so I remained behind. I saw him off at the airport and returned to our home on Park Street, Siparia, feeling singularly alone. As night approached, my apprehension grew. I've never liked being alone, in fact, I hate it. I ascribe this to being born into a family of nine children and always having someone around. I remember lying on the bed with my face down, praying and crying at the same time as I bared my heart to God.

"I'm afraid to be alone. I don't like this. How am I going to stay by myself?"

Instantly I felt someone enter the room. Now, I was lying face down, so I could not literally see anyone, yet I *saw* as if through other eyes. I know now they were the eyes of the Spirit. The person was tall and big, of African descent, and dressed in dark clothing. He laid something like a blanket or sheet over my body, which covered me entirely from my neck to my toes. Then he was gone.

It was not a tangible blanket that I could show anyone, but it was a blanket I could *see* in the spiritual sense. I remember feeling no fear, only curiosity and wonderment. That in itself is significant, given my history of being fearful. I felt there was more to the visit, but I wasn't sure what. It was a new experience, like nothing that had ever happened before. That night I slept soundly, fearless, with no thought that I was alone.

The next day I couldn't shake off the unusual visitation, so I phoned a senior pastor in the PAWI District with whom we were affiliated and asked if I could come in and speak to him. I did not share the details over the phone for two reasons: first, it was too sacred, and second, it sounded like a figment of a person's imagination, and I did not want to chance being dismissed. He agreed to see me and I drove to San Fernando. As I described my experience to the man of God, he did not laugh or scoff or do any of the things I had thought someone might do at hearing of such a peculiar situation.

Instead he remarked when I was finished, "It sounds like an angel, Susan. You've been visited by a warrior angel."

I had not thought of the "warrior" part, but the description seemed to fit. A strong, mighty angel on assignment to protect me. I had not been fearful when he presented himself, but God and His angels represent love and peace, not fear. I needed an angel, for I was vulnerable during that time, maybe more than I knew. The pastor's explanation seemed to be the only one that made sense. Except for him, I did not tell anyone else about the incident.

I stayed the duration of the time by myself until Thomas returned. Sixty-six days after the angelic encounter, I was lying on the bed alone. My eyes were closed. Once again someone entered the room. Immediately I knew who it was—the same big man in dark clothes. He pulled the blanket off me. At the same time the thought came to me that Thomas was my literal and symbolic covering, and now that he was back, there was no need for the angel's protection. But I had needed a covering while he was absent (Ephesians 5:23).

I don't know why the Lord has allowed me to have these experiences, but there is a sensitivity in my spirit that's only matured with age. I've seen angels and I've seen Heaven and Hell. I've walked in the Shadow of the Almighty. I've been to Eternity and I've been healed. God has given me the ability to write and to speak. Could it be that He allows me to see and experience these things for the purpose of sharing them so others can be drawn to Christ?

When I narrated this incident to Tim while writing this book, his first question was, "What is the meaning of sixty-six?"

Tim knew I placed significance on the timing of events, on numbers, names, and words. I firmly believe words especially carry life and death, and that they shape my future.

I turned to the Internet for the meaning of sixty-six. Ridingthe-beast[1] website states that the number sixty-six represents the reduction or the loss of faith in the Divine Plan. That was true of me, for in being fearful, I had expressed faithlessness rather than faith, thereby prompting God to send an assurance.

CHAPTER 20

EXILE

"Call to me and I will answer you and tell you great and unsearchable things you do not know" *Jeremiah 33:3 (NIV)*.

ALTHOUGH I REFRAINED FROM speaking about Heaven, I thought of it frequently. In 2013 I heard of the book called *Heaven is for Real*, by Todd Burpo.[1] In it he tells of his son's visit to Heaven during an NDE. I stayed far from the book, skeptical. I had never heard of someone going to Heaven and coming back besides myself, nor that supernatural happenings like these were taking place across the globe. But a kid? It wasn't until a friend at church talked about it that I ventured to read it. I read, repented for my scoffing, believed, and my experience of 1998 came flooding back. With remembering came yearning. A deep longing overtook me for the peace and serenity of that glorious, incomparable place on high. The depth of my desire surprised me, for it was startlingly like homesickness.

I mulled that over in my heart, and talked about it to my husband and daughter, wearying them with my crushing disappointment of returning back to earth. I was satisfied with my life from the point of view that I desired nothing material, and I had loved ones I was happy to return to. I had accomplished far above what I had ever imagined in this life, and was content.

Still, Heaven began to consume my thoughts. Heaven drew me compellingly. I pondered it by day and brooded over it by night. I began to feel as if I no longer belonged to Earth; I became preoccupied, engrossed with the meadow in Heaven to the point that I phoned my ex-husband who had been a witness the day I collapsed in the OB/GYN's office and peppered him with questions. I was driven to find out the details. I couldn't get enough of what had occurred in that office and what I had said to the two men present.

When I explained to my friends that I didn't have goals, a few raised their eyebrows. They couldn't understand my non-desire for earthly or material things. With good intentions, they urged me to set new goals.

"Go on a boat and put your hand in the water and touch the dolphins," encouraged one well-meaning friend. That was her dream, not mine. If dolphin-touching had appealed to me, I would have done it at SeaWorld in Florida years ago.

"Why would I live other people's dreams?" I replied. She remained silent.

I was frustrated. Would anyone ever understand? I know now that it is impossible for anyone who did not have my experience to truly understand, because their spiritual eyes have not been opened in this dimension.

Other friends interpreted my contentment as complacency, and my desire for Heaven rather than earth as pessimism, which infuriated me. Their short-sightedness only increased my longing for Heaven, to get away from the striving that had once seemed so normal. They knew the ambitious individual I had been, but how I wished they could understand that my perspective had changed. I had held prestigious jobs and earned good salaries, owned lovely homes, and had become an author. Writing for publication had never been on my wish list, it just happened, and when *Little Copper Pennies* and *Little Copper Pennies for Kids* took off in Canada following the removal of the one-cent coin in 2012, I knew I had achieved far beyond what I could ask or think. I, who had never aspired to being a writer, have my books in libraries and homes throughout Canada and on international websites, and a letter of congratulations from our then Prime Minster. I was content.

Through my second marriage, I attained the blessing described in Joshua 24:13: "I gave you land you had not worked on…I gave you vineyards and olive groves for food, though you did not plant them" (NLT). God had given me over and above what I deserved, and I couldn't ask for more. It was as though my desire for earthly accolades and possessions had been taken hostage by the pull of Heaven.

My family, too, would look confused when I talked of wanting to go back. It came across to them as if I didn't love or care for them. They seemed hurt, and did not enjoy hearing about the subject. I love my husband and daughter and my friends and relatives. But it would take someone who had set foot on or seen that glorious beyond to understand why I never wanted to come back to this inferior world, and so far I had not met anyone like that in person.

Inasmuch as I was still living, I identified traveling as something that could occupy my days and allow me to see more of God's creation and how it compared to Heaven. Paris, Monaco, Brazil, the Caribbean islands, and the Hawaiian Islands remained low in the running. I acknowledge the beauty created by the most Holy God, but Heaven surpasses anything considered beautiful on earth. It is in the sky that I see the colors best depictive of Heaven—in the rainbow, lightning, and Northern Lights. God has truly saved the best for last, to be enjoyed forever when the New Jerusalem comes down to the New Earth.

On Sep 21st, 2016, my television was on and The Dr. Oz Show filled the screen. His guest, a pastor named Tony Davis, told his story of being brutally beaten by a gang of youths. Davis died while under medical care and went to Heaven. He described colors, images, and God. But thirty minutes after Davis was declared dead, as the doctor was about to draw a sheet over his body, Davis took a deep breath and opened his eyes. In the interview he said that God told him it wasn't his time to stay in Heaven, and he needed to go back to earth and forgive.[2]

I was mesmerized, glued to the screen, and something stirred in me. My hitherto unknown mission became clear:

Put my trips to Heaven in words so that those who do not believe may hear and perhaps gain Heaven.

I have a good life and a great family, and as sure as I know we love each other, I know with the same certainty that my work on earth is not yet done. I have a huge responsibility. I will occupy my time with writing and travel to tell of God's Eternity. After years of actively obsessing about Heaven, I accepted the fact that I was to remain on earth a while longer, and my purpose was to write down the revelations and speak of them. Those unimaginable, word-defying, mind-blowing, indescribable colors, sights, and wonderment that I had glimpsed. The immensity of its proportions, the bigness of its transparent beings. I pray that I will find the words to create pictures, the concrete illustrations to tell of the abstract, for the unction of the Holy Spirit to do what I am incapable of—bring it all alive and whet a desire for the true and living God in the hearts of the listeners and readers. I know I can do it through His abiding grace, which is continually with me.

I was overtaken with wanting to know who else had been there and what they had seen, so in the new year I borrowed a few books from the public library and read about Marvin Besteman's experience in *My Journey to Heaven*,[3] Dr. Mary Neal's *To Heaven and Back*,[4] and *Proof of Heaven* by Dr. Eben Alexander.[5] And I saw a trend among "us". I noticed that most people who had an NDE or were pronounced dead and sent back found themselves in the presence of Jesus or a light, with loved ones, inside Heaven, or in the garden, while some included a description of their trip to get there. In these authors I found a commonality that mirrored my posture. People who had seen Jesus, angels, or Heaven when near death, often felt as I did when they returned to earth–frustrated, discontented with this world, and wanting to go back. Like theirs, my NDE became the catalyst for writing as it provided material for a book. The spirit of people craves to know what comes after life on earth, for we all are going somewhere when we die. What I write is meant to invite thought and discussion, to build faith in those who do not have it or whose may be wavering, and to encourage those who already believe.

In October, a few weeks after watching that episode on The Dr. Oz Show, our new house would be ready. I took the beautiful house as God's reward for me to remain on earth. The project had been my focus since August, and I had the feeling that once I was settled on the quiet acreage, I'd write about the world above. But although the house was set in place in October, the long wait for water to be hooked up meant we could not move in. Then the new year rolled in and I accepted a full-time job, stifling the call to record my story.

In April 2017 we finally moved to the acreage. That month I also resigned the job.

Putting the house in order in the first few weeks was enjoyable, but as the second month unfolded, the lack of company began to affect me. Some days my husband would leave for the office while I was still asleep, and return from the fields after I had gone to bed.

Even the animals stayed away. In spite of my allergies to pet dander, we brought our Siamese cat, Paris, from the farm in the hopes of making her an indoor pet, but when she hyper-ventilated so pitifully, her normally blue eyes huge and brown, we took her back to the barn and the rest of the cats. She visited on a timetable that was at whim and could not be counted on.

Mournfully, Smokey, my Lynx Siamese whom I had written about in *Chicken Soup for the Soul*[6] and taken on television and to schools, did not darken the yard with his presence, nor did old Strawberry for that matter. An unwelcome plague of tent caterpillars forced me to shut myself inside for weeks, the blinds pulled down against their revolting sight, isolating me even further. For a short time I felt alone, lonely, and dissatisfied.

I had lost sight of my mission.

On June 13th, 2017, I awoke with the pressing desire to fast and pray. I tried to ignore the nudge that I had fallen away from a love, from the routine of fasting that had marked my walk with God for decades. As the hours wore on, I felt a clear sense of peace and purpose. Slowly the realization came that God was drawing me to Himself.

Had I not prayed in despair, desperate to see more of Heaven? Had I not felt in my heart that I would write the manuscript when I came to live on the acreage? Yet here I was, not holding up my end of the bargain. I was failing, flawed as I have always been. Age had not provided the wisdom I needed in a timely manner. In hindsight, I'd waited longer than I should have. Where was the foresight I so badly needed? We did not subscribe to satellite TV, so that distraction was removed. My client's book had been launched, meaning I could relax now and stay away from social media. No other people were around, save for the contractors who came now and then.

God was going to reveal, to speak, and I felt excitement rising. A renaissance was on its way. I sensed this would be a day of change, and fasting would be easy. I lay on the daybed near the window and prayed for several friends whose names came to mind. Later I emailed a few of them about what I'd prayed for, and each was amazed at the leading of the Holy Spirit on issues that I could not have known unless God had revealed them to me.

That day I begged God as I've been beseeching afresh since September 2016—to see more of Heaven. And He heard and answered.

That day I saw the Green Room which I write about in chapter 33. That day I also had the revelation:

I was being reduced to the company of the Trinity only. Alone. In exile. I was in the place God wanted me. He wanted me for Himself. He is a jealous God, but more pertinently, He wanted to show me the great and unsearchable things which have not been revealed to others. Things they cannot search on the Internet or in any earthly resource. He wanted me to call so He could tell me the things unbeknownst to human beings, just as He offered in Jeremiah 33:3.

A place of exile, like where John the beloved disciple was when he saw the vision of Heaven that's penned in the book of Revelation. In exile he saw Eternity. Alone, he saw the details of the life that I had only glimpsed. I begged the Father to show me again. I know now I could only see more when my senses were deadened to this world, for then those senses could be made alive to the next world. The option is binary—there must be a surrender. When my senses compete for earthly things I cannot achieve Heaven.

Except for the short time I saw my husband in the night, I was alone. I had no desire to text or call the workplace. My interest in social media waned. Even finding employment took a back seat. I was driven to pray, to read, to listen, to write. All I wanted was more of Heaven, and to share it with the world.

The evening of the fast it rained. The week before, longed-for rain had fallen on nearby towns but had failed to fall on our crops. How we needed the water! Because it rained, Tim was at home. He decided to put together a bookshelf for me, but instead of doing the charitable act of keeping his company, I began to type the manuscript for this book. I barely made conversation. I was engrossed, joyful as the words flew from my head, through my fingers, and on to the document on my laptop.

The next day it rained again and once more he was at home for the entire evening.

"I'm writing my book and I don't need company," I remarked merrily.

He looked puzzled. Excitedly I shared my revelations from God and how He had spoken to me through the restoration of our trees following the devastation of the tent caterpillars plague. I was persuaded this testimony was worthy of publication, a message to inspire, and pitched it to the PAOC. My joy was boundless when it was accepted for their magazine, aptly named *Testimony*. The article, entitled "Into the Great Unordinary," graced the September-October 2017 issue.[7] My faith zoomed large and my praises to God accelerated.

I described to Tim how God showed me the Green Room.

"Does it sound crazy?" I searched his eyes.

"No," he assured me. "It's not crazy."

"I wish you could see Heaven, too."

"I'd have to be sick almost to dying," he quipped.

Uh oh. Living alone, and living alone on an acreage, poor health was not to be joked about, so I snuffed the idea of him seeing Heaven. I've seen enough for the two of us, and more! The third consecutive day of rain kept him indoors again, and after assembling a second bookshelf, he went to bed and I continued writing into the night.

I had found my purpose. I had plugged into the higher, the solitude, the exile where I was able to meet alone with my God.

CHAPTER 21

POPOPOP

"… I will strengthen you, surely I will help you …" Isaiah 41:10 (NASB).

POPOPOPOPOPOPOPOP.

On August 7th, 2014, my heart was racing at a pace that would put a cheetah to shame. My rational brain instructed me to pull the car onto the shoulder of the highway, but my impulse was to let go of the steering wheel.

Pull over. Let go. Pull over. Let go.

My lids came together as nausea rose in my throat and clamored for a way out. The pounding in my chest drummed copiously in my ears. I was hot and wet with sweat. What was happening?

Pull over and stop!

I maneuvered the red vehicle to the shoulder as my body trembled and rib cage shook.

"Help me, Lord." My whisper was hoarse, the broken kind He hears because He Himself had hung ragged on a rugged cross. The car shook as vehicles whizzed by, then stabilized as they gained distance. But there was no stabilizing for me. Every nerve in my body was on high alert as my heart played its tantrum.

"Jesus, Jesus, Jesus …"

Over and over I repeated that hallowed name. I was twenty-five kilometers from my destination, and all I could do was call on the One who was always with me. Then, as suddenly as it came on, the nausea was gone and my heart settled like a contented baby's into the normal thrum, thrum I was used to.

Praise You, Jesus. Thank You, Jesus. I was weak after the ordeal, but at least I could continue to drive. It was imperative there be no accident, for I was using my employer's vehicle. My car was in the parking lot of the

City of Melville municipal office. My goal was to get the vehicle back intact.

When I had stuck the key in the ignition that morning and the engine had purred to life the last thought on my mind was that *my* life would spiral out of control through a recalcitrant heart. I had planned to start my day by picking up the beautiful signage, fresh and newly-made for the Railway Museum heritage site, and then process some paperwork. This was my first time working with the City and I wanted to be my best.

I checked the mirrors, looked over my shoulder, and pulled cautiously on to the highway. I wished I had used my own car and absorbed the mileage cost, but wishing was as helpful as prairie fog. Thankfully, the vehicle ate the kilometers without mishap, and I exhaled loudly as the city limits came in view. When I parked in front of the Tourism office, I felt like a soap bubble that had withstood the wind.

The summer student assisted me in unloading the signage from the back seat. It had appeared effortless when the artist had placed them inside, but they were heavy and awkward to handle. Now only one task remained—drive the car the final two kilometers back to the City garage. That should be easy enough.

I had barely parked the car when I began to shiver like a leaf. The popopop had returned.

"I don't feel well. I'm going to the doctor's and will return to work afterwards," I blurted to the closest co-worker.

I drove the two blocks south to the medical center. Saliva filled my mouth as I walked to the reception desk.

"I'd like to see a doctor. My heart is racing." The labored breathing was evident.

"We do not accept walk-ins," the receptionist replied primly. "And if your heart is racing you should go to the ER."

My legs were porridge as I trudged back to my car.

Hold me up, Lord. Let me not collapse. Get me safely to the hospital.

The hospital was three and a half kilometers across the highway. Gasping air through my mouth, I fought the urge to slump on the steering wheel. My chest felt as though 500 pounds were pressing on it. Where the ability came to traverse the streets and avenues, get on

Hwy 10, and turn into the parking lot of 200 Heritage Drive, I can only explain as supernatural. Calling on Jesus under my breath and grabbing my chest, I hobbled to the chair in front of the receptionist. The trained eyes of the worker took in the hyper-ventilating, the hand, the crumpled blazer of an otherwise attractively-dressed woman.

"Chest pains?"

I nodded. An EMT rushed to my side.

"Take her to the first bed." The receptionist's request was urgent.

The paramedic took my arm and we entered the outpatient emergency area. Nurses whipped off magenta, black, violet. Blazer, cami, bra. The care team was comprised of males and females, but this was not the forum for modesty. In a blur my blood pressure was taken, colored circles stuck on my skin, and I was hooked up to a machine. Someone connected an oxygen tank to my nostrils and life-giving air filled my lungs.

"Set up an IV."

The head nurse's orders were quick and precise and a staff member sprang into action to give me fluid intravenously. Two bags hung on the pole ready to be connected to a needle on my wrist, but no amount of poking and prodding would locate the stubborn vein. Where, oh where, was my vein? The pain was crippling and the nausea choking when the errant vein was found.

"Owwwwwwwwww."

The discomfort of the needle puncturing my skin was minor in light of regulating my heart rate. The name of my condition is arrhythmia. Heart rhythm problem. The machine with the tubes and color stickers (electrode patches) is an electrocardiogram (ECG). An ECG measures the electrical activity of the heart, its rhythm and rate. A normal heart beats 60 to 100 thrums a minute—my medical record indicated mine was 184.

Within minutes, the doctor was at my side. Vaguely I understood that he was going to administer a fast-acting medication called adenosine into my veins. I would feel a shooting pain and my heart rate would rise higher, then it would drop to normal. If the adenosine failed to bring it down, he would have to use an electrical current to reset my heart. He could have used a car battery as my uncle had to power his black and white television set, and I would not have cared.

I moaned on the bed with tubes on my chest, tubes at my wrist, and tubes in my nostrils. The doctor counted out loud, but I was not prepared for the explosion of pain that rocked my body. I screamed, but thankfully the sensation was short-lived, a couple of seconds at most.

All eyes were glued on the monitor. Silence reigned. Then, in unison a cheer broke from the team as the scratchy ink point of 184 fell to a steady graph of 90 beats. Adenosine had won. I was out of danger, but I would be kept overnight until my heart settled down to my normal rate of 72 beats, or, God forbid, I took a turn for the worse. The monitoring would be done remotely using mobile cardiac telemetry (MCT) where the beats would be transmitted to the station at the nursing desk. If my situation worsened they'd be alerted and come to me immediately. I am indebted for the good care I received at St. Peter's Hospital.

The next morning, August 8th, the doctor informed me that I had experienced SVT—Supraventricular tachycardia. Tachycardia means greater than 100 beats a minute. Supra means above, and ventricle means the lower chamber of the heart. In other words, SVT is an abnormally fast heartbeat that is caused by faulty electrical signals in my heart originating above the ventricle in the atria.[1] He explained that tachycardia—fast beats—occurs when the electrical impulses that coordinate my heartbeats do not work properly. This leads to the fluttering feeling and racing heart. He prescribed Metoprolol, with admonitions to breathe in a paper bag or drink cold pop (soda) if I felt the SVT coming on.

I had a lot of time to wonder and ponder on my condition of irregular heartbeat following my discharge. I thought of my hospitalization for rheumatic fever at age fourteen, and the heart murmur that had been detected when I had taken a physical for life insurance. I recalled how after I immigrated to Canada I continued to ask the dentist for Amoxil whenever I had routine hygiene appointments. Eventually, he decided the improved technologies made dental hygiene practices much safer than before, and I had stopped taking antibiotics for dental work over the last ten years or so. I had replaced the outdoor jogging with walking on my treadmill when I moved to Saskatchewan, so my fitness level was not compromised. I was healthy overall. Where did SVT come from? Was it from the murmur?

At home on my bed, a recollection surfaced and I bolted upright. In 2004 I had secured short-term employment at a company I loved. Two years later I returned to the company. This time, however, the environment and work I had loved slowly became unlovable through overwork and the micro-managing of a noxious boss. Forbes expressed it well, "People leave managers, not companies."[2] I decided to resign the job and found myself a new position halfway across the province. But this job had been so stressful and harmful to my health that just days before leaving, something happened that I had not experienced before. A vice-like pain gripped my chest and my heart raced at a speed I had not known was possible, as if to cop first place in the marathons I had run in my younger days. I opened my mouth to breathe, but I was a captive to the worst feeling I could imagine. I shuffled to the door and stumbled to the office of a co-worker across the narrow corridor. She admonished me to go to the ER department right away.

Another co-worker found a wheelchair and took me to the ER of the hospital where we worked. Although my heart settled to normal before I was triaged, the tests and checks were still done. With the urgency gone, I was told I could go back to work, and I'd receive a follow-up appointment to take an ECG. I was relieved to be told I was all right and agreed to be contacted about the ECG.

I left for my new job and was happily immersed in it when I received the phone call for the appointment of the ECG. That meant driving halfway across the province. Since I had not had a recurrence of palpitations and was my usual energetic self, I declined the appointment. I had no history but for that one occurrence, and was not even taking Amoxil for dental appointments. I was moving up in my career, had just bought another house, and was successful overall. There was no need for the ECG, and in short time I had forgotten about the incident.

But, six years later, the arrhythmia had returned. Although I had not taken an ECG in 2008 when it first happened, I had taken one now in 2014. I was going to be all right.

CHAPTER 22

AT HANAUMA BAY

"He gives strength to the weary ..." *Isaiah 40:29a (NASB).*

WINTER IS OUR FAVORITE time for vacation, and in January 2015, the destination was Oahu, one of the Hawaiian Islands in the Pacific Ocean. A detailed planner, throughout December I created a spreadsheet with specific events and sights, noting each item twice. In case one event couldn't be done on a particular day, there'd be a back up. Pearl Harbour, Island Tour, Diamond Head, Rainforest Hike, Whale Watching, Kailua Turtle Safari, Guided Kayaking, Hanauma Bay, Aquarium, shopping, and football playoffs made the list.

We dissed the turtle safari and kayaking for a luau on the beach. While dinner at the Cheesecake Factory was the highlight of our meals, the assorted new and appetizing dishes at the luau at Paradise Cove took second place. I smile when I remember getting on stage to dance the hula with Radiance and others. Pearl Harbour is sacred and sobering, its historical significance and global impact overwhelming when standing on the actual sites.

Climbing the one hundred and seventy-five steps, going through the tunnels to the top of the iconic Diamond Head onto the crater of the extinct volcano, and gazing at the panoramic view of Honolulu, were spine tingling. The hike to the waterfall was nostalgic—a vivid reminder of the tropical beauty of my native Trinidad. And the blue waters calling my name from every direction could well have been the Caribbean Sea and Atlantic Ocean. Our closets are crammed with the unique fashions of Marshalls and the flea market. The shrimp lunch at the roadside restaurant as we toured the island was again very much in keeping with roadside cafes in Trinidad. The pineapple plantations, gift shops, and even the visit to a religious site I wouldn't usually be interested in but for the sheer use of the bathroom, were satisfying. The glimpses of the hospital where President Obama was born and the school he attended widened my eyes.

Yet, in spite of the charm and uniqueness of each sight, taste, and sound, none marked the vacation as significantly as what occurred at Hanauma Bay. World renowned for its delicate eco-system of coral and fishes, Hanauma Bay is reminiscent of Tobago's coral reef in the twin island republic of my country, Trinidad and Tobago.

It was not the snorkeling, which I was doing for the first time in the crystal waters. Going downhill from the theater to the bay was fun, but tears still blur my vision as I recall the walk up the steep hill after joyful hours of snorkeling. I should have caught the red flags, except one does not know what the warning signs are but in hindsight. The effort and deep breaths required for snorkeling were arduous. My chest had heaved over and over, but I had been okay. The uphill climb in itself was not daunting, as I was used to walking. But three-quarters of the way back up I paused to take pictures. That's when a vicious pain seized my chest, and with it the sickening recognition that arrhythmia had joined the vacation. My body went limp against the thin rod of iron railing separating me from the crevasse below. I pressed a hand against my heart.

"Can't, can't," I puffed to Tim.

The doctor's admonition to drink a gassy pop rushed into my mind. "Pop, Pep-si," I panted.

With a speed eclipsing my heart rate, Tim winged to the café. He was back in record time with a paper cup of Coke without a lid, as the café did not provide lids as part of the plan to reduce pollution. Placing an arm around my shoulder, he held the cup and I sipped the cold, carbonated liquid. The racing did not stop. Nausea surged from my stomach.

Tim quickly gathered the bags we had packed with only the barest of things so that if they went missing our distress would be minimized. But the bags did not hold the tiniest item that could have helped me—the miniscule white Metroprolol pills needed to fight SVT. Those had been overlooked on this, our first expedition in Oahu, safe in my handbag at the hotel in Waikiki.

Nothing mattered now, not even the yellow flippers and orange mask that had screamed fashion faux pas when paired with my mauve bikini, and the discomfiture that had produced earlier on the beach. Before I could choose a yellow mask to go with the yellow fins from the array provided for us, Tim (who had failed to read my mind) innocently handed the yellow mask to another snorkeler when she asked that one be passed to her. I had remained stuck with a mismatched pair. I had looked downright silly and refused to take photos, but now I didn't care.

The chartered bus would be coming in about an hour and we had to walk a far distance down to the parking lot for pickup. Overwhelmed and distraught, I learned that it is possible to feel even more overwhelmed as the moments ticked by. Somehow we made it to the pickup location and onto the bus.

When we boarded, the driver offered me Tylenol, which I declined. The other passengers remained quiet.

"Bag," I whimpered, and Tim passed me a plastic bag meant for the damp bikini I was still wearing.

Breathing into a paper bag was one way to coax the heart back to normal. When a person hyperventilates, she breathes out too much carbon dioxide and "rebreathing" exhaled air helps to restore the imbalance. But no amount of bag-breathing would bring down the erratic beating. I pinched my nose and exhaled. Nothing.

A voice floated through the bus. "I am a nurse. Does anyone need help?"

Why hadn't she come to us instead of calling out? We didn't enlist her assistance, as there wasn't much she could do.

At long last the bus arrived at our hotel; I swallowed a white pill and settled in bed. Finally, after two interminable hours of racing, chasing, nausea, and agony, my heart settled too. For the rest of our vacation the little pill bottle became my BFF. I used two more during our trip as a precaution and did not have any more incidents. Thank God.

In early April, my contract as Manager of Tourism and Economic Development for the City of Melville would come to a close, as the manager was returning from maternity leave. March was a winding-down month, and many days I recalled the joy I had in the position. Managing the office, files, and budget, supervising the students, planning for Canada Day and Culture Days, and partnering with other groups to put on events in the City had been fulfilling. Interacting with the media while promoting the City's events on CTV, filming documentaries with Access7 TV, being the voice on the weekly *Talk of the Town* on The Rock, 98.5 FM radio, being interviewed for newspapers, giving tours, running the souvenir shop, and greeting visitors, were a match made in Heaven for me. It was wonderful doing PR for the City and it was a natural fit with what I did as an author. If I knew one thing, it was that I was good at tourism and marketing.

The economic side saw me reaching out to prospective businesses to partner with our city and networking with peers in provinces across the country. The council meetings with the rest of the staff, mayor, councillors, and the public who chose to attend were a new experience for me, and I count it a huge honor to have worked with such fine people. Personally, it fostered a sense of pride and loyalty, and to this day I look out for the City of Melville. My tenure there stands as a beacon in my job history and memory.

Fridays during winter were not busy, and March 14th was no different. I was alone and enjoying the quietness that afternoon as I watered the plants and drank in the beauty of the little souvenir shop. The shelves were filled with City of Melville pride on aprons, shirts, pens, balls, pins, flags, books, magazines, maps, and a host of diverse keepsakes. The large flat screen television played tours of City Hall, Opera House, and Heritage Museum, along with other clips from Tourism Saskatchewan.

"Thank you, Lord, for the opportunity to have worked here," I prayed aloud.

Then, in that serene office while I gave thanks, it happened. Grabbing my throbbing heart, I hurried to my desk, delved into my handbag, and popped a Metoprolol in my mouth. The rhythm did not slow down. Dizziness claimed my head and my stomach heaved; fortunately I did not bring up anything. The hands of the clock showed quarter to four and the work day ended at 4:00 p.m. In a small city it is soon evident if a worker leaves the job early, and city workers are under particular scrutiny. With my eyes on the clock, I kept praying, "Jesus, help me." I had Diet Pepsi in the refrigerator, but sipping did not help. I blew into a bag, but relief did not come. Pinching my nose merely took the makeup off. The only option was to go to the ER. Four o'clock had never taken so long to arrive, and when it did, I locked the doors and headed to my car.

"You can do it. You can drive to the hospital." I self-talked as, leaning on the steering wheel for support, I drove the one kilometer to St. Peter's Hospital.

The nurse in the ER remembered me from my previous visit. Quickly she hooked me up to the cardiac monitor and confirmed an accelerated rate near 170 bpm. She located a vein on my right wrist and administered fluids intravenously.

"Bear down," she instructed.

I furrowed my brow. "What?"

"Bear down."

When I did not comply, she explained, "It's like going to the toilet."

The penny dropped, and obediently I attempted to bear down and found myself coughing at the same time. Like magic, the number on the monitor dropped to 104, and the pain evaporated. That day she had a student nurse with her. Exultantly she explained to him how bearing down could halt SVT. She was so happy at the outcome, beaming at the chance to demonstrate to the student how the maneuver could prove successful, that I felt my SVT episode had found a worthwhile purpose. Coincidentally, the doctor on call was the same one who had attended to me back in August when it first happened. He was not my primary care physician at that point, but since then I've become his patient, and I affectionately call him Dr. PCP.

Because my situation had been steadied on time there was no need for him to come to the ER right away. The nurse asked me to lie down while I waited for his 7:00 p.m. arrival. It was just after five o'clock, and as our house was a mere two kilometers away, I offered another plan.

"Can I go home and return at 7:00 p.m.?"

The nurse hesitated. "You can stay here. It won't be long before the doctor comes."

I hadn't told my family of the incident. They'd be wondering where I was. Besides, I felt better and I had every intention of returning, albeit with Tim.

"I'd really like to go home. I'll come back. Promise."

"Okay. You'll have to sign a form stating we did not refuse you care and you left voluntarily," she informed me.

I understood that and signed the form. She left the IV in my wrist in case I became worse and needed more fluids when I returned, and I walked out to the parking lot. Regret came too soon. When I turned the steering wheel to back out of the lot, the needle jabbed into my skin. Tears rushed to my eyes. An IV hook-up was meant for certain positions, and turning a wheel at seven corners was not one of them. But amidst jabs, tears, and ouches, I made it home.

At seven o'clock, Tim and I made our way back to the ER. Dr. PCP explained how the Metropolol pill would have taken effect within half an hour, not right away as I had expected. I recounted to him the episode I had in January in Hawaii and he wrinkled his forehead. Snorkeling required exertion, but the other two times the arrhythmia had occurred I had not been exerting myself, yet I had chest pains.

He told me of a procedure called ablation. If I chose ablation, I would never have irregular heartbeats again. He described the break-through and success of a new electro-cardiologist in Regina. It was incredible to think such a treatment existed, but what did I know of heart treatments? I was new to this. Yet I was super excited. Deep down I felt ablation was for me. My arrhythmia was debilitating and life-threatening as I could have a heart attack with it. Moreover, panting and gasping were humiliating.

"I want to die dignified," I reasoned to Tim. "Do you know how humiliating it was in Hawaii to gulp for air while people looked on? My heart has acted up three times in eight months. It's getting worse. I want to do this procedure."

He understood. He had witnessed it firsthand. Although ablation was a very low-risk procedure, I set my mind to the fact that I could die and be free from this imperfect human heart. How I hungered for the meadow I had visited in 1998. Maybe this time I would go back for good.

We agreed to ablation, and on March 16th Dr. PCP faxed a letter to Dr. Wojcik, a cardiologist in Regina, seeking his advice on whether I could be sent to the new EP specialist, the shining Dr. Sultan.

CHAPTER 23

DOUBLE DELIGHT

"In His grace, God has given us different gifts for doing certain things well ..."
Romans 12:6a (NLT).

B EFORE THE DECISION TO send me for ablation could be made, I had to undergo a series of tests to ensure I was a candidate for it. An ECG had be taken to show which parts of the heart muscles might be damaged.

On June 25th, 2015, Tim took the day off to accompany me to my two appointments. The first one was at Dr. Wojcik's office on Dewdney Avenue in Regina. There, his assistant took my vital signs and performed the ECG. When it was over, we drove to Regina General Hospital (RGH) for the treadmill exercise stress test. The stress test would detect any abnormal heart rhythms that might occur due to exertion.

By then it was noon, and while driving to RGH my stomach gurgled. I don't usually eat breakfast, and it had completely slipped my mind that I should eat something that morning, given the crucial nature of the tests. I could have eaten up to two hours before the test, but it was too late now. My last meal had been seventeen hours ago and I was uneasy about doing a strenuous test on an empty stomach.

In the hospital, I met the brilliant Dr. Wojcik with his gentle sense of humor. He reviewed my history and asked more questions. My ECG results from an hour earlier showed that I was indeed able to take the stress test. Praise God for that first positive step. Dr. Wojcik talked about the low-risk ablation process and explained that if I passed my stress test, it would be an excellent option for me. I was excited, albeit hungry, and couldn't help wondering how that would affect the results. As the saying goes, "empty bags can't stand for long." I might not be able to walk as long as I would have had I eaten. Silly me! I'd be my own undoing at that one chance on the stress test. To be well again and not have a palpitation would be a medical miracle, and here I could mess it up because I had been plain stupid and not eaten.

I changed into a hospital gown and my own running shoes, which they had asked me to bring along. A technologist attached electrodes to my chest and explained the process. I would begin to walk, and after a few minutes the speed would be increased. I was to let her know when I wanted to stop. There was no set time for the test—it was only an endurance test to record my heart rate as the speed was increased and the incline became steeper.

When the initial set time expired, she increased both speed and incline, talking and informing me of what was going on at every stage. All the time I walked, she watched the jagged line on a monitor that displayed my heart rhythm. I watched some of it too but thought it was best to focus on the walking and not dilute my energy with a preoccupation of graphs.

The technician was caring, for even though she encouraged me to walk as long as possible, she also kept asking if I was dizzy, or felt short of breath, or was too tired to go on, or was experiencing any pain. Once I stopped, the test would be finished. I walked for eleven minutes and then nodded my desire to stop. I might have gone on longer had it not been for hunger. I changed into my clothes and drank some grape juice before leaving the hospital.

I realized then the necessity of Tim being the driver that day. I could not have driven home after the test, for I was worn out. We stopped at Earl's Bar on Victoria Avenue for lunch on our way back and talked about possible outcomes based on the success of the treadmill test. Only when the results were sent to Dr. PCP, though, would he advise me of the next stage.

The results were exhilarating.

Dr. Wojcik had written, "On examination, blood pressure 120/70, pulse 52, respiration 14. Head and neck were normal. Chest clear. Normal heart sounds. No murmurs, gallops or bruits. Peripheral pulses were palpable. Musculoskeletal and neurological exams grossly within normal units. Resting ECG showed sinus rhythm was within normal limits."

His clinical impressions read: "History of SVT. Stress test was negative for angina and ischemia. A 2-D echo was reported as normal. I will ask Dr. Sultan, EP specialist, to review the patient in consultation regarding EP studies, and possible ablation."

It was only while writing this chapter that I became aware of another healing miracle. Requesting my health records has not been a norm for me. In fact, were it not for purposes of accuracy for this book, I would never have asked for them. When I read Dr. Wojcik's notes, goosebumps overtook my body … "No murmurs, gallops or bruits" he had written.

No murmurs?

I had developed a heart murmur following rheumatic fever when I was fourteen. I had been denied life insurance when I was twenty-seven because of murmurs and bruits. Yet here was a brilliant, renowned cardiologist assessing my most recent ECG and declaring my heart murmur-free. How could that be? When did this miracle happen?

I reclined my head on the Ikea chair I was sitting on while I typed, and the answer dropped like a dead bolt from Heaven.

When I was touched by Eternity in Heaven's meadow on October 16ᵗʰ, 1998, not only was I healed of hyperemesis gravidarum, I was also healed of a murmuring heart. God healed my heart murmur. I was touched by Eternity for two healings that day, making it my third miraculous healing overall!

Holy, holy God. How good He is to me. This was a double delight.

How I wished I had known that my heart was healed earlier. I'd have spared myself untold unnecessary doses of antibiotics. For years I had insisted on Amoxil for my dental cleanings, because the risk of contaminated blood with corresponding infections in my heart was not to be treated frivolously. But my heart did not need it. The murmur had been healed. Praise God, praise God, praise God.

I turned to the Childbirth diary on the coffee table with the burgundy writing and picture of a mother and baby. It's a sacred document, a standing stone, my testament of the doings of God. Idly I turned the pages, still crisp and clean after nineteen years. I wasn't sure what I was looking for, why I lifted one sheet of pink paper, and let it drop before lifting another. Suddenly I felt as if I had touched electricity, that quickening when God is about to reveal something. I experienced it with both spiritual Head and Heart—Heart searching for the blood-pumping organ called the heart.

I paused on page 31. The blue scribble arrested me even though I had read the words many times since I began the manuscript. "No evidence of heart affected. Listened for heart murmurs." The date was January 11th, 1999.

No evidence of heart affected?

At the bottom of the page was the recommended treatment in my cursive penmanship, "Ultrasound of heart, echocardiogram on 20th January."

I was in the kind of moment where I felt my soul expand so it could fit an ocean. Paper rustled gently and page 33 came into view with its date of January 20th. January 20th was the same day the cardiologist had given the prediction that my child would be a boy, but what popped in carbon ink was not the echocardiogram results, although that was all good. Instead it was my question in parentheses to Dr. Im of the cardiologist that grabbed my attention, and the answer: (Maybe Dr. _____ detected a very small murmur? No, he said.)

That ever-vigilance to guard my heart had its reassurance in a resounding NO. The cardiologist had not detected anything. No murmur in 1999. Not even a teeny, tiny one.

I had been healed as sure as the sun had continued to rise.

But God was prodding Heart. *Murmur-free. Murmur-free ...* Holy, holy God. That was about the words of my lips and the meditation of my heart, in the words of King David in Psalm 19:14. My heart complaint had been healed (literally), wasn't it then my reasonable service to examine myself and make a change of my words so that they would be pleasing to God?

I'll try.

No, I'll intentionally live murmur-free.

Quantum physics informs us that a void cannot exist—it must be filled with something. What must replace murmuring? Thanksgiving sounded like a probable option, yet I paused.

Then suddenly a zing in my spirit. *It's the opposite of murmur.*

I turned to the thesaurus to find an antonym. *Quiet.*

Holy, holy God Almighty.

In the peaceful quietness of Heaven's meadow, not only was my emaciated 95-pound body freed from the disquiet of hyperemesis gravidarum, but my heart had been quieted too.

The day I wrote these words in our home in the quiet countryside, I made a pact with God to live murmur-free. Finally Head and Heart had aligned.

When Dr. PCP told me I could expect a call from Dr. Sultan's office, my elation was like a helium balloon cut loose from its anchor. Not long after, the anticipated phone call came. I was so excited I half expected to go into arrhythmia, but fortunately I didn't. On August 7th, a sun-drenched Friday, Tim and I drove to Regina for a consultation with the specialist. My feelings were mixed—this was do or die. I hoped I'd have the procedure before our trip to Trinidad in January. That would be the first time Tim had visited the island of my birth, and I was ecstatic to show him the paradise twin republic. But even without the trip, a new heart made an unsurpassed present.

Dr. Sultan is an EP, an electrophysiologist, a physician who specializes in heart rhythms. His business card lists him as, "Cardiac Electrophysiologist and Cardiologist, Medical Director, Electrophysiology and GMS Cardiac Rhythm Device Clinic." His reputation preceded him, and he was highly esteemed by his peers and physicians in general, so I'd be in good hands. But I was unprepared for his youth and looks. That was another double delight, to be in the good hands of one so good looking.

He quoted the success rate and changed lives, as testified by patients, and explained the process in great detail. I didn't remember the science he so competently described, so I researched it on the Mayo Clinic's website to help with this writing.[1] First, an electrophysiology (EP) study would have to be done to find the best treatment to control my arrhythmia. There are two kinds of ablation procedures, both used to destroy the cells that cause arrhythmia. With radiofrequency ablation, referred to as RF or heat ablation, a special catheter is placed in the heart and used to "burn" the cells responsible for irregular beats. Cryoablation, also known as cyro or cold ablation, "freezes" the cells that cause arrhythmia.

Dr. Sultan determined that RF would work well for me. He showed me images of my heart captured in Dr. Wojcik's office and using those and the ECG findings, described the space where the electrical pathway was missing a beat or beats. I understood that space was responsible for the short-circuiting that triggered the arrhythmia or irregularity. He would join the two ends together to eliminate the space, thereby producing a full and uninterrupted circuit.

"How did this space come to be?" I asked him.

"You were born with your heart like that." His simple and concise answer was a revelation. I felt as if my head had grown larger and was spinning like a ballerina on steroids. But I could not give my thoughts the luxury of retrospection. I willed myself back to the calming voice of the young specialist in front of me. He was describing how I'd be sedated for the process, not anesthetized or put out cold. I would be awake and aware of what was going on. He would use a non-invasive process called catheter ablation, not open-heart surgery. A catheter, a long tube, would be inserted in the large vein in my groin and linked to my heart to deliver heat energy that would correct the cells causing the irregularity. The success rate was 95% for those who qualified, and if the ablation was not successful, a pacemaker could be used.

"What's a pacemaker?" I looked at Dr. Sultan then at Tim and back at the clean-shaven genius.

He explained that a pacemaker is an electrical device implanted under the skin to help manage irregular heartbeats. I had never seen a pacemaker, but I knew someone who had one implanted just below his shoulder blade. I had remarked how well he looked, after not seeing him for a year or so, and he had explained how the pacemaker had given him new life. I didn't know who had done his procedure, but I could see the device projecting against his skin and that memory surfaced in the EP's office. It was vanity speaking, but I shuddered at a pacemaker being visible if I wore a tank top or swim suit.

"What does a pacemaker look like?" My eyes were focused on the EP specialist in the armchair opposite us. The luxurious leather, dark cherry wood bookcase, and neat office created the perfect background for one as renowned as he, and served to heighten my confidence in him. The ambience seemed indicative of his fine brain and skill.

He pointed to the little device on the desk in front of me and I jumped. I had not even noticed it, but when one does not know what to expect, one is taken by surprise. I picked it up and examined it closely. The pacemaker was silver and shaped like a wide, big comma. There were ports for tubes to be inserted, which would lead to the heart. I rested the device lightly on my shoulder blade.

"Does it protrude through the skin?" Oh vain, vain me. I wanted the reassurance.

He assured me it could be placed in a way so as to not be visible, but I kept picturing the gentleman's pacemaker bulging against his skin. I did not want a pacemaker. I passed it to Tim who in turn scrutinized it. He also was seeing one for the first time.

I asked Dr. Sultan about the pain factor with the ablation procedure, and he replied that, though I'd feel a slight soreness in my chest because the heart would be exposed to trauma, in a day or two my chest would feel fine. The spot where the catheter was inserted would take a few more days to heal and I'd have to clean it so as to not develop an infection. Barring an infection, I would not need anything more than Advil for any pain I'd experience. I asked whether he had ablated hearts from patients of my people group and whether my being of East Indian descent could cause any issues. After all, the population in Saskatchewan was mainly Caucasian and First Nations. That, and a number of other questions, Dr. Sultan answered efficiently and easily, and I was reassured.

"Think about it and call my receptionist if you decide you want to go through with it," he concluded. We all stood as the consultation came to a close. "I'm booking into April 2016. If you decide to go through with it, you'll have to sign a consent form."

So much for October and my birthday. I had thought about the ablation for months. I was one hundred percent certain—more, if possible—that I wanted to have the procedure in order to put an end to the unwelcome irregularity that showed up whenever it felt like it. With a successful ablation I'd be able to lead the normal, active lifestyle I was used to. The only new element in the consultation was the pacemaker. I wanted to think that over a little more. Knowing that when I made the decision I'd have to sign the form and Tim would have to take another day off to drive me and there'd be the problem of finding parking in the congested streets of Regina, we took the form from the receptionist with us. I'd mail it in. But how I wished I could get in earlier than April.

Then a thought struck.

"Do you have a waiting list in case someone cancels?" I asked the receptionist.

Unfortunately, she didn't as she was not the one who set the dates. The EP Lab at Regina General Hospital scheduled the procedures.

"They will contact you with a date." She shuffled some papers on the desk. "But I'll put a note in your file that you'd like to be placed on a wait list."

"Thank you very much. I appreciate it." I smiled my way out into the summer air. If no one canceled, I'd still be scheduled for April and have a proper, working heart for spring.

CHAPTER 24

BIRTHDAY GIFT

"Every good and perfect gift is from above ..." James 1:17a (NIV).

THE 155-KILOMETER DRIVE HOME was punctuated with discussions about the ablation procedure and periods of silence. The second step had been successful. I'd been declared a candidate and only a date stood between me and my renewed heart. Leaning against the headrest, I gazed at the fields in which swaths lay in neat rows. Some acres had already been combined and the grain harvested. Others were untouched. But my perusal of the fields was short-lived. At last I could give in to the luxury of retrospection that had shaken me in the office.

"How did this space come to be?"

"You were born with your heart like this."

For years I had reasoned that my heart murmur was caused by rheumatic fever. The decline of the life insurance policy had been a result of the murmur. But the cause of the murmur may have been a birth deficiency, not the result of rheumatic fever. Never had I given credence to the idea that I had been born with a defective heart through inherited genes.

A tear slipped sideways, wetting my ear. I should have known, or at least suspected, yet it had never entered my mind. I had heard stories of a cousin, a "blue baby," the description given to children whose complexion has a bluish tinge because of poorly oxygenated blood.[1] Sam was only twenty-seven when she went to Heaven. Then there was Kam who had died when she was six years old (from another sickness). The girls were sisters. How could one family bear so much grief?

It could have been me. My heart could have given way and my family would have had one girl short.

But I had lived. God had allowed me to enjoy and excel on His earth. Psalm 118:17 drummed in my head, echoing as God's voice had in Eternity when I was told to come back: "I shall not die, but live, and declare the works of the LORD" (Psalm 118:17 KJV). (This verse is in the Dedication.)

I bit my lower lip to prevent the tidal wave building behind my lids. I didn't want to distract Tim's driving or for him to know my distress. I don't understand why God allows some to die and others to live. I am an ordinary woman who had given my life to Him, taught and preached His Word from young. He was not yet done with me. My purpose in life is to declare the works of the Lord. Some things come but once in a lifetime, and if I could point out my once-in-a-lifetime-moment, it is to know my purpose after being in Heaven then sent back. This book is a declaration of that purpose.

Over the weekend I prayed that I would not need a pacemaker. Nonetheless, I checked the box on the form stating that I agreed to one if needed, and mailed in my consent. Now I just needed a date.

I didn't have to wait long. Three weeks later, in early September, a letter arrived in the mail informing me that my procedure was set for November 19th. I was surprised and pleased, for although it was not October, November was close enough. And when April came, I'd be all new for spring instead of having to go to the EP Lab.

On Tuesday, October 27th, three weeks before my procedure date, my phone rang. I recognized the code of 766 and knew it was Regina General Hospital. I used to be an employee there and the code had been on my business card.

"May I speak to Susan Harris?" a female voice inquired.

"This is Susan," I replied.

"I'm calling from the EP Lab at Regina General Hospital. A cancelation has opened up a spot for ablation on Thursday, October 29th. Would you like to be scheduled?"

My heart beat picked up in excitement, but in a good way, as when adrenaline pumps, not in palpitations.

"Let me check if my husband can get the day off, and I'll call you back."

I phoned Tim. Without missing a beat, he cheered, "Accept it. I'll take the day off."

Praise God for family and emergency leave in his job. I called the nurse and the date was fixed. God had answered another prayer. I'd wanted the procedure in October, and it had been moved from April 2016 to November 2015 and then to October 2015. Later that evening, another nurse telephoned with specific instructions for the procedure and the preparation I needed to make on my end. She asked if I had questions and left a phone number in case I needed to contact them. There was not much time for we would be leaving home the next day to stay at a hotel so we could be at the hospital on the morning of the 29th.

I was going to have a new heart, a gift in October for my birthday.

On Wednesday evening, Tim and I checked in at the Ramada hotel in White City, a small town twenty kilometers outside Regina on Hwy 1. We had to be at the hospital for 10:00 a.m. on Thursday, after which we'd return to the hotel to spend another night following the ablation. I needed to be near the hospital in case I had a reaction and had to go to the ER, but White City was close enough.

At the hospital I was prepped for the procedure in the Post Cardiac Intervention (PCI) unit. Tim stayed with me the entire time. A bevy of tests was performed again—renal panel to measure kidney function; APTT and PT panels for blood clotting; glucose fasting test for sugar; glomerular filtration for kidneys; CBC & auto differential for the cells in my blood; calcium, magnesium, and phosphates.

It was critical that my blood clotted properly, because the catheter would be inserted in a major vein, and with that came the risk of bleeding to death. An IV was set in my wrist in anticipation of the procedure. I was treated gently and with great care. Repeatedly I was asked the same questions by different members of the team to ensure they did not overlook any information or treat me for something other than catheter ablation. When the time came to be wheeled in to the EP lab, Tim kissed me and settled down to read my book, *Remarkably Ordinary: 20 Reflections On Living Intentionally Right Where you Are.*[2]

The EP lab was divided into two parts, an area where staff did their work adjacent to a couple of other little offices and the section where the X-ray machine and patient bed were. A glass partition separated me from the staff area. There were a number of hi-tech screens and medical equipment. I had never seen such attention paid to creating a sterile environment. Every single surface was attended to. Everyone's head was covered and they wore extra coats. The machines were covered too. The technicians explained that there must be no germs at all because the doctor was going into my heart, hence the heavy coverings. I chatted a bit with the team as they did the sterilizing needed for the ablation. I mentioned to one of the technologists that I used to be employed at the health region and we struck up a more significant conversation.

"What are you doing now?" he asked.

"I'm an author."

He looked puzzled, and I added, "I write books."

"You write books? That's so cool," the employee enthused. "What kind of books and how many have you written?"

I told him and a few seconds later he blurted out. "I'm feeling nervous. My hands are trembling. I can't believe I'm attending to a celebrity."

"I'm not a celebrity." I laughed hard just before the nurse hooked on the IV for my sedation and pain medication.

"I'm going to tell the others," he said.

My laugh faded. The reality was here and ablation was about to begin—writing books was the furthest thing from my mind. I did notice, though, that a few more staff members peeped at me through the glass partition.

Dr. Sultan came in and talked to me. He reviewed what he was going to do, even asked again if I would take the pacemaker should it be necessary. I assented. He cleaned the area on my right groin with something that burned like turpentine then placed a heavy material, similar to what covered the X-ray machine, over the warm blanket that covered me. More precautions for sterility.

I remember crying out as he injected a local anesthetic into the groin area. The research describes the catheter as a soft wire threaded through a needle and sent up the vein.[3] It was guided to my heart through X-ray. I wish I could have seen how it mapped the abnormal electrical pathway in my heart tissue. It was surreal to know that right then and there energy was applied through the tip of the catheter to remove the abnormal electrical pathway that caused the irregular beats. The catheter paced my heart at different speeds and recorded the electrical signals, and the speed and recordings showed on the monitors.

I wished I had been put to sleep instead, coward that I am when it comes to needles and pain. I could feel a slight pressure as he applied energy to my heart, and the nurse increased the pain dosage in the IV in response to my groans. She stayed by my side during the entire process and held my hands when I cried out. But I knew that with each application the pathway was coming closer together until it was a full circuit.

After a couple of hours, it was over. The staff smiled in relief. Dr. Sultan had done it again. My heart was fixed. For the first time in my life, I had a perfect heart.

Yet I remember that grace and mercy had piled blessing upon blessing in spite of my imperfect heart.

It was a win for everyone. I felt ashamed that at one point during the process I had moaned pathetically to the shining star, "I don't like you."

The machines were shut down and the catheter removed. The nurse pressed on the insertion site to prevent bleeding. The blanket and heavy sterile covers were removed, and I was wheeled back to the PCI unit for observation. I had to lie on my back for six hours to reduce the risk of losing blood from my leg. The vein that had been catheter-ed was a large one, and if I stood up, or even sat up, gravity might send too much blood to the area and my life could gush out.

The experience is one I will never forget. I received excellent care at RGH. The nurses were very attentive, and I was more than surprised that the meal came in insulated trays so the food remained hot. I joked to Tim that instead of soup in the recovery unit, I could have been eating manna in Heaven. Some things I'd rather forget, such as having a bedpan brought for me. My gown and the bedding got wet enough that they required changing, and I was impressed by how the nurses replaced both the blanket and gown while I remained horizontal. Another moment of gratitude came when I remembered a conversation I had heard a while back. Someone wanted to know if ablation works for palpitations caused by anxiety and depression. Sadly, ablation does not work if the heartbeat is irregular due to anxiety.

"Thank you, Lord, for making me a candidate for ablation."

Dr. Sultan popped in to check on me. I was recovering nicely and was more in control of my senses.

"I'm sorry I said I didn't like you while you were treating my heart," I apologized. "That was pain talking." I flashed him a wide smile. "I like you a lot, and I think you are marvelous."

It was his turn to smile. He was not at all offended. He looked different now that his green cap and surgeon gown was off. In his brown suit he looked debonair and dashing. Double delight again. We talked a bit and I thanked him again for my heart.

As the six hours drew to completion, the nurse suggested I walk around the ward slowly to regain my stance. Resting my weight on Tim, we did a couple of rounds. Then we signed the discharge papers and drove back to the Ramada. I was still under observation.

When I had laughed with the technologist in the EP lab, what I didn't know was that it would be weeks before I laughed again.

CHAPTER 25

BACK HOME

"Do not be afraid or discouraged, for the LORD will personally go ahead of
you…" *Deuteronomy 31:8a (NLT)*.

I SLEPT WELL THAT night at the Ramada, choosing the side closest to
the wall so that the insertion site on my right leg would be undisturbed.
Tim lay on my left. The next morning I woke up feeling fine. Thankfully,
the danger was over and we could drive home to Melville. I urged Tim to
go down for breakfast as I was somewhat groggy from the anesthesia and
was moving slower than usual. He went ahead, and a few minutes later I
decided to join him. I opted to go down in my red silk pajamas, the ones he
said looked better than what some people wore to work. They were decent
and attractive, and to change them would take me too long in my post-ab-
lation stupor.

I could see Tim's head in the breakfast nook so I inched up quietly,
but said loudly enough that others could hear, "Would you like company?"

Tim is Caucasian and I am a brown girl, so my little flirtation drew
curious eyes.

"I thought I'd pick the best-looking man to have breakfast with," I
crooned coyly. He got up and kissed me, his face red at the attention the
flirting had attracted.

"I'll get you a cup of coffee," he replied, pleased in spite of the blush.

That's when I noticed how perfect the beautiful red teacups looked
with my red PJs. Forget flirting. I wanted a red teacup to take home.
"These are gorgeous." I turned to the breakfast attendant. "Usually teacups at hotels are white."

"We get lots of compliments on them," the lady answered. "The
owner of the hotel insisted on having them."

"He has fantastic taste," I gushed. "These are so attractive."

Next to the hotel was a farm equipment dealership and auction site, patronized largely by males. I gleaned from the attendant that the men liked the red cups as much as the women did. Unfortunately, she couldn't sell me one.

Tim brought my coffee to the table, but as I sat down I whimpered and promptly straightened up. My thigh where the catheter had been inserted was stiff and sore, and my leg couldn't adopt the 90-degree angle required for sitting. So much for being coy. That brought breakfast to a quick halt, and we packed our things and set off for home. I had to recline the seat as far as possible since my leg needed to be extended straight. I groaned as the car turned out of the lot.

Tim frowned. "Are you okay?"

"Lying down in a moving car is making me nauseated, but I know you can't do anything about it," I whispered.

His goal was to get me home quickly, and it could not be a minute too soon. We pulled into our driveway about 1:00 p.m. After settling me, he went to the post office to fetch the mail.

"There's a box for you," he announced upon his return.

"From whom?" I asked.

He read the name of a high school friend who now lived in Edmonton. That was a nice surprise. The contents of the box produced great joy—snacks and condiments from Trinidad. My friend's wife had visited and generously brought me back the much-grieved-for items which I couldn't get in Saskatchewan.

"Channa!" I exclaimed at the bottle of fried chickpeas. "And lime pepper sauce, coconut milk powder, Maggi seasoning cubes." All made in Trinidad.

I was touched by the timing the Lord had orchestrated for this gift of love to arrive. What a welcome back home with my new heart! Satisfied that I was okay, and with the added pleasure of the chickpeas I began to snack on immediately, Tim set off for the farm to feed the cats and to check up on things after being away.

As Friday afternoon wore on so did the lingering sedation, and I began to feel a slight discomfort in my chest. That was expected, though.

The leg would be sore for a few days more, but I was prepared for that. I swallowed some Advil and was able to sleep comfortably that night.

On Saturday morning I woke up late, cognitive of the date. Would it be another cold Halloween as the past years had been? Given the turn the week had taken, with the unexpected call for ablation, buying candy had been the furthest thing from our minds. Not that I gave out candy, but Tim did. My preference was popcorn, hot chocolate, pencils, or emblems that promoted Jesus. I reasoned that children did not need more sugar. But the needs of children flew through the roof as my own need asserted itself when I tried to get off the bed. My left side stung with red hot pain. I couldn't move my arm without screaming like a banshee.

"Oh God, help me," was the gut-wrenching moan that came out instead. I had no strength to scream.

Tim brought me more Advil, and Tylenol. They did not even dent the torment that congregated on my chest and left side. My neck and shoulders, arms and chest, burned with fire, escalating even more when I thought it had reached its zenith. That was not supposed to be happening—hence I had no prescription for painkillers.

"My ... my arm," I stuttered.

Speaking in full sentences was impossible. When I glanced in the mirror, my eyes looked like pieces of dark brown glass from broken Smalta bottles, a drink made from molasses in Trinidad. Something was happening and it was not my heart. But what? My neck, shoulders, and arm had not been touched during the catheter ablation.

The only position that brought relief was holding my arm against my chest, as if I was wearing an imaginary sling. The moment my arms dropped, blinding, white hot agony shot up with a speed that could shame lightning.

Tim was dressed, ready to go do the many chores that demanded attention on the farm.

"Don't ... leave ... me ... a ... alone. Don't ... leave ... me ... a ... lone."

My whimper was barely audible. I had no energy to talk. No volume to beseech. That wretched, wicked pain was worse than childbirth, for an epidural had helped with that. I huddled on the daybed, head bent over my body, my forearm on my chest at right angles to my upper arm. If I lifted my head the torment intensified. Tears rained down my face.

"I'll make you a sling," Tim announced proactively. His shrewd eyes had noticed that I kept my arm across my chest, but I was losing strength in the arm and could not hold it in place.

As I type this scene, I think of Moses praying as the battle raged against the Amalekites in Exodus 17. While his arms were raised to heaven, the Israelites prevailed, but when his arms drooped as he got weary, the Israelites began to lose. Then Aaron and Hur held up his arms until the sun went down, and the Israelites won the battle.

I needed something to hold up my arm.

Folding a towel across my right shoulder and under my left armpit, Tim made a knot around my neck, but the thickness of the towel scrunched awkwardly, and required effort to keep it in place. I let it fall.

"I'll go and buy a sling at the drug store." He picked up his keys and my wail intensified.

"D … o … n …'t go. Don't … go. Don't … leave … me … alone."

I wept like a child, terrified to be alone.

He wrapped his arms around me, those strong arms that carried the strength we would need over the upcoming months.

"I'll be back soon. I promise. But I must get you a sling."

I could not hold on to him. I had no will, no power. I had nothing. Gently he extricated my feeble body from his and I heard the door shut behind him.

"Oh God, help me. Help me, God." I prayed piteously.

Huge tears plopped down my cheeks, soaking my blue silk shortie with the black lace and thin ribbon straps. My daughter had given that nightgown to me as a Christmas present. She was in Saskatoon, oblivious to everything. She didn't even know I'd had the procedure. No one knew except Tim and the medical teams. My condition was private and I guarded my secret. I closed my eyes as I waited for my husband's return, propped against the paisley cushions in the living room dominated by the picture window. The glass throughout the house made it all sunshiny, but today I was oblivious of the brightness and comfort I enjoyed on a regular day–the cathedral ceiling and fireplace in the room that flowed L-shaped to the dining area and out to the deck; the bedrooms and bathrooms and master en suite, the kitchen with its oak cabinetry, stainless steel appliances, and rectangular window; main floor laundry; the spacious recreation room that doubled up as main-floor basement with an office and an extra bed for sleepovers.

I heard the key in the door and Tim entered. He had been as quick as he'd promised. In a trice, he had removed the sling from its packaging and tried to fit it on me. But it was a not as easy one might have hoped.

"Dang," he muttered in frustration. While my pain mounted, he tried to follow the picture on the model's arm and finally managed to get the sling on. Immediately I felt a reprieve. I had won my fight against gravity and could keep my wrist against my waist. I hadn't eaten and Tim coaxed me into having coffee, but pain had reduced my appetite to nil.

I took more Tylenol and positioned myself on my right side on the daybed with my left arm in the sling—the same daybed on which I would lie dying with wisdom tooth pain in 2017. Then he would use a different chair and we'd be in a different house. Curled up fetal style, I was very small. Tim covered me with my favorite blue blanket with the snowflakes on the corners. My moans faded as the pain came down to a tolerable level. Moving the wicker coffee table from the middle of the living room, he drew up an armchair and sat facing me.

Within an hour the water I'd sipped with the Tylenol demanded I go to the bathroom, and as he helped me up, boiling pain scalded my left side and arm. My legs buckled.

"Take ... me ... to ... the ... E ... R."

Tim grabbed my fuzzy blue housecoat and purse from the bedroom and slipped the robe over me. Then he carried me to the car where he drove the two kilometers to St. Peter's Hospital.

CHAPTER 26

"ADMIT HER!"

"I, even I, am he who comforts you ..." Isaiah 51:12a (NIV).

TIM PULLED UNDER THE awning of the hospital and hurried in to fetch a wheelchair. In record time I was registered at the desk. Words like "heart" and "ablation" whirled staff into action. Assessing the gravity of my condition, the nurse asked kindly, "Why didn't you come in earlier?" I remember feeling a rush of gratitude at her concern, for I had not wanted to be a bother by coming to the ER. She assured me I was not a bother if I was sick. She set up an IV with Toradol to treat the pain.

My health record indicated I arrived at 13:51 on October 31, 2015. As it turned out, Dr. PCP was on call that weekend. I marveled at how each time I went to St. Peter's he was on call.

As soon as he laid eyes on me, he exclaimed, "I'm admitting you!"

Hospitalization was not what I had foreseen, and I resisted. "I don't need to be admitted, Dr. PCP. I can feel the pain subsiding. I'll be fine at home." How naïve I was. When asked about my level of pain,[1] I had indicated it was about 7.5 when lying down, but it shot up to 9.5 when I moved.

Level 7 pain is described as "severe pain that dominates your senses and significantly limits your ability to perform normal daily activities or maintain social relationships. Interferes with sleep."

And level 9 is, "Excruciating pain. Unable to converse. Crying out and/or moaning uncontrollably."

On the pain scale,[2] the numbers 0 through 10 are assigned a description to help a person communicate the intensity of what they are feeling. 0 means pain free and 10 is pain that makes one pass out. When I was moving in and out of consciousness on June 24th, 2017 due to pain from my tooth extraction, I had been experiencing level 10 pain, according to the scale. Childbirth pain is considered an 8. But pain is personal and it varies with individuals, and mine felt far greater than the number 10 could express.

I had been in pretty bad pain, but the Toradol was working. Still, Dr. PCP shook his head. "You need to be here."

"I'll tell you what, Doctor," I negotiated. "Let me go back home and if I don't feel better I'll return."

I would be as comfortable as could be in our beautiful, spacious abode. The good doctor acquiesced. Back at home I laid down for a rest, sleepy, as the Toradol did its magic to my body and the agony diminished. I must have dozed off for when I woke up I was hungry.

"What would you like to eat?" Tim inquired.

"Nachos," I replied immediately.

The Waverley Hotel served the best nachos with beef and melted gooey cheese, green onions and olives, sour cream and salsa. Tim phoned in the order, and in ten minutes he went to pick up the meal. But the nachos were never eaten, for when I rose to wash my hands, savage pain snarled again. If eager children rang our bell for their share of treats on Halloween night, we'll never know. (We still had no candy, but then we did not need it.)

We left our darkened house and returned to the ER where a wheelchair was waiting at the entrance. Tim had notified them of my coming.

Dr. PCP was there when Tim took me in again shortly after 7:00 p.m. He took one look at me and gave the order: "Admit her." This time I didn't object. In a blur I was given more medicine then taken to a room where I thought I'd spend the night for observation. The nurse from the day shift was gone and in her place was another nurse who had a trainee with her. I met a second nurse whom I recognized as a personal friend. She did my registration paperwork while I lay on the bed and answered the questions. The bed was angled until I was in more of a sitting position. The rails on both sides had been raised so I was able to lean on them.

My main memory of the first night in the hospital is that my pain seemed worse than it had been during the day. I was restless. My upper body throbbed in spite of the powerful medicine I had received. The pain accelerated faster than the medicine could keep up, and every cell in my arm screamed for relief within an hour after being given the meds. My chest felt as though it was being pounded with hammers. I sobbed. Every hour I buzzed the call bell, begging for more pills. My medication administration record for the night of October 31st showed that I was given morphine at 21:25 and the "PRN" Tylenol as the need arose after that. (PRN is a Latin terms that stands for "pro re nata" which means "the thing is needed" Medicines that are taken "as needed" as known as PRN medicines.)[3]

When I sounded my buzzer, a nurse inquired over the intercom as to what she could do for me.

"Can you come?" I asked. I was naïve to the fact that I could give my request over the intercom. When the nurse and her trainee arrived, I asked for more medicine. The RN told me what the other nurse had explained, that morphine could not be given before six hours had passed, but I could get Tylenol. I did not want the "PRN" Tylenol, as it did not even dent the pain I was feeling, but I accepted it. Eventually, at 1:30 a.m. on Nov 1st, I was given more morphine. Later, when the duo made their rounds, they stopped in again.

"Try and get some sleep," the nurse admonished. I had been looking at my phone in the dimness of the night.

I shot a glance in the direction of my yet-unseen roommate behind the curtain. "I would if she would stop snoring," I replied wryly.

The nurse conceded that it was impossible to sleep with such sounds. As it provided a diversion from my own plight, during moments of relief I timed the snoring on my phone and looked for patterns. A heavy nasal sound built up to a crescendo, then changed into a whistle, then slowed down to gasps that tapered off quietly. The long heavy one occurred every three minutes, with dimmer sounds in between. I mentally constructed a graph as the nasal noise built, peaked for a number of seconds, then plateaued off with the whistle. It was the weirdest snoring I had ever heard.

To be fair, I heard her telling her husband the next morning how poorly she had slept because I was in pain, moaning, calling for nurses all night, and the lights had been switched off and on. That was true and I was sorry to have been a poor roommate. Fortunately, it was only for two nights, as she was discharged then.

Around 2:30 a.m. the morphine wore off, and so did my ability to listen to my roommate's snoring. I pressed the bell again.

"Give me more medicine," I begged. "Please give me more."

"I've given you all I can for now," the voice answered kindly.

That didn't make sense. If they had given me all the medication they could give, why was I tormented this way?

"But I have so much pain." My voice was ragged.

"I'll come and see you," she replied.

The nurse who came in was my friend.

"Why do I have so much pain?" I asked again.

It was a rhetorical question. She consoled me with gentle words, but I did not sleep a wink that night. I moaned and buzzed and prayed and couldn't understand why so much medicine could not bring my pain level down. That is not how life should be. How many hours needed to pass before I got morphine? Only morphine mattered. A lifeline that could be thrown only every six hours leaving me floundering, drowning during the other hours.

I was able to use my right arm and decided to note the time when my medication was administered so I could know when to ask for more. Morphine must not be second late! With my iPhone tucked in the crook of my left arm, I one-finger typed the precise time I was given meds, and the name of the meds into Notes. I asked the nurses the names of every pill they were giving me, though at that time the idea of using the records for publication was as probable as me going to the moon. I could not have known I'd see the other world. For this book, I would request my health records and compare my own file in Notes with the Medication Administration Record. But it was the Notes app on my iPhone that showed the correct times I received pills. And it was the proof I needed of another visit to Eternity.

It was now the darkened hours of Sunday, November 1st. I typed in Notes that I had been given Toradol at 4:30 a.m. At 7:30 a.m. I received morphine.

Dr. PCP visited me on daily rounds and I naively asked if I could go home. Although I had only been admitted about thirteen hours, the calendar had crossed from Saturday to Sunday, so I was going on to my second day here. Save for the maternity ward, I had never been in a hospital for two days as an adult.

He shook his head. "No, I'm sorry. You can't go home yet."

My nurse friend reinforced this. The amount of paperwork they had done for me was not typically done for a one-night stay. I would be there at least three days.

Three days? My heart felt cold. I did not look forward to this. I did not look forward to anything actually. Especially visitors. Truth be told, I was adamant against visitors. In a small city of five thousand everybody seemed to know everybody else's business. Prying eyes and wagging tongues held as much appeal to me as kissing a snake. My condition was private, and I would fight for it to remain that way.

My walls against visitors included the chaplain. In my most serious tones I requested he not visit me. Yet he did, twice, in spite of the fact that my admission form indicated that I did not want clergy services. I told the nurses not to let anyone visit me except my husband. I asked that the curtains be drawn to keep me hidden from the curious eyes of those walking in the corridors. Except for the hospital staff, I had told no one of my condition. Not my pastor. Not my family in Trinidad. Not even my daughter. More than once daily I reminded the staff that I wanted no visitors and to please draw the curtain around my bed after they checked on me.

I alternated between Toradol and morphine all day Sunday. Toradol every eight hours, morphine every six, with Tylenol thrown in for good measure. But the Tylenol could not compete with Toradol or morphine. It was more of a placebo, a psychological comfort that I had been given something and it would make me feel better. My iPhone record lists:

1:30 a.m. Morphine

4:00 a.m. Toradol

7:30 a.m. Morphine

12:00 p.m. Toradol

2:30 p.m. Morphine

5:15 p.m. Tylenol

9:10 p.m. Toradol

11:15 p.m. Morphine

But while Tylenol may have produced psychological relief, my agony was not psychological. It was the harsh reality of human flesh tortured. Eight times that day I swallowed pills and relief was short-lived at best.

"Can you lend me a Bible?" I asked a nurse. She brought me one, emphasizing, "You must give it back to me."

"I will," I assured her. Straightaway I texted Tim to bring me my Bible and a notepad. He did, and I returned the borrowed Bible.

I needed the nurses' help to get to the toilet. One had informed me in clipped tones that if I wanted a shower I had to do it myself, even though I could do nothing unassisted. I was used to showering at minimum twice a day, but once would be satisfactory. Tim took it upon himself to help me, and leaning on him I'd shuffle to the shower. He would do this nightly for the duration of my stay. His routine was to go to work, to the farm to feed the cats, then to the hospital to help me shower.

"Look, there's shampoo and conditioner," I had exclaimed.

I was surprised at the pleasure the shower brought me. It provided me with a sense of my regular life, and soon I had luxuriously clean hair. The morning of the ablation—four days ago—was the last time I had washed my hair. My husband brought my brush and blow dryer and for the first time attempted hairdressing. Tim's experience with a blow dryer up to that point involved de-icing the keyholes of his vehicles in winter. I was touched by his care and felt like a model when he was done. Move over, *Glamour* magazine! How taxing all this was for him, yet he did it without complaint.

In Trinidad, patients usually take their own nightwear to the hospital, so I carried on with the practice. Tim packed up pajamas and nightgowns, shorties and negligee sets. I remember his astonishment when he brought the bag to the bed.

"I've never seen these before. Why don't you wear them at home?"

I had long stopped wearing PJs because the pants felt constricting, but they were good for the hospital and helped keep me warm. I wore shorties at home so the long gowns and sets had remained closeted. We had been married for four years, and Tim had never seen the dozens of pieces he had sorted through.

The nurses, too, took interest in my lingerie and paid me many compliments. Statements such as "I love your PJs," "Those are beautiful," "I've never seen a style like that," or "Where do you buy your stuff?" were frequent lines of conversation. My responses became automatic:

"My daughter gave me this for Mother's Day," referring to the purple silk pair with the lacy top and thin straps.

"This is from La Senza," meaning the short green silk nightie.

"I bought this online at Victoria's Secret," of the short pink set with the lace straps.

"This is from La Vie en Rose, it was a piece for my honeymoon," referred to the yellow silk negligee set that my husband said produced the aura of an angel when the recessed light cascaded on me as I sat writing on the bed. Wearing my own sleep things was a huge comfort during my hospital stay, as were my little blue blanket with the snowflakes and the fluffy blue robe with the white trim on collar and sleeves. But how I longed to go back home and wear them there.

CHAPTER 27

TOURIST IN ETERNITY

"Thine eyes shall see the king in his beauty: they shall behold the land that is very far off" Isaiah 33:17 (KJV).

"TOO MUCH PAIN."

The email I struggled to type shot into cyberspace in a nanosecond, landing in my husband's inbox at 11:21 a.m. It was Monday, November 2nd, 2015, and the relief I hoped for was nowhere in sight. Within seconds my phone rang, bringing his comforting baritone.

"Did they give you pain killers?" Tim's question was rhetorical— perhaps reflecting the helplessness he felt at not being able to assist me— for I had been on a strict regimen of the addictive pills since admission.

"Yes." The word was feeble, almost inaudible across the forty kilometers separating us.

For the third consecutive day my 112-pound body lay limp and defeated. The doses of narcotics had to be measured against my weight, and any excess could send me in a coma. But I needed stronger drugs. I had not touched the breakfasts since I was admitted. I could not lift the lids off the trays nor pour water nor remove the foils from the juice glasses, but with patience the staff assisted with the lids and coaxed me to eat. The apple I'd received on the first morning decorated the table, though not because I thought it was poisoned like Snow White's apple was.

"It hurts when I eat," I had murmured to Dr. PCP.

I couldn't understand why for three days now I had taken the best pills prescribed for the aftermath of a procedure like mine, yet torture zoomed through my left side, paralyzing my arm and shooting pain into my body.

"Did they say what they'll do next?" Tim prodded across the miles.

"The nurse said she would tell the doctor." Deep sighs accompanied my words.

Broken and tearful, I had whispered to the nurse as she made her rounds earlier, "No one should have to live with so much pain." She assured me she'd inform the doctor right away that my pain was not going away. Although pain level is measured on a scale of 1-10, I believed a new scale ought to be created for mine—it felt like 1,000.

"Did you get any medication or do you have to wait for her to call the doctor?"

"I got Toradol and morphine this morning and the pain eased a little bit, but when it started again, they gave me Tylenol. Tylenol doesn't do anything, but they can't give me more morphine or Toradol until a certain amount of time has passed." I puffed the words as more torture ripped through my left side, from neck through shoulder, down the arm, and into my legs. Interestingly, there was no pain in my chest as Dr. Sultan had predicted. He'd said my heart would be fine in a day or two and it appeared to be, but what was going on with my neck, shoulder, arm and leg?

No doubt sensing the effort it took me to speak, Tim ended the conversation with, "Let me know what they say. I'll see you tonight. I love you."

The nurse returned to tell me that the doctor would be prescribing me new medication and she would let me know more soon. Meanwhile, it was time for the morphine and I swallowed the offering before sinking into the pillows.

The Notes app showed the record for that day:

2:26 a.m. Tylenol

3:20 a.m. Morphine

6:00 a.m. Toradol

7:45 a.m. Morphine

9:45 a.m. Tylenol

12:10 p.m. Morphine

I did not get much relief. A couple of hours later it was time for Toradol.

2:20 p.m. Toradol.

The pain was rising above the 1000 threshold on my scale.

The nurse came in to tell me that the doctor had instructed her to add 3 mg of Hydromorph contin, which was to be taken every twelve hours. I mumbled the strange words, wondering if I would ever master this language that rolled so easily off the medical team's tongues.

2:35 p.m. Hydromorph contin

4:20 p.m. Morphine

8:30 p.m. Toradol and Morphine together

10:25 p.m. Hydromorph contin

"They're giving me a new 'hydro pill'," I explained to Tim when he visited that night. It would be a few days before the nurses spelled the unfamiliar word to me, and a few more before I could sound the name properly. I opened Notes and showed him the log, which he read with interest. On Monday, November 2nd I had been given four different medications eleven different times to treat my pain, an average of meds every 2.18 hours. Yet the pain was unstoppable.

"That's a good log," he observed.

"I'm a writer," I responded matter-of-factly. "It comes to me naturally."

But the log had not been created with the intention of "writing". It was merely to ascertain that morphine was not administered a second late. I had zero inkling, as likely as emptying the Pacific with a cup, that a year later I would be indebted to the recordings I had made on my iPhone, for what happened next fast-tracked the decision to write this book.

6551957. 6551957.

I mumbled the numbers again and again as I strained to position my phone in the crook of my elbow.

6551957. Was it 7 or was it 9? Actually, it was both. The 9 had flashed first and then settled to 7.

Pressing the circular button at the bottom of the phone, the screen lit up silver in the dim hospital room, announcing the time as 2:33 a.m. and the date as Tuesday, November 3rd. I touched the button again for Home and it opened to Notes, the last page I'd used to record my dose of Hydromorph contin at 10:25 p.m. the day before. I whispered the numbers aloud again, and at the same time the name John came to mind, and I wrote:

Phone Number 655-1957 and the Book of John.

I studied my typing. *There's a clue here, I know. I have to interpret these numbers.*

Is it John 6:55?

Is it John 19:5-7 or John 19:5-9?

In the darkling hours of the night—literally in the early morning of November 3rd, 2015—this is what happened:

I am taken up in a narrow tunnel, traveling at an incredible speed, and someone is with me. I whoosh upwards, faster than any rides I have taken at theme parks. My head goes first and my arms are at my sides. My posture reminds me of Jesus' ascension when He was taken to Heaven, in an upright position with His head first. I am aware of being guided upwards by a big, strong person. I can see his shadow but not his face or body. He is alongside me on the outside of the tunnel, which is a cylindrical tube about five feet in diameter. The walls of the tunnel are transparent, as if made of glass or clear crystal, and it is cool inside. It appears to be early night or late dusk.

It is dark in the tunnel but not black. I can see clouds with a hint of gray swirling on the sides as I go higher and higher into the sky, and I begin to see what looks like topography emerging through the clouds. It reminds me of being on an aeroplane at 37,000 feet altitude and going through the clouds. The first time I traveled to Canada I had been struck by the way the cloud formations had looked like the landscape of another world.

I see the number 655 stretched across the air in burnished gold, like when the sun is setting and it reflects brown-gold. Before I can wonder at its significance, I have the answer through thoughts filling my mind. The thoughts are that I am in Eternity and 655 is a clue to the title Prince.

655 is a telephone code of a place called Princes Town in Trinidad. *The Prince's Town.*

I have entered the kingdom of the Prince, the town where the Prince reigns.

The Town of a Prince. The Prince of Peace.

I have a heightened sense of awareness. I know things I have not learned, as if God's omniscience, His all-knowingness, has filled me.

It is still, quiet. There is no verbal communication, no noise, only this messaging system whereby thoughts enter my mind. I seem to know everything naturally, intuitively, and I know I am on Jesus' turf. It is not strange to think that God will give us answers before we ask. Isaiah 65:24 holds a precious assurance, "Before they call I will answer; while they are still speaking I will hear" (NIV). I believe individuals can certainly share in God's omniscience as He sees fit.

Wonder wells in me as the kingdom unfolds before my eyes. I feel I am being given a tour, a peek into the other world, seeing things there that are alluded to in the Bible, if not directly recorded. Knowledge permeates my being—that just as there are landmarks on earth, there are air marks in Heaven. There are actual markers of location and position. The words *location* and *position* are emphasized, as there is more to learn about them. I do not know what they mean just then, but I will later.

I liken what I see to a vacation I had taken to California several years before. We were going to visit Universal Studios, and as we drove down the freeway, the famous HOLLYWOOD sign loomed into view. The gigantic white letters were nestled high in the mountain. Until then I had only seen the sign on television and movies and had shivered at the beholding of this impressive landmark. Likewise, excitement filled me in the tunnel.

More numbers come into view, stretching across the space like a shallow concave. 1957 or 1959. I feel as if I first saw 1959 but it settled to 1957. As I pondered this on my return, the story of the hand writing on the wall that appeared to King Belshazzar came to mind. The words that the Hand of God wrote were Mene, Mene, Tekel, Peres (Daniel 5: 25-28). Then Peres had changed to Upharsin. Similarly, 1959 had changed to 1957. Four words, four letters, with the last one changed.

Without warning, the speed drops, but there is no slowing down or jerking at the abrupt halt. I am standing in space at the top of the tunnel with the clouds at my feet. I am suspended in air, weightless. I sense I am a tourist adventuring into unknown territory. I am being shown the other world. I know almost everything there is to know and I am given knowledge as I need it.

I know I am on the edge of Eternity.

Awe swells in me. This is an entry point to the afterlife with God.

The scene is clear and endless, stretching as far as my eyes can see. The atmosphere of Eternity, "eternosphere", as I termed it. This view of Eternity is a marvel, an adventure that confounds me. It's limitless. Boundless.

The clouds are only at my feet, not above or at the sides. There is no sky or stars, just transparent, clear air in an expansive outdoors. I have never seen anything so immense, so overpowering in size. There is a sense of time being still, as if it does not exist. The knowledge enters my mind that time stands still because there are no schedules to demand time in Eternity. A year or a minute feels the same, and I am living out the seeming paradox of 2 Peter 3:8, "But do not let this one fact escape your notice, beloved, that with the Lord one day is like a thousand years, and a thousand years like one day" (NASB).

I stand stationary, not floating, suspended above the tunnel, observing and drinking it all in. I am aware of being taller than my five feet two inches, but I am not human flesh. Instead, I am a large, transparent human silhouette. I have no organs, only a clear, distinct form. My mind has grown proportionate to the vastness, and the vastness and I blend into one.

Ahead of me in the distance is the likeness of a castle. The castle is golden, with lots of turrets and towers rising high into the eternosphere. The tops thin out to points similar to castles with turrets I've seen in pictures and in countries I've visited. The gold looks brown, rather than the lustrous yellow gold of the midday sun. The castle is mammoth, stretching far into the distance, but I can only see a fraction of the front. I am not very close to it and I only view the exterior, just as I have gazed at prominent buildings on earth from the outside. I am not allowed to go into the castle. It is reinforced that I am only to be shown an overview, because I am a tourist and I am not there to stay. If I go in I will remain there, but I am not given the choice to enter.

There is no other building or habitation here except that of the Prince. Isaiah 33:17 tells of this Eternity: "Thine eyes shall see the king in his beauty: they shall behold the land that is very far off" (KJV). I am viewing the land that stretches afar off. This is the place Jesus went to prepare a mansion for those who accept His salvation on the cross.

Closer to me, and on the same level where I am standing, is landscaping. Gardens with curvy green sculptures as if pruned by the most expert of hands. John 15:1 enters my mind, "I am the true vine and my Father is the gardener" (NIV). We use this verse as a symbol of spiritual growth, but Father God as a gardener in Heaven was literal to me. This is an exquisitely cared-for place—lush and green, manicured and pristine. Shades of bright green on the edge become more yellow-green closer to the castle. Such a vivid shade of green I have not seen on earth, and therefore no word to describe it has been created in English. The beauty is stunning, beyond my ability to relate.

There are no flowers on the perimeters of the castle grounds at which I gaze, only lawns with low-lying shrubs and flat green grass. Beyond the grounds is space, more eternosphere. It feels exactly like I had experienced in the meadow in Heaven on October 16th, 1998, calm and idyllic, with the same tranquility and overwhelming peace and stillness, except it is more far-reaching.

In front of the castle is a huge sign set in a curved design with "KINGDOM OF THE PRINCE" in the same polished gold as the castle. I am aware of having perfect vision and the ability to record and remember what I see, a small part of this infinite, indescribable eternal world. I look and look, taking it all in, a witness, a tourist, a video journalist whose recording device is burned in her memory. My proof is my memory.

Then, as suddenly as I entered the tunnel, I found myself awake on the hospital bed mumbling the numbers. I had been brought back to earth in a wink. I don't recall coming back down, but I imagine I would have come feet first and straight down. I felt sad, annoyed that I had not been allowed to remain in the Kingdom of the Prince, in spite of knowing that I was in Eternity as a visitor. I know it is my flawed sinful nature to feel petulant at God, but I could not assimilate the crushing disappointment of being sent back. That was my second visit (the third being my tooth surgery in 2017), and the wistfulness of my first visit in 1998 came rushing back like waves at high tide. Tears filled my eyes in the dim ward.

If I compare my 1998 experience to this one in 2015, I can note peculiarities of my trips and routes of getting to Heaven.

1. I was not aware of a trip up to Heaven's meadow, but I was aware of my trip up the tunnel to Eternity.

2. I was aware of my return from Heaven in 1998, but I was not aware of my return from the tunnel.

3. Simultaneous to collapsing in the OB/GYN's office, I was walking uphill on soft green grass. Simultaneously from gazing at the castle in Eternity, I was back on the hospital bed.

4. I did not argue to stay and no voice told me to come back, as had happened in 1998. I surmise God wisely made the decision to send me back abruptly to spare me from begging to stay where I was not supposed to be.

I surmise, too, that perhaps I am not allowed to remember all the details of the trips, or that I may remember them in parts as time unfolds.

I came back from Heaven's meadow with feet in the direction I was moving (towards Earth), and may have returned with feet first again this time, but I have no recollection of it. I may have returned down the tunnel or I may have been whizzed back as in 1998, but I have no memory of it.

I believe God wanted me to have different experiences so I could share them with you. After all, just as a person can travel using air, water, or land options, so too God has options of routes to get us to Heaven. In the same way as someone can enter a country through different ports, so too, God can take us to different points of entries before we reach the pearly gates. That could be the reason so many NDErs tell of varied routes and what they saw. If I entered Canada through Lester Pearson airport, I would immediately step into the metropolis. If I entered via Regina, I'd be surrounded by prairies. The landscape is so different that a person might question if she were in the same country. So too, I believe it is in Heaven.

Back in the ward, I tried to gauge the time my out-of-the-body experience (OBE) may have taken, and how long I remained in the world to come. After taking the Hydromorph contin at 10:25 p.m., I had lain awake until midnight and may have gone to sleep shortly after. In the notebook Tim had brought me, I'd jotted that I had dozed off at around12:30 a.m. on another night. When I returned to my bed it was 2:33 a.m. Extrapolating from those timeframes, the length of my visit to Eternity could have been up to two hours long.

Later that morning, an implication of the visit to the other life would materialize.

CHAPTER 28

DDD

"The LORD sustains them on their sickbed ..." *Psalm 41:3a (NIV)*.

I pushed my rendezvous to Eternity to the back of my mind. At 2:51 a.m. I buzzed the nurse and she brought me morphine. I fell asleep and remained asleep until I was awakened at 6:00 a.m. for Toradol. That was the first time I'd had to be awakened for meds; usually I was calling for them. My pain was at level 5, the most manageable it had been since it started on October 31st. In fact, it was my best day since the ablation procedure.

I had a cup of coffee for breakfast. At 9:00 a.m. my nurse friend came to ask if I'd be interested in answering some questions for accreditation, a process for maintaining standards of excellence in healthcare.[1]

"Sure, I'd love to," I replied enthusiastically.

I was happy to be able to serve the hospital that had cared for me. The No-Visitor-Not-Even-Clergy mode was still red, but the accreditor was not a visitor, and she definitely would not invade my privacy. The nurse came back with the interviewer and introduced us.

As the accreditor pulled her chair closer to my bed, I remarked, "Today is the first day my pain has broken since I came here on the weekend. If it had not broken, I wouldn't have been able to speak to you."

Later that day I replayed my remark in my mind, and a revelation shot into my brain.

My pain broke after my visit to Eternity. I was touched by Eternity for a fourth healing!

That is significant because I had not actively noted the improvement in my pain until I made the comment to the accreditor. I attribute this reprieve from pain to an association with Heaven, as had happened in 1998 with HG, and in 2017 with my dental surgery. (Because the pain would return, I do not count this healing in the same vein as the other three which were permanent.) I remained on the same regimen of painkillers that day—morphine, Toradol, Hydromorph contin, and the "PRN" Tylenol.

Wednesday, November 4th 2015 was memorable for two reasons. The first was that it was the inauguration of Prime Minister Justin Trudeau. I had not subscribed for television, because my condition begged for a quiet environment. I could not focus on the screen and its happenings. From the start my roommate's television bothered me; she turned up the volume saying that she was deaf in one ear. Seniors were given free television, whereas non-seniors like me had to pay.

I'd never consider entering a Miss Universe pageant, but for a soundproof booth—instead of linen curtains between our beds—I might have auditioned. I mentioned the noise factor to Tim, and he bought headphones and suggested I offer them to my roommate. She refused them. Fortunately, the nurses were sympathetic and requested that she use the headphones. After tunneling up to Eternity, I began to feel so much better that I took a subscription for television on Wednesday morning to watch the inauguration of the new government.

The second reason the day was notable was that I had woken up with tingling in my left hand and two of my fingertips were numb. When I told this to Dr. PCP, he sprang into action.

"I'm sending you for an X-ray. Tingling and numbness are associated with nerves." Ding, ding, ding. It turned out that the true cause of my pain was a pinched nerve in my neck—Degenerative Disc Disease, or DDD. Little wonder that my neck, shoulder, arm, and leg on my left side had been in white pain, but my chest had been fine. The onset of DDD coincided with the ablation, but the ablation had gone perfectly, whereas the DDD had not been diagnosed yet.

That morning, Gabapentin was added to my medication slate. 100 mg to be taken four times daily.

Four days after the reprieve from Eternity, the pain asserted itself again, and on Saturday, November 7th the dose was increased to 300 mg. That's 1200 mg a day! It was a crazy dosage, but I had crazy pain. The dramatic increase was effective, and for the first time in a week I felt I could go home and be okay.

The Gabapentin produced involuntary jerks to my body, and I logged the times and observations in my foolscap writing pad. I typed emails to my daughter, describing little antics around me and what the cats might have done. I missed the darling pets. I began to eat a bit more at meals. I looked forward to the afternoon snack of coffee because real coffee was served from the kitchen instead of the instant packets that were kept handy on the ward.

I had two roommates during my stay, both of whom were senior women. After the trip up the tunnel I was able to sit up for short periods, so I decided to have coffee with Roomie #2, as I called her, one afternoon. Our conversation had been routine as she divulged it was her second visit to the hospital that year, the first being in the spring.

"I almost died back in April," Roomie #2 recalled. "The doctor said there was a time I had no heart beat."

I wondered if that was an exaggeration but politely said nothing.

"I knew I had died," she continued. "Because I was in Heaven."

At the word *Heaven* my hand shook and I rested my cup on the table.

"The peace …"

I snapped to full attention.

"The peace in the garden …"

Her voice trailed off again, as if she were back in the garden absorbing something that could not be expressed in words. Then and there I was convinced that this woman had experienced the other life as I had. I felt the connection immediately in my spirit. When I was growing up, our pastor used to emphasize that, when seeking God's will on a decision, we would know it through experiencing peace. Peace is the hallmark of God. I had absorbed peace in Heaven and so had this roommate. Her description, or rather her lack of it, matched mine. The garden, the grass, the temperature, the beauty.

"I can't describe the colors I saw or the peace I felt," Roomie #2 explained apologetically, shaking her head at the inadequacy.

"Don't worry," I assured her. "I've been there too."

I related my experience of 1998. We agreed that nothing on earth could compare to what we felt and saw; like me, she had not wanted to come back. I found an inexpressible comfort knowing I was not alone in desiring what I had seen and wanting nothing but to go back to its glory. At long last I had met a real person who understood what I was talking about. I did not tell her about my tunnel visit a few nights ago. I had to process it first, and besides, I was tired from the coffee chat.

I got to know the staff in nursing, housekeeping, dietary, lab, X-ray, and other support services, as well as the doctors during the eight days I spent in the hospital. I was grateful for the care I received, and towards the end of the week, with my pain down to level 3, I asked my husband to bring me thank-you cards to give the staff. I had copied their names from their ID tags and inquired about those I was unsure of. I could barely scribble and got tired quickly, but I spent several hours persevering to write meaningful words on dozens of cards that weekend. Then on Monday, November 9th, I was discharged.

After sharing a bathroom and living in eighty square feet of curtained space, I was ecstatic to be back in our beautiful home. Tim filled my prescriptions, including a new medication, Keterolac. I was managing my meds, and I set the alarm so I could take the pills at the required times as directed. I was wary of becoming addicted to the painkillers, especially Gabapentin.

All went well on Monday, Tuesday, and Wednesday, but on Thursday evening the pain started to rise again. On Friday I was at the level 1000 mark on my pain scale, just like in the early days in the hospital. The nurses had cautioned against letting the pain get above level 6, as it is difficult to bring it down. I had taken my doses carefully, like a religious ritual, paying attention to time and amount and entering them in Notes. But as the day wore on, I became more and more debilitated.

"I have too much pain," I said to Tim over the phone. "It's so easy to want to take more pills."

He cautioned me not to take any more than prescribed. Upon leaving the hospital, my maximum dosage of Gabapentin was 300 mg, but only if I needed it. The pills had been dispensed in 100 mg caplets, so I could be flexible with how much I took. The lower the dosage, the better. I was keenly aware of the effects of 1200 mg of Gabapentin on my body taken in doses of 300 mg each, its addicting power, and the fog I lived in because of it. I was eager to bring that number down and get off all the pills as speedily as possible.

"Take away this pain, Jesus," I prayed over and over, at times in a whisper and other times silently in my heart.

And in the form of Reason the Lord spoke to me, "Do not take another pill. You will overdose. Go back to the ER."

And then I understood why sick people ought not to manage their own pain medication. For taking a maximum dose does not equal pain removal. I know the desperation of looking at several bottles and wanting to swallow them all so that the wicked pain contorting my body would go. I also knew that I would go with it. That my husband would return home to a corpse. So I moaned and fought the pain alone, with Reason cheering me on.

When Tim came home, we discussed going back to the hospital. I was loathe to return, because I had been given all the tools to manage myself … all except the willpower not to swallow the entire bottles. I had kept a record of the meds I took and the times so as to prevent overdose, especially of the Gabapentin. In the twenty hours spanning Friday and early Saturday morning, I had taken:

Friday Nov 13

2:00 a.m. Gabapentin 300

6:00 a.m. Keterolac, Gabapentin 200

8:00 a.m. Hydromorph Contin

12 noon Gabapentin 200

2:00 p.m. Keterolac

6:00 p.m. Gabapentin 200

8:00 p.m. Hydromorph Contin

10:00 p.m. Keterolac

Saturday Nov 14

12:00 a.m. Gabapentin 300

1:30 a.m. Gabapentin 100

I had taken 1300 mg Gabapentin in twenty-four hours instead of the pre-scribed 1200. The extra 100 mg was an overdose. With my pain increasing, sometime after 1:30 a.m. Tim took me back to the ER.

CHAPTER 29

SECOND ADMISSION

"In God I trust and am not afraid ..." Psalm 56:11a (NIV).

T HE NURSE ON DUTY at St. Peter's Hospital was one I had met the week before. Of all the nurses, she's the one I would characterize as sour. She knew my condition well, for she had attended to me while I was in the ward. She fidgeted with the computer at the registration desk and pronounced she could not use the new software upgrade, which would delay me getting attention. Tim offered to help (he worked with the health authority), and so I was able to get my patient ID band and hasten the attention I needed.

The doctor instructed the nurse to give me a shot of Toradol. As she prepped my arm for the needle, she remarked rudely, "You have chicken arms!"

I had been sick for over two weeks now, hardly eating, delirious with pain, and she was mean and spiteful. That kind of behavior is grossly inappropriate for a healthcare worker. My eyes grew moist. I looked at Tim but did not say anything. Like most vulnerable people, I felt afraid to anger the one who had power over me, especially one with a needle in hand.

The medicine did its magic—I was still aching and hurting, but at a lower level.

About 4:30 a.m. on Saturday morning the nurse announced matter-of-factly, "You can go home or you can stay over."

Tim looked at me, but I left the decision up to him. The nerve that was touching my bone kept sending shocks down my left arm and side. I could only lie on my back. The bed at the hospital, with its position settings, would give me the support to relieve pain in a way that my bed at home could not.

"I'd like her to stay over," Tim replied. His response seemed to take her by surprise, even anger her.

"What is your pain level?" the nurse demanded.

"Four," I replied.

"Only four?"

I felt as if she wanted me to say zero.

"Yes," I replied softly, drowsy from the Toradol. Level 4 pain is a lot of pain to someone who has been as ill as me. My reply did not please her.

"If your pain is going down then you don't need to stay over," was her caustic comeback.

Later, I mused on the culture that exists in certain careers where employees seem to think they own the department and the resources. They act as though they can chase out whomever they want at will. But their salaries—and resources like beds, medication, supplies, and food— are budgeted from taxpayer dollars, and I am a taxpayer.

Tim gripped the bed rail. "This is the most comfortable she's been in over forty-eight hours, and I would hate to disturb her. I'd like her to rest where she is."

That was not what the nurse wanted to hear. I imagined placing a patient in the ward for observation was extra work.

"If I take her home, we may have to come back as we did before." Tim was referring to October 31st when we had made two trips to the ER on the same day. No, staying in a hospital is not our first choice, or second, or even third, but sometimes it is necessary.

"All right," the nurse huffed, and I was taken to the ward.

While writing this book, I came across an article on MSN entitled, "33 Secrets Hospitals Don't Want to Tell You."[1] Secret 32 reads, "One can request a full night's sleep at the hospital."

Later, when the doctor on call made his rounds, he declared that I was too ill and needed to remain in the ward until my doctor visited me on Monday.

So, on Saturday, November 14th I began my second stay at St. Peter's hospital. Upon reviewing my medical records, I chuckled at the comments the sour nurse had written, "Although [patient] rates arm discomfort at a 5, does not appear in distress."

Secret 18 of the MSN article read, "Admitted? Log everything." Thanks iPhone. I had logged it in a foolscap pad too.

Secret 28 was, "Take notes especially at discharge." I had been taking notes years prior to reading the article.

I was in the smaller section of the shared room this time. Did the nurse think I wanted to live in 60 square feet of space when I could live in 1600? She had judged me on my appearance, but it was not the first time I had been judged; it seemed to be an ongoing pattern. Back in 1998, few people believed I was as poorly with morning sickness (hyperemesis gravidarum) as I was, until I collapsed in front of my OB/GYN.

Even when I was hospitalized in Trinidad as a teen I was judged on my appearance. Patients could not see the doctor unless freshly cleaned, and I chuckle at the memory of the nurse's voice admonishing us to, "Tidy up, tidy up. Doctor's coming at eight." I was the only child in the ward for female adults, and in spite of my swollen wrists and knees, which were visible to all, many invariably concluded, "You look too good to be in the ward." It was my face that had been scrutinized. This nurse in Canada had made the same judgment in her record of "does not appear in distress". Most recently, after throwing up on Hwy 16 the day after my daughter's graduation, the nurse at Lanigan hospital had entered my condition as "normal". Explain to me how one who cannot walk unassisted, has thrown up six times in two hours, can't even keep down water, and cannot speak is deemed "normal"? Of course, that same nurse had incorrectly written my sign out time as 14:25 when in fact my blood test was taken at 15:40.

From the first morning at St. Peter's I had done the "tidy" routine. My handbag held everything I needed, so after the nurses helped me to the bathroom, I'd neaten my hair and apply powder and lip gloss using my right hand. With Tim's help I showered nightly. As long as it's in my power to do so, I will look and smell clean. But while I chuckle at the sour nurse's comments, I know that if I have a third visit there, I'll wear pretty lingerie and be my best me.

The highlight of the treatment of my second admission was the introduction of physiotherapy. My first discharge report had noted that I should enrol for physiotherapy, but when I had phoned for an appointment, the wait time was six weeks with bookings into January 2017. On Monday, November 16th Dr. PCP visited me and ordered physiotherapy. No matter how much medicine I'd taken to mask the pain, it was imperative that the nerve impingement be addressed. I was on the same medications as before with one exception—Toradol had been replaced with Diclofenac.

Being back in the environment where the tour to Eternity had taken place, the memories flooded afresh. I had time and paper, so in halting penmanship I wrote down the details. It was Sunday afternoon and when a pair of nurses came in shortly after their shift started, they appeared surprised that I was back. One was a nurse with whom I had developed a deeper relationship, and she remarked, "You must be writing about something good. You look happy."

"I'm writing about Heaven," I replied, astonished that my countenance reflected a joy they could discern. I would have thought my expression would be one of concentration as I tried to capture words for things that are far better experienced than described.

"I went up a tunnel on November 3rd." My tone was matter-of-fact, as if I had said I ordered pizza. "And I saw Heaven."

Both women stared at me, adopting statue mode while I described in general terms what I had seen. Whether they believed or not, they did not indicate, nor were there jottings on my records about my story.

The in-house physiotherapist did an assessment on me and provided four sessions over the next few days. The second session stands out as memorable—it produced so much relief that I slept for an entire afternoon and awoke pain-free. That was noticed by all.

My roommate said to me, "You were out all afternoon. I wish I could sleep like that."

A couple of the nurses said, "We did not awaken you when we checked in, because you needed to sleep."

And the staff member who delivered the afternoon coffee said when she brought supper, "You didn't look as though you'd be awake soon, so I didn't leave coffee." I agree—cold coffee is no good.

I kept taking pills for the pain, which was worst when lying down at night, but it was the intervention of the physiotherapist's capable hands and professional knowledge that got me on the healing track. I'll not forget how she placed her fingers between the C3 and the C4 and on my C7 and pried my neck bones apart. They had been touching each other and squeezing the nerves between the bones, producing that horrendous pain I'd had for two weeks now. I owe my recovery to that wonderful woman and the ever-dependable Dr. PCP.

By tracking the times when my meds were given, I began to see a pattern. I was having pain 24 hours a day, but my meds were not spread out to accommodate the night hours, namely between 11:00 p.m. to 6:00 a.m. That was due to staff handovers, which occurred at the end of the shift, and frankly, to some nurses not willing to bring medication outside "scheduled" rounds. If a dose has to be given every six hours to control pain, it would be more patient-centered if the medicine was given around-the-clock in an equi-hourly schedule. Certainly budget cuts and staff shortages do not make it easier for nurses, but if pain management is the reason for a patient being at the hospital, then flexibility must be accommodated.

Once when I had asked for a pill during the dark hours, the same sour nurse had brought it and made it clear she was not happy about delivering it. Usually the nurses would switch on the lights and pour the water as I couldn't handle the jug. They'd also ensure I swallowed the pill before leaving. Not the sour one. She plopped the little white paper cup with the pill on the table and stormed out the room. She did not turn on the lights, nor pour the water, and certainly couldn't be bothered if my pill fell on the floor or if I took it at all.

I was discharged on Monday, November 23rd. While I was waiting for my papers to be written up, the CEO of the hospital walked my way and we struck up a conversation. I had been embarrassed by the sour nurse's comment about my "chicken arms" and did not want similar insults to be thrown at patients by a bully employee. I took the opportunity to discuss it with the CEO. She listened and promised to follow up. She mentioned the thank-you notes I had given—forty-five cards on both visits—as some of the staff had drawn it to her attention. She expressed her appreciation of my gesture, because it had been very motivational to the staff. I was thrilled that my presence had made a difference in the eighteen days I had been hospitalized.

On that second stay there was no shampoo and conditioner, only the generic wash the hospital provided. When I inquired about shampoo, a staff member explained that the hospital does not provide shampoo—the bottles I had used were left behind by a patient. I recalled how special it felt to have real shampoo and conditioner, so after I was discharged, I purchased a set of the TreSemmé brand I use and donated it to the hospital.

~

At home I pondered further on my trip into Eternity. C.S. Lewis has said, "If I find in myself a desire which no experience in this world can satisfy, the most probable explanation is that I was made for another world."[2] God has wired into us the desire for more than what this world offers, and I have seen the more. Not only has God wired humans, but all His creation is equipped with desires and impulses that we call "natural instincts", but which I deem are supernatural inklings that transcend the natural.

Take Canada geese, for example. They migrate each year when winter approaches. The government of Canada's website describes this instinctive migration in these words: "Northern-breeding Canada and Cackling Geese overwinter mainly in the United States. Migrating geese are present in spring beginning in late March and usually depart for northern breeding areas sometime in April. They usually begin arriving in southern Canada in late September and may stay around until freeze up."[3]

The geese conduct these rituals seasonally, because their DNA is coded that way.

We humans, too, are coded by the Master blueprint. Coded for Eternity.

Although the natural beauty of this earth takes our breath away and renders us silent, it is but a resemblance of the above-natural beauty of Heaven. Earth is a foreshadow, a foretaste, a peek into what we shall see in Eternity. It is like the dim reflection in a mirror that is spoken of in 1 Corinthians 13:12: "Now we see things imperfectly, like puzzling reflections in a mirror, but then we will see everything with perfect clarity. All that I know now is partial and incomplete, but then I will know everything completely, just as God now knows me completely" 1 Corinthians 13:12 (NLT).

Whenever I read this verse, a memory surfaces. One of the houses we purchased had a mirror with stains, which I tried to clean with Windex. But when I wiped off the Windex, the spots were still there. Those marks were embedded in the glass. I couldn't see my face properly, only partly where the spots did not cover the mirror. Earth is a mirror with spots that cannot showcase Heaven. Another comparison I draw is the tabernacle in the Old Testament. God had instructed Moses to design it after Heaven's blueprints, which God gave him on Mt. Sinai (Hebrews 8:5). By extrapolation, I infer that earth was likewise designed after Heaven, similar, but after the fall it became inferior to the original.

I was born and raised on one of the most coveted locations on earth, an island in the Caribbean Sea. The turquoise waters with foamy tips, sandy beaches, swaying palms, balmy breezes, rugged coastlines, valleys and imposing mountains, waterfalls and rainforests, and picturesque fauna and flora, are second to none in natural beauty. Throughout this earth nature is resplendent, yet these awe-inspiring creations are dark compared to what exists in Eternity. The best is where God Himself reigns! The heavens *do* proclaim the glory of God and the skies His craftsmanship as Psalm 19:1 (NLT) declares.

In March 2016, I had an MRI done on my head and neck to learn more about the DDD. The findings showed mild degenerative changes in the mid to lower cervical spine, and fusion of some C-joints. I made some lifestyle change to cope with DDD, including physiotherapy and exercise. I've reduced the number of hours I spend on the computer and use dictation where I can. In fact, I used dictation software for half of my first draft of this manuscript. Overall, I am happy that the MRI showed all is well with my head.

CHAPTER 30

IS EVERYTHING WRITTEN IN SCRIPTURE?

"Things which eye has not seen and ear has not heard, and which have not entered the heart of man, all that God has prepared for those who love him"
1 Corinthians 2:9 (NASB).

As described earlier, on November 3ʳᵈ, 2015, I had been taken up to Heaven via a tunnel. En route I had seen the numbers 6 5 5 1 9 5 7 splayed in the air as I approached the Kingdom of the Prince, stopping at the outskirts of the kingdom.

I questioned the Lord about it: "Why am I here? What am I yet to do?"

And the answer that came to me in thought was to this effect:

There are many who have entered Heaven and seen the interior and Jesus, angels, loved ones, and such like, and have talked about it, but few tell about the outside. You will tell them. Some believe that Heaven is real, but others don't. It has signage and boundaries like earthly kingdoms, but it is not shared with any other kingdom. What you saw lines up with the Word. The numbers correspond to verses in Scripture.

Stop. People who haven't had an NDE are quick to point out that we who have say things that are not written in the Bible. Let's explore this further.

To begin, the word near-death-experience and its acronym NDE are not in the vocabulary of the Christian church. I never heard the term during my studies in Biblical Theology or in any sermon, teaching, or talk over fifty years. It wasn't until my third NDE in 2017, which I described in a post on Facebook, that my friend Alan Anderson, a retired pastor and chaplain, gave the name to my experience. (Even when I saw the Dr. Oz clip in September 2016, the term had escaped me.)

Second, people regularly exclaim that they "nearly died" if they had a narrow miss on the highway or experienced a similar occurrence. This exaggeration has made it confusing at best for those who have literally "nearly died", where we get out-of-the-body and experience the other world. The exaggeration "nearly died" is not the same as "near-death experience". In this book, my context of NDE is of individuals who have literally died or been on the brink of death so that their souls leave the body, as defined by Dr. Raymond Moody.[1]

Third, my details about Eternity are alluded to in the Bible but not enumerated in Scripture the way I describe them. Before you drop the book, however, I urge you to consider Paul's wisdom of the mysteries of God in 1 Corinthians 2.

"Eye has not seen ..." Could it be that you *see* words with your eyes when you read them, and those words are not meant to be "seen" yet? Or the more obvious context—human eyes have not seen it, but in God's time we will see?

Likewise "ears have not heard ..." If it's in the Bible and is read aloud then it would be heard, wouldn't it? Did God intend for some to hear when it is the right time?

"Not entered the heart of man what God has in store ..." This speaks to the inability to imagine or think up something. The phrase suggests a built-in barrier set up by God regarding what humans can imagine. As I mentioned in the Introduction, I simply cannot fabricate what I've written, because the ideas, concepts and notions cannot "enter" my heart. And if they cannot enter, I cannot express them on paper. The only way these mysteries are made known is if it pleases God to reveal them.

In fact, the most gifted writer with the most active imagination cannot access what God has for us in Heaven. But God raised the veil and permitted me to see and hear a miniscule amount through visions and NDEs. One of my goals is to help normalize the conversation in religious circles concerning near-death experiences. As a non-fiction writer focusing on facts and research, and a trustworthy speaker for three decades, I believe God had this planned all along. He was building credibility for when I would make public the facts of Eternity that had been entrusted to me.

Fourth, some pastors have told me that they are simply not trained in the subject of NDEs in seminary, and are therefore not equipped to handle it. I understand how difficult it could be for those who have not experienced an NDE, or known of anyone personally who has, to speak concisely on the subject. And it could be particularly sensitive for pastors and leaders who suddenly find they are not the voice of authority on theological aspects of death. After all, they are chosen to be the "experts" on the Bible in their congregations.

Yet many members of churches truly do want to hear about NDEs, because they have been exposed to them. I know this because since I made my NDEs public many have approached me with, "Can I tell you something ...?" and launched into an account that they'd been too hesitant to voice for fear of being dismissed with unflattering adjectives. The Christian church already believes in Heaven and Hell, and therefore focuses on missionary outreach and social justice to bring more to Christ. That is good, but there is more. In the pews are believers who need hope and encouragement, whose experiences must be validated and not ridiculed. I've been in church leadership, and I get it completely. It's one of the gaps I pray that I can fill. And the Lord wants me to fill the gap and has been leading the way for me.

While reviewing the manuscript for this book in October 2018, I was pleased to update it to include an avenue He opened for me to share broadly about my experiences. Access7 Television in Saskatchewan granted me an hour-long slot to host my own show that I've entitled *Eternity*. I will share my own experiences and those of others, and research and answer questions on "Where Will You Spend Eternity?". Praise God for seeing my heart and opening a door. I pray that many men and women, boys and girls, will come to the saving grace of Jesus Christ as I teach and lead the prayer for salvation each week. Only in Eternity will I know the impact of *Eternity*.

Christian churches refrain from using numerous terminologies—and I had avoided them as well. But I have become more open since my experiences, and hence more comfortable with this vocabulary. Take the word "being" for example. Saying "Being" with reference to God is generally associated with eastern religions. I heard it a lot among my Hindu relatives, so I understand the raised eyebrows when NDErs speak of the

Being of Light they encounter. (I actually encountered that Light as described in chapter 3.)

The Oxford dictionary defines "being" as "a real or imaginary living creature or entity, especially an intelligent one."[2]

We are human beings and identify with the term. Check.

Spirit beings exist. Check.

And God is a spirit, making Him a spirit being. Check, right?

At this point someone who does not want to continue the logic may excuse themselves. *Susan, there's a lion on the porch. So sorry. Gotta go.*

Not sorry at all. Uncheck.

The most real, living, intelligent entity is GOD. And newsflash ... He can be termed "entity" just as we can be termed human entities. God does not mind if He's called Being because He *is* a being—a spirit being. It's really about semantics, friend. It's language. I use the terms others use for the ultimate purpose of leading them to Christ. And I humbly say that almost everyone I share Christ with give their lives to Him.

One fact that does not change is that God is masculine gender, a Father. And this should not be allegorized otherwise. I've not seen His face, but I've seen His shadow and sensed His presence. We can describe Jesus as a person when He appears to us in human form. The Bible calls Him the Light of the World, and He approached people in death through light. A spirit light being cannot be touched, just as the sunlight cannot be touched. People who have not read the Bible do not have the language of Father, Son, and Holy Spirit to describe what they see, so they use the simple description Being of Light. Note that I am not speaking of counterfeit light, that's a whole other discussion. I'm merely articulating the word Being in describing the true and living God.

He appeared to me in Light form on June 24th 2017, first a brilliant orange Light that changed into a soft champagne color in umbra style, radiating dazzling white at the core. Many individuals have seen the Light take on the human form of Jesus and pull them out of darkness into a place of joy and peace. I did not see His human form, but I believe the accounts of those who say they have.

There are too many other terms to list and expand on but words like consciousness, out-of-body, and depending on which evangelical group one belongs too, "tongues" included, are words that are avoided like the plague.

Along with the numbers 6 5 5 1 9 5 7, the Gospel of John had come to my mind. Focusing on the first three numbers, I turned in the Bible to John 6:55, "For My flesh is true food, and My blood is true drink" (NASB).

Jesus is the one speaking in John 6:55. The Prince. The verse verifies His identity. It is not an angel or a man speaking, or a random description in those verses. What are the odds of that happening in the 31,000 plus verses in the Bible? I'm convinced my interpretation of what I saw was not coincidence, it was God-prompted.

The remaining digits of the number were 1957. I felt this referred to chapter 19, verses 5-7. The New American Standard Version of John 19:5-7 reads, "Jesus then came out, wearing the crown of thorns and the purple robe. Pilate said to them, 'Behold, the Man!' So when the chief priests and the officers saw Him, they cried out saying, 'Crucify, crucify!' Pilate said to them, 'Take Him yourselves and crucify Him, for I find no guilt in Him.' The Jews answered him, 'We have a law, and by that law He ought to die because He made Himself out to be the Son of God'" (NASB).

Goosebumps took over my arms, and I felt the prompting well up in my spirit:

Look at the words that point to Jesus' identity:

Crown ... a crown is worn by royalty—kings and princes, queens and princesses. Jesus is the King of all kings, and the Prince of Peace.

Crucify him, crucify him ... whom did they crucify?

Purple is the color of royalty ... a third clue.

Son of God ... another proclamation that is common knowledge.

Just as there are indicators and addresses on earth, so there are in Heaven. You saw it and it is consistent with the inbreathed Word. Just as there are name plates and signs on Earth to tell you where you are, so the kingdom of Heaven has symbols and words.

I looked again for parallels in what I had seen. Both John 6:55 and 19:5-7 talk of the flesh and the blood, the covenant of the crucifixion. The call to crucify Christ.

Chapters 6 and 19, so far apart in the Bible, yet they carry the same message of the crucifixion. This is the internal consistency and thread of truth.

I remembered how the number 9 had flashed before it changed to 7. That would make the original number 1959. I decided to read John 19:5-9. (Verses 5-7 are above.)

Verses 8-9 read, "Therefore when Pilate heard this statement, he was even more afraid; and he entered into the Praetorium again and said to Jesus, 'Where are You from?' But Jesus gave him no answer" (NASB).

"Where are you from?"

My hands were shaking ... Holy, holy God!

I know, Pilate. Jesus is from the Kingdom of the Prince. You take a crystal tunnel to get there.

Awe settled over me as I took in the enormity of what I had been shown. The description, the numbers, the Bible verses, the messaging ... to be entrusted with these was too immense for my mind. But it was not by my mind or by my might, it was by His Spirit, as Zechariah 4:6 reminds. "Father, let me find the words to impart what I've seen and heard," was my prayer.

Another parallel that intrigued me was the word "kingdom". When the number changed from 9 to 7 it had brought to mind the writing on the wall in the book of Daniel. What is interesting is that the translation of Peres/Upharsin contains the word "kingdom" (Daniel 5:26). I too had seen the word "kingdom" on the sign KINGDOM OF THE PRINCE.

If I created a mind map with all my experiences, I'd find they converge in Eternity. I've read in the works of Dr. Moody[3] and Dr. Long[4] that many NDErs went up a tunnel of clear glass. Jesus went up before the eyes of the disciples with the same body posture as I did, straight up with his head upwards before He disappeared (Acts 1:9).

Consider this: Is it possible that Jesus was in a glass tunnel that could not be seen by those around him? Transparent, clear glass could easily camouflage in air. Is it that the tunnel can only be seen through spiritual eyes? I do not infer truth in speculating—rather I invite thinking to a possibility based on what so many of us have experienced while transitioning.

And what about Elijah who went up in a whirlwind? (2 Kings 2:11). The Oxford dictionary defines a whirlwind as a column of air moving rapidly round and round in a cylindrical or funnel shape.[5] I describe my return to earth from Heaven's meadow in chapter 10 like this: "Faster than any speed I could imagine, I found myself receding from Heaven, sucked back to somewhere. Someone is at my side, but he's not as close as when we walked in the meadow. The way back looked like a dark road spiraling as in a drawing—widest at the Heaven top, but fish-tailing to thin nothingness at the other end. I feel as if I am flying backwards, my face towards Heaven, my feet pointing in the direction I am traveling back to. I am in a horizontal position, whizzing through the air at this speed which I cannot measure but which feels like the twinkling of an eye as described in 1 Corinthians 15:52."

"Wide at the top and thin at the other end" describes a funnel shape. There appears to be a parallel between Elijah's going up experience and my coming back one. I zig-zagged the route like the prophet in the Old Testament.

It is my prayer that you, the reader, will not dismiss what I've experienced simply because it is not divulged this way in the Bible. Each of my experiences is grounded in Scripture, with added details. God shows NDErs more about Heaven than is stated in Scripture as part of the mystery unfolding. Oh, the blessing to see these aspects of Eternity.

A skeptic may argue that every detail ought to be written in the Bible. I touched on this earlier in the chapter and invite such skeptics to consider this: Since Eternity cannot be grasped or measured in earthly mentalities, the best way to condense it in a practical volume is to give highlights and glimpses. I believe if Heaven is to be described in detail, that vast, infinite world prepared to accommodate every person ever conceived, animals, the mind-blowing colors, and all the glorious things spoken of in Scripture, it would be so gigantic a volume that it could not be held by a single person. Such a Bible would be un-liftable, unimaginable, un-readable, and all the "uns" that go against being read-

206 | TOUCHED BY ETERNITY

er-friendly. A hard copy book of that magnitude would not be used. It would have to be broken down into volumes, like encyclopedias. (And what if the sermon text was taken from another volume than the one I carried to church that day?)

I believe that the Lord allows us to peek into Heaven and Hell to help us understand what is contained in the Bible.

Additionally, the vocabulary needed to describe Heaven is, frankly, beyond the human capability to relate, as I have mentioned several times. I say, respectfully, that even the most brilliant writer could not sufficiently describe the wonder of Heaven and the vastness of Eternity. Those who have returned to speak about it *know* the frustration of grappling with language to impart what has been seen. The names of colors, for example, simply do not exist. At best we compare colors to the closest they come on earth, but what is seen cannot be spoken of adequately. We are acutely aware of how short we fall in conveying the glory we glimpsed. A thousand pictures and more thousands of words cannot do Heaven justice. I believe God allows us the frustrations so that we would not steal His glory or become prideful, as the shortcomings in communication maximize our reliance on Him.

It is my opinion that the Lord has highlighted in the Bible what He wants us to know of Heaven, a general overview rather than numerous specific details, but those details can be made known in His time to whom He chooses.

To simplify the concept further, consider the word "house". In John 14:2, Jesus says, "In my Father's house are many mansions: if it were not so, I would have told you. I go to prepare a place for you" (KJV). Bible commentators differ on the meaning of house and mansion. According to Vine's Expository Dictionary, the Greek word for house is *oikia*,[6] a dwelling, the eternal dwelling place for believers. House is a singular noun.

The Blue Letter Bible puts it this way, "The Greek word for mansion is μονή, which is translated monē, meaning manor or manse. This mansion is a permanent staying place, not a tent, inn or temporary resting place on the road. The house, the dwelling place will be as glorious as a mansion and there will be many such dwelling places and there is nothing in the word to indicate separate compartments in Heaven."[7]

Matthew Henry Bible Commentary explains mansions as distinct dwelling places or apartments for each saint.[8]

Another body interprets mansions and the Father's house as Christ's mystical body, that is, a divine organism composed of the Triune God mingled with his chosen people.[9] Other scholars suggest that there will be literal buildings in heaven, not a single mansion, but many (plural) mansions (John 14:2).[10]

The Bible states its truth in a few words, but the interpretations by people are different. Fortunately, as long as someone believes in Jesus' death on the cross, houses and mansions become irrelevant. When one gets to Heaven, he or she will realize the truth. From my experience of seeing Heaven, I like to think of mansions as individual dwelling places—in my 2007 vision I saw separate houses as in a suburban area; in 2015 I saw a gigantic golden castle; in 2017 I saw a smaller blue castle.

The royal residences of the British monarchy are a close parallel to the "mansions in Heaven comprising the multiple buildings theory" in my opinion. Again this is my personal belief. A search on the official Royal website[11] revealed over a dozen residences occupied by the royal family of Britain: Windsor Castle, Balmoral Castle, Clarence House, Kensington Palace, to name a few. In Heaven, I believe there will be more buildings than we can imagine for both individual habitation and collective gatherings.

If one were to accept the interpretation of Heaven as one house with many rooms, the Palace at Versailles presents a model like this. In 2016 Radiance and I visited the chateau, as the luxurious country residence is called. It is a single building with many rooms; the official website states that the palace contains 2300 rooms, a few examples being the Hall of Mirrors, the Royal Chapel, the Congress Chambers, and the King's Apartments.[12]

The secrets of Heaven are revealed to those who call on God, and to those whom He chooses, even if such individuals never desired the information. As someone who has had many unforgettable, unsought experiences, I can vouch that such knowledge comes through deep, dark moments, through times of excruciating and unbearable pain, and in sickness. Which individual wants to be broken to the point of being useless, a burden to the ones closest to her? Who wants to risk losing the love of a husband because he is depleted by an invalid wife? And if it happens once, would I want it to happen twice? Or twice to the same husband in a short space of time? No. Those of us who've had an NDE do not wish this on ourselves. But when it happens and we realize that many can miss this spectacular place called Heaven then we want to tell it to the world so that they may be saved.

My message is to hearten those who hope, but more so it is for the lost that Jesus came to seek (Luke 19:10). All I can do is attest to what I've seen, to encourage any who want to know more concrete details of the afterlife, and pray that hope in Jesus rises in their hearts. Human experience cannot displace God's Word, but God uses humans to build His kingdom on earth. Like a vessel of water, I am the vessel and He is the water, the life, and the hope.

CHAPTER 31

THE MAP

"I am the way, the truth, and the life" *John 14:6 (KJV).*

Two weeks after my NDE on June 24th 2017, when I saw the blue castle, I had a vision. It was about 6:45 a.m. and I was still in bed. Tim was preparing his breakfast in the kitchen. It was my first full night of sleep since the tooth extraction, and the dull ache suggested that I should take a painkiller. The pain was still bearable at level 3, so I chose to snuggle a little longer.

I pulled the bamboo sheet over my head and closed my eyes. The movements in the kitchen had slowed down, so Tim must be eating oatmeal while he browsed the Internet.

My thoughts ever God-wards, I prayed, "Show me Heaven, Lord." And instantly it happened.

Darkness appeared, zooming towards me then lightening to gray.

My heart picked up speed because I could tell that this was Eternity, and I was about to see a mystery, something secret from the Lord as promised in Jeremiah 33:3.

A room comes into view. It is dark, but as my eyes grow accustomed to the dimness I can recognize items. It's as if I'm in a newsroom with a small television with an old-time-looking screen instead of the snazzy flat screens of present day. A Caucasian woman walks eastwards towards the television and flicks it on, then moves to the left and exits the room. Her face is shadowed, but I glimpse it as she leaves—she is attractive and polished, and her hair is pulled back from her face in a bun. Her riveting, intense blue eyes are the most prominent feature in her face.

The monitor flickers to life with black and white zebra stripes appearing in the middle of the screen such as when a poor connection is made. It flashes twice, like ragged lightning, and then the screen takes on Technicolor. As it does, I feel it whizzing into my face, gathering momentum and expanding in a nanosecond. Everything is huge. It is Infinity.

A yellow-brown background— more yellow than brown—lies under me, and as it whizzes by I see it is a map. Lines crisscross the paper, if it is paper, and the huge map races under my gaze. I seem to know direction. It is coming to me from the west going eastwards. Then the map stops as a close-up before my eyes. Unlike the typewritten names on the maps we buy, the writing is in script, a loose kind of handwriting.

Is this how the writing on the wall looked when the Hand had appeared and written Mene, Mene, Tekel, Upharsin? (Daniel 5:25 KJV). Did the handwriting look like this on the tablets of stone of the Ten Commandments? When Jesus wrote in the sand before the Pharisees and the woman taken in adultery? (John 8:6-8). Did the same Hand draw the lines and dots I am looking at and write the names of the places on it? How intimately He knows the earth from His vantage point in the heavens!

The places are written as proper nouns—the first letter is uppercase and the rest are in lowercase. The area I am shown is on an edge, on the east boundary of a land mass where land ends and the ocean begins. I cannot determine yet if beyond the land is an ocean or space. It looks hazy as water appears in the far distance, and could have been interpreted as space too, but it is definitely a demarcation.

The map settles in place under my view. The area has a definite triangular edge resembling a rough horseshoe. Around the shape a half circle arc is drawn in pencil, as if someone had used a protractor, and horizontal lines extend from both ends of the arc. The lines and arc around the triangle are not part of the original map—it looks as if Someone has highlighted a place for personal use.

A clue for me to distinguish a comparable place on a map.

The protractor drawing is at the top of the map. The location that is significant to me, however, is not directly below the horseshoe-triangle, but lower down, and could be either to the right or the left.

The names of places flash before me, but I only recognize four letters of one name, Wght. The rest of the word is obliterated, but my first thought is *Washington*.

At the bottom of the map is marked "110% 5%". A legend. I get the impression it is a measure of scale. For example, the maps we use may show 1-1,000, which can be interpreted as 1 cm represents 1,000 km, but I can't help wondering if percentages are used in Eternity. I could not say if it was akin to latitude and longitude. Or perhaps God has unknown cartographic elements in the blue yonder?

Suddenly I feel myself receding from the map. It grows smaller in the distance at lightning speed as I'm being drawn back to earth. I do not want to go back, I want to see more.

"Show me more, Lord," I beg.

The communication returns, *You will forget what you see. This is enough.*

I do not hear a voice as I had when I was leaving Heaven's meadow. God shares His ability to know thoughts with me, and I am allowed to know His thoughts. But not everything is made known to me, or perhaps I am not allowed to keep that knowledge and it is forgotten when I return to earth.

I could hear Tim approaching the bedroom door and I called out to him. It was as if I had been awake all the time and knew what had been going on in the house.

"Yes," he replies, and comes close to the bed.

I tell him of the vision, ending with, "I was not asleep because I could hear you in the kitchen. And I'm not making this up, really."

He nods and heads off to the shower, leaving me to brood on the parting words: *You will forget what you see.*

Why would it matter if I forgot? For whose benefit should I remember?

Even as I mulled it over, I knew the answer. Recording is the antidote to not forgetting. I must leave a document trail similar to the way the Israelites left standing stones—to remember what God has done. It is for the benefit of the generations to come, for looking back at God's covenant and supernatural acts, His protection and favor, His mercies and love, His goodness and faithfulness. The Israelites did not have computers or dictation software to hold their memories, so stony pillars were erected and the stories passed down in oral tradition from generation to generation. But I have digital and hard copy media.

I ruminate on the traditions. Oral practice is still evident among the First Nations people of Canada. And long before the Israelites entered Canaan, sacred stones were erected to pagan gods in the Middle East. Archaeologists have uncovered the Gezer stones, huge, impressive stones at Tel Gezer that testify to the use of monuments to depict memorable happenings. I once taught a series at church called *That the World May Know* with Ray Vander Laan and one of the topics was standing stones.[1]

Examples abound in the Old Testament. Jacob set up stone pillars at Bethel in order to remember the powerful dream in which God reaffirmed his covenant with him (Genesis 28:18-21, 35:14-15). Moses placed twelve standing stones at the foot of Mount Sinai after receiving the Ten Commandments (Exodus 24:2-4). The Israelites erected standing stones to remember their miraculous crossing of the Jordan River (Joshua 4:2-9). Joshua built a standing stone when the covenant was renewed at Shechem (Joshua 24:27).

The practice of standing stones carries on in the New Testament, where Peter describes believers as "living stones" (1 Peter 2:5). We, believers in Christ, are symbolized as living standing stones. We are to be people who live our faith so fearlessly that it captures the attention of others. As living stones, we testify to God's faithfulness in our lives. Jesus is the chief cornerstone in the Body of Christ, and I am a living stone in that Body. My visions and near-death experiences captured in writing are standing stones. Implicit in "not to forget" is a charge, a responsibility to record. My heart rate quickens as I absorb the implication.

I must not forget, because how will they know?

I will be shown more if I write down what I see, but I will not see more until I am obedient in keeping the memory alive.

My *Little Copper Pennies* series captured the history of the iconic Canadian penny when it was removed from circulation in 2012. Those books grace homes, schools, and public libraries across Canada. I must do the same for the other world.

All day long I pondered the map vision. Was it a map of Eternity? Of another specific place? Where? What did it represent?

Obediently, but not without trepidation, I started to write what I saw. But how does one write about such things when they seem so unreal? I was convinced there might be a physical description somewhere on earth that would add to the understanding. I was willing to trust God, like Noah, when he heard from God to build an ark. Noah built, I will write. Like John on the Isle of Patmos, who saw and wrote, I had seen and would write. Oh, for the wisdom of Daniel to interpret. For the ability of Joseph to give meaning.

I pray out loud, "God of Daniel and Joseph, you are my God and I trust you to prompt me with the meaning."

The Lord spoke through a recall of Jeremiah1:9: "Then the LORD reached out his hand and touched my mouth and said to me, 'I have put my words in your mouth'" (NIV). I realized that if I open my laptop, He will put the words in my brain. Slowly, line by line, episode by episode, He is showing me the mysteries of Eternity, and how much I see will depend on my faithfulness to write it line by line. This responsibility, being entrusted with the Kingdom, requires faithfulness, and I do not want to be found lacking.

Here am I Lord, I'll write. I don't want to forget.

Trembling, but at peace, I opened a browser on my laptop and typed *Wght*. A list came up with the first word: weight. I refined my search to countries, towns, and cities, and another list came up. I scrunched my forehead as I scanned the list. Only one word contained all four letters. *Washington*. The initial word that had been dropped in my spirit during the vision. George Washington, the first president of the United States of America, has the most places named after him in the United States of America.

My next step was to research Washington D.C., the most notable place with the word *Washington* and the capital of the US. But as soon as I looked at Washington D.C., tucked in securely by land masses, I knew it was not the one. The place I sought was located on an edge of a mass, and if such a place existed on earth, it was in a north-easterly direction with a boundary of water.

My third step was to narrow down "Washington" to the northeastern US. This time the Borough of Washington in Warren County, New Jersey was among the choices. My body felt warmer for I knew New Jersey was in the northeast US. But first I had to consult a map for its location. Over eight tabs were opened on my browser as I performed search after search on Google, pulling up maps of New Jersey showing counties, maps of New Jersey in relation to the wider US, and maps showing boundaries and oceans.

Then my mouth opened and I gazed transfixed at the screen. The county of Monmouth[2] in New Jersey has a horseshoe-like triangular shape jutting into the Atlantic Ocean. Had I found my state?

I scrambled to the next task, to locate the Borough of Washington. I found it situated in Warren County. My mind boggled as I located the county about forty-five degrees northwest of the protracted area I had seen on the map in Eternity. The blood rushed in my ears, drumming in rhythm to my thrumming heart. Then calm rose in my spirit, a settling that I'd hit the target.

I could not keep up with the steps as I clicked and opened more browsing tabs—CIA World Factbook, History of the Borough of Washington, Britannica, were but a few. I was hungry to read the history.

"Washington Borough, named for America's first President ..."[3]

Although I knew it was named after the first president, my breathing quickened again as a question popped in my mind: *Like locales in Eternity are named after the Son?*

My heart was still pounding as I devoured another line: According to the Borough's website, Washington has a total area of 2 square miles (5.1 square kilometers).

Something inside me went ping.

Area. I searched for a conversion tool. Perspiration formed on my neck and I wiped it with my cotton dress. My mouth was dry. I was about to discover something significant, but what? The conversion table showed up on the screen—there are 1280 acres in 2 square miles.

Something in Eternity measures 1280 acres, or 2.0 miles².

My heart was still buffeting as I continued. "The borough also served as a hub center for the farmers of the surrounding townships."

Farmers. My husband is a farmer and we live among farmland in a township. Our house is set on an acreage with fields around, the highway a mere 135 meters away. I understand the "hub for farmers". The parallel jumped at me. The information seeping into my spirit from God and ancillary research were both in a context of farming.

Nature. Jesus had used parables of nature to teach and draw illustrations, thereby making concrete the abstract, unknown secrets of the Kingdom of God. The sower (farmer) and the seed, the wildflowers and birds, the gospel and the seed dying to bring forth harvest—all are farming themes. And God was using everyday farming to help *me* convey the unknown of Heaven. That was also true of the concept of land location and its correlation to the numbers I had seen in my trip to Eternity as described in chapter 33.

What does 1280 acres represent?

"Lord, fill in the blanks."

Immediately the blanks filled as the thought swelled in my heart:

The size of 1280 acres, the two square miles, represents the area of the domain of the blue castle with gold trim that gleamed white that had appeared as I lay dying on June 24th, 2017.

Holy, holy God! I cannot contain this but for You. Oh Jesus! You tell us in John 14:2, "In my Father's house are many mansions. If it was not so I would have told you. I go to prepare a place for you ..."

The castle with the towers and the turrets with a shade of blue I had never seen before, the brilliant luminescence I stared at, spellbound, in the distance beyond my husband's shoulders, one like Steve Jobs may have wowed at, is one of the mansions Jesus has gone to prepare. I believe through the revelation the Lord gave me that the Borough of Washington shares the common factor of size with the blue mansion in the sky. The castle in the sky probably rests on a mass of 1280 acres.

The tag line on the upper left corner of the Borough of Washington's website, and the final line of information on the home page is its motto, "Hometown Friendly". When I had sat in Heaven's meadow, I felt that it was where I belonged. I was home. But there's even more. The downloads from God come over time. As I reviewed the manuscript in 2018, the Holy Spirit took me back to October 16th, 1998 in the OB/GYN's office, and the word "home" leapt at me:

"You need home care." Dr. Im's tone was urgent and he picked up the phone to arrange for a nurse to come to our address ... I never knew if he got a hold of the department. For at that moment, I slumped forward on his desk. Simultaneous with my memory of slumping on the doctor's desk, is one where I am walking on soft green grass going uphill ... "

I had gone HOME for my home care!

Holy, holy God.

I HAD RECEIVED THE CARE I NEEDED IN MY HOME IN HEAVEN AND WAS SENT BACK TO EARTH HEALED AND WHOLE.

On July 7th, 2017, the day I had the vision of the map but prior to doing the research, I had posted about my NDE of June 24th on Facebook and commented, "This world is so not my home."

I pine for the peace and space, the joy and wonder of the perfect life I had tasted. As Christians we believe this world is not our home. Hometown Friendly. What a comparison and revelation of my home in Heaven. That mansion in the sky covered an area similar to the Borough, and its motto was also applicable. As discussed in the previous chapter, I believe the blue castle is my home.

I am aware not to project my vision and interpretation as anything other than my own experience, but I hope it will invite introspection about Eternity. God has not given us in the Bible as many details as I've written, but He has promised to show us new things.

CHAPTER 32

WHY SEE HEAVEN WHEN IN PAIN?

"God chose the weak things of the world ..." 1 Corinthians 1:27b (NIV).

I WAS NEVER INTERESTED in the topic of pain until writing this book, and for the first time I asked the question: Why do I see Heaven when I'm weak, sick, and in pain? And a related question: Was Jesus sick like I was?

Scripture uses the specific words of hungry, thirsty, and tired when speaking of Jesus, but does not state that He was sick. Yet the evidence is there. The night before the cross He sweated blood. On the cross He was tortured, experienced agony and unimaginable pain. He was battered, bruised, dehydrated, exhausted, and weak. His blood flowed and His flesh was ripped into an unrecognizable mass of tissue. That horror is unparalleled and makes my being "sick" a garden party.

Pain comes from the Greek word *odin*,[1] meaning birth pangs. My heavenly visits first started in 1998 when I was in a literal "birth" state, pregnant and afflicted with HG.

Paul says of pain in 2 Corinthians 12:10, "... for Christ's sake, I delight in weaknesses, in insults, in hardships, in persecutions, in difficulties. For when I am weak, then I am strong" (NIV). Weakness is a theme in my life and therefore is the perfect context for becoming strong in Christ.

On Saturday, July 9th 2017, the Lord had spoken to me with words coming up as if from my stomach and fastening themselves in my brain. "Do you prefer to be weak and see Heaven OR to be healthy and not see it?"

Oh, why must there be a choice? Why one or the other and not both? Self-absorbed me, daughter of the fallen—I wanted the health and the sightings of Eternity too. I knew my answer, the binary choice, but I could not bring myself to voice it. So instead I wrote to my friend, Helen, on Facebook. She understands pain too.

"I totally understand that thought and impression," Helen wrote back. "When we are weak we experience God in a special way because we are so helpless and dependent on Him."

My 112-pound pain-plundered body makes me the paradoxical and contradictory "strong". In *odin* the *paradoxos* takes on enlightenment. In *odin* I am nearing perfection. In the weak, frail state I see the celestial city; I sit on the grounds and watch children who worship before the throne.

My wealth is in ill-health. If I am healthy, I will focus my attention on outside things that take me away from God, but when I'm indoors literally confined to a bed, I find Him more and more. God is a jealous God, and He calls us to holiness by loosening the ties to this world—this world that worships the brilliant and the beautiful, the successful and the rich, the famous and the athletic. They are splashed on television and social media, larger-than-life in their extravagance. The world rushes to admire them, make them our heroes, emulate them.

But the *paradoxos* calls from 1 Corinthians 1:26-28, "Brothers and sisters, think of what you were when you were called. Not many of you were wise by human standards; not many were influential; not many were of noble birth. But God chose the foolish things of the world to shame the wise; God chose the weak things of the world to shame the strong. God chose the lowly things of this world and the despised things—and the things that are not—to nullify the things that are" (NIV).

A post I wrote on Facebook on the theme expressed this:

> Jesus was attracted to the lowly, the poor, the marginal, the hungry, the weak and sick. His heart tore at the vulnerable ones, and tore for them. Is it that I hear from God most clearly when I am sick because He always draws near to the sick? Is He closest to me then? Did He not hang on the cross weak, sick, and helpless? That vulnerability brings me into a unifying oneness with him. I will take up my cross and offer it to Him who hung on a cross. This cathartic relationship of crosses, bridging the oneness of mortal me and matchless God, is the essence of the gift of sickness to allow us to serve Him fully. We partake in the fellowship of His sufferings when we are weak and vulnerable, sick and in need. For we raise as a banner the reason He came – to seek

and save. As Mark 2:17 says, "They that are whole have no need of the physician, but they that are sick" (NIV).

He came to me on my sickbed, healing me not once, not twice, but three times.

I feel the heaviness of His presence. The *kavod*[2] as the Greek states, the weight of His glory. My surrendered heart will do as the prophet did in Habakkuk 2:2, "And the LORD answered me, and said, Write the vision …"

Helen continues, "The Scripture says in Isaiah 45:3, 'I will give you treasures in the darkness—secret riches.' These riches come to those who have walked in the valley and called out to the mighty God who saves, because there was no other way."

It was in the literal darkened hours between night and morning of November 3rd, 2015 that I tunneled up to Eternity with my arms at my side and a large unseen companion. Metaphorically, in the dark state of nausea and anguish my treasure was to see and hear unsearchable things like the tunnel, which is not even mentioned in the Bible.

I swallowed her words, "The treasures of the darkness come slowly and at His timing."

1998, 2015, 2017. Twenty years to the date of this writing. How slow is that?

Helen directed me to a quote from *The Problem of Pain* written by the notable C.S. Lewis: "God whispers to us in our pleasures, speaks to our conscience, but shouts in our pain; it is His megaphone to rouse a deaf world."[3] I had indeed become deaf, but my mandate now was to be a crier. Awaken them to what had been revealed during the periods of pain.

I had messaged her concerning Jeremiah 33:3 and what I was interpreting of the spiritual life. "The NIV states the word 'mysteries' as 'unsearchable things'. It hit me last year that what I will discover will not be things one can search on the Internet or in books. The map that I saw recently, for example, and the trip I had back in 2015 in the hospital, I've not read about or heard anything from the angle I present."

Hungry to know the experiences of others, I had read a few books and watched several movies. They contained descriptions of green grass, the peace, the lights, the colors, the tunnel, and the magnificence of the mansions that people saw as they neared death, but I had not read of the gushing water from the belly, or the signage in Eternity, or the map, or the location numbers similar to the land location of the countryside, or the Green Room (in chapter 33). Those are unsearchable, untold, and new revelation from God to me.

Helen wrote back, "That's an excellent translation for unsearchable things. Google is the go-to place to search for everything. The things of the Spirit cannot be had quickly, easily, or on the cheap. It takes years to form a diamond and so it is with God's people."

The confirmation in the mouth of this witness, this gentle woman of God, fueled my desire to keep typing the manuscript.

There was more to her message. "Line upon line, precept upon precept, a little here and a little there is how it comes. When we think we have arrived we do not realize we have barely begun. This is the one whom He esteems—he who is humble and contrite in spirit and trembles at His word. Oh for a trembling at His word, and to become humble as a little child."

I halted. The confirmation of building the book "line by line" could only be revealed by the Spirit. When I had found myself receding from the map vision, I had begged, "Show me more, Lord." And the answer was, "You'll forget if you see more." Bit by bit, one snippet at a time, as one idea unfolds I record it, and then another piece comes. Eternity cannot be grasped by the human mind—it must be broken up into small pieces and captured alongside a concrete analogy on Earth. Then will the comprehension come. And even so it may still be vague.

The reproach reverberated in my heart. *I am my only barrier. I stand in the way of my future. I am responsible for my failure if I do not write.* I knew the pace of the revelations would depend on my obedience. My action determined my outcome. Then and there I made a pact with God that I would write whatever He showed me and not be afraid.

I turned back to Helen's wisdom, stark black on the white screen. "I know something is brewing within you. We start out as at the beginning ... the earth was formless and void. Then the Holy Spirit hovers over us and speaks, and life begins to form from the nothingness. It is so amazing and exciting."

The very beginning in Genesis ... "In the beginning God created the heaven and the earth. And the earth was without form, and void; and darkness was upon the face of the deep. And the Spirit of God moved upon the face of the waters" Genesis 1:1-2 (KJV). I contemplated the verse, zeroing in on "darkness". From darkness is spawned the light, the new. From the nothingness comes the everything-ness. I saw darkness before I saw the map. A blog I'd written had read like this:[4]

> In the darkroom the negative takes form, losing identity as a picture emerges. This aptly named negative belongs to the darkness and can only be developed there. It is a shifting paradigm to conjure the dark as anything but an evil swirling abyss, empty and threatening, where God is absent. Yet a shift there must be that dark gives birth to life. In the inky womb the baby sleeps and is perfected. In the stygian underground, seeds laced in black soil defy gravity to shoot up green. The clefts of rocks are dark; He hides us and we are safe.
>
> The old hymn sings, "When Jacob met the Lord upon that lonely night ..." A dark night for the repentant thief.
>
> The chorus trills, "I want, I want, that kind of blessing."
>
> Really? In the ebony night? When the markets turn and the favor runs low and the words we strive for hover in sight, but dance frustratingly beyond reach? And the shame—as we fight until morning light breaks when dawn shows God was, and is, closest to us in the dark?
>
> The blessing in and of the dark is only found in the darkroom. The place where the negative surrenders.

My pain will not be in vain if the unsaved will be saved.

CHAPTER 33

THE ALFALFA FIELD AND THE GREEN ROOM

"Write down the revelation ..." Habakkuk 2:2a (NIV).

IN AUGUST 2016 WE made the decision to build our house on an acreage close to the farm. For six years Tim had made the 120-kilometer trip daily—from home to work to farm and back home—and it was draining him.

The farm is a bustling operation that must respond to a short and unpredictable timeline. In its simplest form, planting the crop involved cultivating, harrowing, seeding, spraying, and adding fertilizer. Harvesting includes swathing, combining, filling trucks, and emptying into bins. Marketing involves contacting buyers, and it is common to load grain in semis in brutal January temperatures. Then there's the administration and management with its library of paperwork. Winter crops must be seeded before the ground freezes, and disasters bring their own intricacies. The alfalfa fields require a different kind of work. After the hay is cut, it must be dried and compressed into bales, which then must be moved to accessible storage sites.

We discussed the house-building. "If we begin the foundation preparation this summer we can be moved in by fall," I reasoned. Tim felt dubious, but I was confident in my project management skills.

We decided on a modular house. For a few years I'd been looking at models, attracted to the craftsmanship and designs. The huge island dominating the kitchen/dining space had been the first feature that drew me to the one we purchased. The triple bar lights and skylight through which I could see the sun and stars were unmatched in any home we'd lived in, and the jetted tub with shower stall in the master en suite had sealed the deal of the choice of the Savanna as our dream residence had been named.

On August 1ˢᵗ Tim and I scouted the final spot for the house. Five years earlier we had built a well. Modular homes looked best on large plots of land, and ours would be set against trees on a high location to avoid flooding. The contractor cleared the land, leaving most of the L-shaped grove of trees that formed a natural windbreak. The foundation was prepared, the septic system installed, and all was ready for the new house to arrive in October for my birthday.

We had to apply for a permit with the rural municipality (RM), and it was during the application process that I really became acquainted with land location. Unlike the city, where houses are assigned streets and numbers, countryside addresses are derived using land location. I'll use the location of one of our alfalfa fields as an example–NE 20 22 03 W2. The letters and numbers identify Quarter, Section, Township, Range and Meridian as follows[1]:

NE is the Quarter on the North East side

20 is the Section

22 is the Township

03 is the Range

W2 is West of the Second Meridian

Therefore the land location reads as, "The north east corner of Section 20, Township 22, Range 03, west of the 2ⁿᵈ Meridian." (The first meridian begins in Manitoba.)

Shortly after completing the form for the building permit, I began to mull over the location numbers. It would soon be my address and I needed to remember it in the correct order, especially for emergency services. (I could not have projected how soon that would be!) But I had an unshakeable feeling there was more to the numbers.

A month later the revelation came:

Our location contained seven numerals. *The number I had seen in Eternity contained seven numerals. 6 5 5 1 9 5 7.*

Is 65-51-95-7 the location of the Kingdom of the Prince?

Akin to Section 65, Township 51, Range 95, Meridian 7?

There was no need for east or west cardinal points, for Jesus is the Star, the *north* star. As the north is the default for direction, He is our direction and compass even in Eternity. There is only one Meridian, and it's in Christ himself, the chief cornerstone.

I recalled the prompting in my spirit when I had studied the numbers I'd seen in Heaven. *Just as there are indicators and addresses on earth, so there are in Heaven. You saw it and it is consistent with the inbreathed Word. Just as there are name plates and signs on Earth to tell you where you are, so the kingdom of Heaven has symbols and words.*

A shiver went up my arm and Jeremiah 33:3 rose in my spirit again, "… I will tell you great and unsearchable things that you do not know" (NIV).

"Location" in Heaven as I've established before is not spelled out in the Bible. That was unsearchable information the Lord showed me as I called on Him. I had remained tight-lipped about my trip up the tunnel into Eternity, but now I wondered, *Could it be that I first had to learn the significance of location on earth in order to draw the parallel to Heaven?*

I believe so. I needed a framework for reference and the new build provided it. Jesus' parables were earthly stories with Heavenly meaning, and my understanding of Heaven's location had to be derived from the concrete understanding on Earth. People would be able to think more about Heaven if they could hold on to an earthly concept.

I fizzed like live electricity. The meanings of the numbers must be explored.

Like names, numbers have significance and traditions—twenty five marks silver, fifty marks golden, and so on. I speculated on the Biblical and symbolic significance of the numbers in the land location format, 65-51-95-7.

A Google search brought up the following:

65 is associated with the Israelite tribe of Ephraim.[2] Isaiah 7:8 reads, "Within threescore and five years shall Ephraim be broken . . ." (KJV). The website also identified 65 to mean "shattering". The significant words in both references are "broken" and "shattering"—fitting descriptors of Jesus, the Prince of Peace, who was broken for our redemption.

51 has the meaning of repentance in the Bible.[3] Repentance of sin is the first step to eternal life.

95 means The Voice of God.[4] God's voice had spoken to me in Eternity.

7 is God's perfect number.[5] It represents completion, divine perfection. In seven days He created the earth. He rested on the seventh day. Bible Study website noted that number 7 is the foundation of God's word, and *foundation* was noteworthy to me because I had stood on the edge of the kingdom, on its foundation in His perfect, complete world. And the number I had seen had 7 digits.

The associations and meaning were sobering, because each correlated to what I had been shown in Eternity and Scripture. Again, I'd like to underscore that my beliefs are meant to spur thinking.

At home I have 360 degree views of God's land. The acres of green soothe my mind, and the yellow canola and golden wheat bring unfailing pleasure. The animals and birds, the changing landscape of the seasons, even the dust devil that shook my car in a field, unfold marvel. The sweeping panoramas of the sky, clouds changing from cumulus puffs to angry tornadoes with tails, fascinate me. The brilliant lightning shows are unmatched. But the most coveted is the blue above that separates me from my deepest longing—Heaven.

On June 13th, 2017, one week before my wisdom tooth was extracted, I was praying on the day bed in our living room with its beige walls and white ceiling, when suddenly I had a vision of being in a room filled with what looked like green and purple Northern Lights.

The purple looks like the rainbow shade between blue and violet. The green is dominant and intense, punctuated intermittently by streaks of purple, and both colors are true to the Aurora Borealis I've witnessed. The green has more yellow than the rainbow shade. The lights look like opaque gossamer, and they dance thick and heavy in a rhythm. The room is massive, as everything is in Eternity, but where I am feels small because I cannot see beyond the lights. I'm reminded of fog, thick white prairie fog that reduces visibility to mere meters, except this is green, impenetrable, riveting fog. Where I stand is all green. I am spellbound by the living, moving curtains of light that appear 3-dimensional. Green glory. I do not know anything more nor do I receive any special knowledge just then.

The vision faded, and I recalled a blog I had written after my first sighting of the Northern Lights a few years before.

> It was winter and as the darkness fell, the Northern Lights came out. A wave of sea-green interwoven with purple and blue, rising and falling in rhythm to an invisible beat. I stood transfixed in my backyard, the snow deep around my boots, gazing at the shimmering, magical, dancing lights. The colors frolicked as the lights soared and fell, then appeared again as if in hide and seek with elfin comrades. A treasure for my eye.
>
> God, who staged this spectacular display, is at work in us to stage His will and good pleasure (Philippians 2:13 NIV). Each day brings new opportunities to show His glory, be that through our behavior, our speech, or our writing.

I contemplated the vision over the following days and prayed for revelation. Then, as if shot from a quiver, the meaning pierced my spirit. *I was in a preparation room, not unlike the Green Rooms of television houses I'd waited in to be interviewed. The Green Room at CTV is literally painted green, and guests wait there until it's their time to walk onto the set under the hot, bright lights to go live on air. I was in a Green Room in Heaven, the Preparation Room, waiting to go into the presence of the Son who is the Light.*

Holy, holy God!

The Northern Lights are not duplicated by man, nor is lightning, and they reflect the true colors in heaven from what I've seen. Sunsets and sunrises offer striking examples too, but the drawback is that one cannot look at them without hurting one's eyes, whereas one can look at Heaven's brilliance directly without being blinded.

I delved into the significance of green and purple and discovered some fascinating facts. Green is a secondary color on the color chart and is produced by mixing blue and yellow. It is the most common color in the physical world and is found everywhere in nature. It is the color of awakening, of resurrection and rebirth in spring, and there's a guarantee that life will go on while things remain green. Green symbolizes fertility and harmony. Researchers have found bodily benefits to green, such as improving vision—watching green soothes the eyes—and alleviating stress through the relaxation of the body. A Harvard study showed that people working in green offices are more productive and satisfied[6]. Further, the green light on the traffic trio equates to safety.

I was in a safe place, in Heaven.

The color purple is also a secondary color and is a blend of energetic red and stable blue. Purple is associated with royalty, nobility, and sophistication, and speaks of wealth and luxury, creativity and mystery.[7] I had been swaddled in purple lights in the mysterious after-world created by our Lord for those He will receive as His own. Putting the significance of the two colors together, I wondered if I was getting close to the Throne Room of God.

I did not have to wonder long.

Eleven days later, on June 24th, 2017, I saw Jesus, the Light of the World. I am convinced that I had indeed been in a "waiting" room!

Much later in 2018 as I add this paragraph (and others) to the book, I am surprised, yet not really surprised, as connections are made among my experiences. This leads me to believe that the Holy Spirit will continue to show me things at a later date and that none of my experiences and encounters is exhaustive. On October 16, 1998, when I visited Heaven, I had been wearing a lilac (a shade of purple) dress with iridescent sequins in the bodice that sparkled green and purple. Had the Lord lined that up so I was in my "royal color" for my Heavenly visit? Nineteen years later in a vision the same colors again appeared in Heaven. Did that indicate His presence? I believe the connections are significant rather than coincidental. Everything that happens to me is intertwined and scheduled by God, and far from finished.

CHAPTER 34

HE REMEMBERS THAT WE ARE DUST

"... for he knows how we are formed, he remembers that we are dust" Psalm 103:14 (NLT).

On July 7th, 2017, I shared my NDE and seeing the blue castle publicly on social media for the first time. The responses from around the globe were fascinating. A comment succinctly expressed by a friend summed up the sentiment of many: "Outside of salvation itself, I think these kinds of encounters are the greatest miracles humans can experience. I cannot wait to read about yours."

Most individuals who experience NDEs are changed and find themselves with a renewed mission and message. The theme of God's compassion was uppermost in my spirit after my June 24th experience. The verse from Psalm 103:14 rang in my ear, "for he knows how we are formed, he remembers that we are dust" (NLT).

Friend, I wish you could feel the empathy and kindness of God that I felt. He is truly *mindful* of our human weakness. I emphasize the word "mindful" because not only does God remember, He intentionally keeps at the forefront how fragile we are. He knows how our inclinations contradict—indecisions, temptations, and weaknesses versus the desire to do what's right. So often we fail, as Paul expresses, "For what I am doing, I do not understand; for I am not practicing what I would like to do, but I am doing the very thing I hate" Romans 7:15 (NASB). Father God is tuned in to our vulnerabilities, our secret thoughts and feelings, and He keeps them in the forefront of His mind.

We judge each other, forgetting that we too fall, though it may be in a different category. We are fallen like the one we condemn. But God does not condemn, for He knows that He formed us from the pliable dust of the earth. He held the dirt in His hand and squeezed it and rolled it and drew lines on it. He is ever aware that dust is blown by the wind and melted by the water. Winds of temptation, waters of sin. We are murmuring dust, disquieted dust. But He is ever merciful to us, because we are so frail. Father God is overflowing with compassion towards us.

He does not berate us even when our behavior makes Him sad. As a mother feels for the child she bears, a father for the one he raises, so too God feels for each of us, because He shaped us inside a womb of dust. Think of a baby whose finger is squeezed and who is bawling in pain. The parent feels for the child and wishes it had not happened, but the parent does not push the child into further pain. Instead, she takes measures to avoid the finger being squeezed again. So too, we ought to be like God and not take every opportunity to harp on the misdeed. Forgive and let it go. Would you like God to continually chide you? No. Similarly, we must treat others as He treats us. And His compassion to us is never ending. He is long-suffering, not quick to anger, because He remembers that we are weak and broken, that we are useless dust.

Friend, the ability to live compassionately lies in the remembering. We must remember the weaknesses of others and deal with them gently, patiently, mercifully, because each of us will have a moment when we need another to overlook the wrong we have done, and to forgive. To be gentle, patient, and merciful with us.

I came back from the other life changed. My ability to empathize has increased with my NDEs. I welcome diverse views, eager to discuss so I can point another to Christ. I am more open-minded than I used to be.

Our bodies of dust are temporary. When we enter Heaven they will be changed even if we look like our present human self. That's why some spirit beings are seen as figures made of light. We may have the option to present in both forms until we are fully transformed into immortality in the new Heaven after the resurrection of the dead.

In August 2017 I gave a partial testimony to a group at a Home on the Range event on the ranch of award-winning singer, Rachel Dancsok. You could have heard a feather drop as I talked. Eyes filled as the presence of God hooked the listeners. I had never met any of the attendees, but one woman kept nodding and nodding as I spoke. When it came to question time, she shared that she'd had a similar experience of the afterlife. I had prayed for confirmation and got it.

After the meal, a former pastor and Bible scholar held me in discussion for three hours, questioning and cross-questioning me on my NDEs and doctrine. At the end he seemed satisfied with the veracity of my encounters. People are driven to know more of Eternity. While many believe in Heaven, it is still strange to hear of details not spelled out in the Bible. I am eager to spread the messages of hope, healing, and glimpses of Eternity, to inspire believers and make proselytes of skeptics. To point all to Heaven.

When people ask, "Why me?" I reply, "Why not me?"

Firstly, God is looking for someone ordinary so He can do the unordinary through them. Just a simple, flawed individual that He can work through. Like me who post too many pictures of kittens on social media. Like you. On June 13th, the same day that I saw the Green Room, I penned an article on the regrowth of the trees—also green—in the windbreak after the plague of tent caterpillars had stripped them bare. A mere ten days after spraying, the shoots were back, a miracle unique to our property. I felt God was stirring a parallel rebirth in my spirit, and the trees were the evidence in the natural. That was a week before my tooth was extracted, before my third NDE. The extraordinary, the unordinary is mine, but I believe my experiences could happen as easily to anyone.

Secondly, God charted my path before I was born. He knew me long, long before I was made human. Similar to the way heirs are groomed to carry on royal traditions, God has a "royal priesthood" to carry out His work. From childhood I had been trained in the ways of the Lord. When I fell God forgave, lifted, and restored me. He has invested in me for half a century, showing me things, speaking to me, healing me, building a platform in the Caribbean and Canada before launching me into the wider world. He has given me the tools and the visibility, which, though small compared to others, could be multiplied exponentially like the loaves and fishes. The alignment of my skills and education with the heavenly trajectory of my NDEs is a plan, not a coincidence.

I've experienced more disruptions to my health over the last four years (2014-2017) than I have during the rest of my life put together. Those disruptions have forced me to shelve critical elements of my life. I could not have everything at the same time (though I can have them all over various periods of time).

Economics postulates the concept of opportunity cost, which is the value of what must be given up in order to acquire something else. I acquired the subject matter for this book through ill-health, lying on a bed. I would not have seen Eternity had I not been at the point of death. Looking back, my experiences can be seen as blessings, but I see them more as a responsibility to draw the unsaved to Christ and to uplift believers. I would not be a testament of healing but for the suffering I had to undergo. Still, I never asked for it, or suspected that it would occur, nor did I recognize it until long after.

I spend a lot of time thinking about Heaven. I have peace. I pray for wisdom to answer and assure people. I pray for longsuffering to deal gently with those with a differing or antagonistic opinion. I pray for the Holy Spirit to do what I am incapable of doing. I study the Bible more and I devour literature from scientific sources about NDEs as well as personal accounts of NDErs. I want to remove the fear of dying from those who are afraid. I want to travel and tell of the mansions that await us. I want to shout out my testimony of healings and point all to the Living God. Without compromise. Without fear.

I have always been bold in sharing my faith, but now I am unstoppable. Funnily, I longed to go home to Heaven until I started writing this book. Not yet. I am convinced that my best days are ahead of me, and I want to live, and live out my responsibility to lead as many as I can into Eternity.

For I've never felt more alive than when speaking of death.

ACKNOWLEDGEMENTS

I WROTE THIS BOOK to avoid another NDE. After not one, or two, but three NDEs that took me on the other side, I'm afraid that if I don't share what happened, a fourth one might occur again. I'm convinced that God wants me to yet remain on earth and tell my story, and so draw many more to Him. I hope my experiences with death, angels, Heaven and Hell, miraculous healings, and visions will impact the reader for the glory of God. In telling my story, the events, locales, and conversations are portrayed to the best of my memory, and documented records ensure the accuracy of the content. I wrote the manuscript in 2017, updated it in 2018, and published it in 2019.

To my primary care physician Dr. PCP, the shining EP Dr. Omar Sultan, cardiologist Dr. Wojcik, Dr. Stephen Im, other specialists and medical teams, and the staff of the various hospitals who attended to me in both Trinidad and Canada, thank you from the depths of my heart.

I owe a huge debt of gratitude to God's people from the many churches and organizations who invited me to speak over three decades, and to those who prayed and took care of me when I was unwell.

Thank you to my endorsers, and friends on social media who followed my story, believed in me, and showed their unwavering encouragement as I wrote this book. The validation by many who felt safe in sharing their own encounters of the supernatural or the experiences of others with me reinforced the "everyday" nature of glimpses of the life to come.

I am grateful for the safe and God-fearing home in which I was raised. I acknowledge the sacrificial support of Rev. Thomas Harris in helping to build my ministry, and being a witness to my first NDE. Thank you for your input, prayers, patience, and friendship to this day.

My daughter Radiance, you are above special. My first NDE started with you, and I saw you in Heaven before you were born. Never forget that you are named after the fruit, gifts, and grace of the Holy Spirit—charisma. I know that He who began a good work in you is faithful to complete it (Philippians 1:6).

My husband Tim, who went through what no husband should go through in such a short space of marriage. Only you know the degree of suffering I endured. Thank you for faithfully tending to me and sharing the writing journey. Because you witnessed my illnesses and, most notably, my third NDE, I was able to interpret my experience of how the body crosses over to Eternity upon death. And that no one can refute! This book could not have been completed without your love, help, and cheerleading. I love you.

To Jesus, the Light of the World—I shrank from baring the details of my life, but I surrendered my pride and privacy. I am a trophy of Your grace. I pray that the Holy Spirit will quicken my words so that many will turn to You and our Father in Heaven will be glorified. I will tell of Your saving power with my last breath. I will go where You want me to go, for You are with me. We will do this together. Amen.

NOTES

Introduction

1. Raymond Moody Jr., *Life After Life* (New York: Harper Collins, 2001).

Chapter 4 Paramedics

1. Vagus nerve. *Medical Definition of Nerve* (May 13, 2016). http://www.medicinenet.com/script/main/art.asp?articlekey=7631 (last accessed September 8, 2018).

Chapter 5 At the Hospital

1. *Government of Saskatchewan Lean Contract come to an end.* (March 31, 2015). Retrieved from http://www.cbc.ca/news/canada/saskatchewan/government-of-saskatchewan-s-lean-contract-comes-to-an-end-1.3017218 (last accessed September 8, 2018).

Chapter 7 OH WOW!

1. Mona Simpson (October 30, 2011). *A Sister's Eulogy for Steve Jobs.* The New York Times. https://www.nytimes.com/2011/10/30/opinion/mona-simpsons-eulogy-for-steve-jobs.html (last accessed September 8, 2018).

2. MacBook Pro with Retina Display. https://www.apple.com/ca/macbook-pro/ (last accessed September 8, 2018).

3. David Guzik. *Study Guide for John 3.* Blue Letter Bible. https://www.blueletterbible.org/comm/guzik_david/studyguide2017-jhn/jhn-3.cfm (last accessed September 8, 2018).

4. *What does it mean to be born of water?* Got Questions. https://www.gotquestions.org/born-of-water.html (last accessed September 8, 2018).

5. Todd Burpo and Lynn Vincent. *Heaven is for Real* (Thomas Nelson, 2010).

6. Mary Neal, M.D. *To Heaven and Back: A Doctor's Extraordinary Account of Her Death, Heaven, Angels, and Life Again: A True Story* (WaterBrook, 2012).

7. Dr. Jeff Long. http://www.nderf.org/NDERF/Research/number_nde_usa.htm (last accessed September 8, 2018).

8. Raymond Moody Jr., *Life After Life* (New York: Harper Collins, 2001).

9. Neal, *To Heaven and Back*.

10. Don Piper and Cecil Murphey. *90 Minutes in Heaven: A True Story of Life and Death*. Revell; Anniversary edition (Revell, 2014).

11. Burpo and Vincent. *Heaven is for Real*.

12. Howard Storm. *My Descent in to Death: A Second Chance at Life*. (New York Doubleday, 2005).

13. David Gocking. *The Glory of God*. Blue Letter Bible. https://www.blueletterbible.org/comm/hocking_david/attributes/attributes16.cfm (last accessed September 8, 2018).

14. Paradoxos. *NAS Exhaustive Concordance*. https://biblehub.com/greek/3861.htm (last accessed September 8, 2018)

15. Moody, *Life After Life*, p 129.

Chapter 8 About the Heart

1. *Rheumatic Fever*. Mayo Clinic http://www.mayoclinic.org/diseases-conditions/rheumatic-fever/home/ovc-20261251 (last accessed September 8, 2018).

Chapter 9 Pregnancy Woes

1. *Hyperemesis gravidarum: Duchess of Cambridge morning sickness condition explained*. The Telegraph. https://www.telegraph.co.uk/news/0/hyperemesis-gravidarum-duchess-cambridges-morning-sickness-condition/ (last accessed September 8, 2018).

2. *Apgar Score*. Medline Plus. https://medlineplus.gov/ency/article/003402.htm (last accessed September 8, 2018).

Chapter 12 Class of 2017

1. Kathryn Kuhlman. *I Believe in Miracles*. (Bridge Logos Publishers 2001).

2. Kathy Troccoli. *Go Light Your World*. Lyrics. https://www.lyrics.com/lyric/2708991/Kathy+Troccoli/Go+Light+Your+World (last accessed September 8, 2018).

3. NewYorkDress. http://www.newyorkdress.com/Tony_Bowls/TB117139.html (last accessed September 8, 2018).

Chapter 14 On Tour

1. Howard Storm. *My Descent into Death: A Second Chance at Life*. (New York Doubleday 2005).

2. *How Tall is Mount Everest?* The New York Times. https://www.nytimes.com/2018/02/03/world/asia/mount-everest-how-tall-nepal.html (last accessed September 8, 2018).

3. *How Deep is the Grand Canyon?* UStravelia. https://ustravelia.com/how-deep-is-grand-canyon (last accessed September 8, 2018).

Chapter 18 Angel at Trump Hotel

Susan Coolidge. *What Katy Did* (Purnell Books, Maidenhead, 1965,) 39-40.

Chapter 19 Angel at Park Street

1. Properties of the number 66. RidingThe Beast. https://www.ridingthebeast.com/numbers/nu66.php (last accessed September 8, 2018).

Chapter 20 Exile

1. Todd Burpo and Lynn Vincent. *Heaven is for Real* (Thomas Nelson, 2010).

2. *Tony Davis Interview on The Dr. Oz Show* https://vimeo.com/205140242 (last accessed September 8, 2018).

3. Marvin J. Besteman and Lorilee Craker, *My Journey to Heaven: What I Saw and How It Changed My Life.* (Grand Rapids: Baker, 2012).

4. Mary Neal, M.D. *To Heaven and Back: A Doctor's Extraordinary Account of Her Death, Heaven, Angels, and Life Again: A True Story* (WaterBrook, 2012).

5. Eben Alexander. *Proof of Heaven: A Neurosurgeon's Journey into the Afterlife* (Simon & Schuster, 2012).

6. Susan Harris. Smokey's Lockout. *Chicken Soup for the Soul The Cat Did What? 101 Amazing Stories of Magical Moments, Miracles and …Mischief* (Chicken Soup for the Soul Publishing 2014.) 115-117.

7. Susan Harris. Into The Great Unordinary. *Testimony.* Pentecostal Assemblies of Canada. September-October 2017.

Chapter 21 Popopop

1. *What is Supraventricular Tachycardia?* WebMD. https://www.webmd.com/heart-disease/what-is-supraventricular-tachycardia#12 (last accessed September 8, 2018).

2. Victor Lipman People leave Managers, not Companies. https://www.forbes.com/forbes/welcome/?toURL=https://www.forbes.com/sites/victorlipman/2015/08/04/people-leave-managers-not-companies/&refURL=https://www.google.ca/&referrer=https://www.google.ca/ (last accessed September 8, 2018).

Chapter 23 Double Delight

1. *Cardiac ablation.* Mayo Clinic. https://www.mayoclinic.org/tests-procedures/cardiac-ablation/about/pac-20384993 (last accessed September 8, 2018).

Chapter 24 Birthday Gift

1. *Blue Baby Syndrome.* Healthline. https://www.healthline.com/health/blue-baby-syndrome (last accessed September 8, 2018).

2. Susan Harris. *Remarkably Ordinary: 20 Reflections On Living Intentionally Right Where you Are* (White Lily Press, 2015)

3. *Cardiac ablation.* Mayo Clinic. https://www.mayoclinic.org/tests-procedures/cardiac-ablation/about/pac-20384993 (last accessed September 8, 2018).

Chapter 26 "Admit Her!"

1. Karen Lee Richards. ProHealth. *What The Pain Scale Really Means..* http://www.prohealth.com/library/showarticle.cfm?libid=20019 (last accessed September 8, 2018).

2. Ibid.

3. Christina E. DeRemer. Safe Medication. *Using PRN or "As-Needed" Medicines Safely.* http://www.safemedication.com/safemed/PharmacistsJournal/Using-PRN-or-As-Needed-Medicines-Safely (last accessed September 8, 2018).

Chapter 28 DDD

1. Accreditation Canada. https://accreditation.ca (last accessed September 8, 2018).

Chapter 29 Second Admission

1. 33 *Secrets Hospitals Don't want to Tell You But Every Patient Should Know.* http://www.msn.com/en-ca/health/wellness/33-secrets-hospitals-dont-want-to-tell-you-but-every-patient-should-know/ss-AArPrVc?li=AAggNb9#image=30 (last accessed September 8, 2018).

2. C.S. Lewis. Brainy Quotes. https://www.brainyquote.com/quotes/c_s_lewis_714960 (last accessed September 8, 2018).

3. Handbook. *Canada and Cackling Geese.* Environment Canada. https://www.ec.gc.ca/mbc-com/6D2B893B-C671-41AF-8439-713305DB384C/Handbook_Canada_Cackling_Geese_e%5B1%5D.pdf (last accessed September 8, 2018).

Chapter 30 Is Everything Written in Scripture?

1. Raymond Moody Jr., *Life After Life* (New York: Harper Collins, 2001).

2. Being. https://en.oxforddictionaries.com/definition/being

3. Raymond Moody Jr., *Life After Life* (New York: Harper Collins, 2001).

4. *Near Death Experience Research Foundation*. NDERF. http://www.nderf.org (last accessed September 8, 2018).

5. Whirlwind. *English Oxford Living Dictionary*. https://en.oxforddictionaries. com/definition/whirlwind

6. W.E. Vine. *An Expository Dictionary of New Testament Words*. Chicago: Moody Press, 1985.

7. David Guziak. *Study Guide for John 14*. Blue Letter Bible. https://www. blueletterbible.org/Comm/guzik_david/StudyGuide2017-Jhn/Jhn-14.cfm (last accessed September 8, 2018).

8. *Matthew Henry Commentary*. Bible Study Tools. John 14:2 https://www. biblestudytools.com/commentaries/matthew-henry-complete/john/14.html (last accessed September 8, 2018).

9. Witness Lee. *Not a Heavenly Mansion*. https://www.ministrysamples.org/ excerpts/NOT-A-HEAVENLY-MANSION.HTML (last accessed September 8, 2018).

10. Ron Kangas. *In My Father's House*. The Unleavened Truth of John 14. http://www.affcrit.com/pdfs/2000/02/00_02_a3.pdf (last accessed September 8, 2018).

11. *The Royal Family Official Residences*. http://royalcentral.co.uk/residences/ the-royal-familys-official-residences-1717 (last accessed September 8, 2018).

12. Château de Versailles. *Welcome to Versailles*. http://en.chateauversailles.fr (last accessed September 8, 2018).

Chapter 31 The Map

1. Ray Vander Laan. *That The World May Know* https://www.thattheworldmay-know.com/standing-stones (last accessed September 8, 2018).

2. New Jersey. https://www.mapofus.org/wp-content/uploads/2013/09/ NJ-county.jpg (last accessed September 8, 2018).

3. Borough of Washington. Borough of Washington History. http://www.wash-ingtonboro-nj.gov/town-history.html (last accessed September 8, 2018).

Chapter 32 Why See Heaven When in Pain?

1. W.E. Vine. *An Expository Dictionary of New Testament Words*. Chicago:

Moody Press, 1985.

2. Glory. http://www.ancient-hebrew.org/vocabulary_definitions_glory.html (last accessed September 8, 2018)

3. C. S. Lewis Quotable Quotes. https://www.goodreads.com/quotes/1180-pain-insists-upon-being-attended-to-god-whispers-to-us (last accessed September 8, 2018).

4. Susan Harris. *The Darkroom* https://twgauthors.blogspot.com/2015/06/the-darkroom-by-susan-harris.html (last accessed September 8, 2018).

Chapter 33 The Alfalfa Field and The Green Room

1. *Land Descriptions and Where They Come From.* ISC. https://www.isc.ca/signed-inhome/help/land/pages/landdescriptions.aspx (last accessed September 8, 2018).

2. *Bible Numbers 65* http://www.1260-1290-days-bible-prophecy.org/bible_numbers-13-60-65-130-390.htm (last accessed September 8, 2018).

3. *Properties of the number 51* http://www.ridingthebeast.com/numbers/nu51.php (last accessed September 8, 2018).

4. *Number 95* Voice of God. https://biblenumbersforlife.com/tag/meaning/ (last accessed September 8, 2018).

5. *Meanings of numbers in the Bible. The number 7.* http://www.biblestudy.org/bibleref/meaning-of-numbers-in-bible/7.html(last accessed September 8, 2018).

6. *A Green Office Equals a Productive Office.* Forbes. https://www.forbes.com/sites/adigaskell/2017/02/15/a-green-office-equals-a-productive-office/#61449a0f7ca5 (last accessed September 8, 2018).

7. *Purple Color Meaning.* Colours Meanings. https://www.color-meanings.com/purple-color-meaning-the-color-purple/ (last accessed September 8, 2018).

ABOUT THE AUTHOR

Susan Harris is an author, television host, speaker, and a teacher of 12 years. From the age of nine, she has stood in front of audiences, and over three decades has inspired thousands in schools, churches, conferences, and youth groups to find fulfillment in life. Her beliefs and experiences have helped women in particular to discover practical ways of leading positive and intentional lives. Her messages of hope are presented with clarity, conviction, and humour.

Susan obtained her Bachelor of Science in Management Studies from the University of the West Indies and then completed a post graduate Diploma in Education. She went on to earn a Diploma in Writing from the Institute of Literature in Connecticut, and a Certificate in Human Resources and Industrial Relations from Athabasca University.

Susan held the designation of Certified Human Resources Professional (CHRP) in Canada from 2008-2014, and is a member of the Saskatchewan Association of Human Resources Professionals. She has worked in various management positions and is active in several writing groups in Canada.

Susan was the valedictorian when she graduated from the Certificate in Biblical Theology course at the West Indies School of Theology. She held leadership positions in churches, and co-pastored with her husband for 19 years, serving as an itinerant preacher in her own capacity. She volunteers on a few boards and reaches out compassionately to persons with disabilities.

Susan is a hybrid author of 14 books, and has been published by Borealis Press in both English and French. Her writing can be found in several publications including *Chicken Soup for the Soul* (which features her cat Sir Smokey), and the *Sage* and *Testimony* magazines of the Pentecostal of the Assemblies of Canada. She also writes children biblical literature for Sunday school curricula.

Susan can adapt to audiences and geographic conditions, and she attributes this to the exposure of city living, island living, and rural living. Winter seasons have seen her interchange a briefcase and a shovel, tossing snow in high-heeled boots and executive suit. No matter the wear or the place, kindness and compassion are displayed in her demeanor. Prayer is the cornerstone of her life, and she would advise that you cannot cut corners with prayer.

Born and raised in the sparkling island of Trinidad, Susan now makes her home with her family and Sir Smokey and the rest of the gregarious cats on the lush prairies of eastern Saskatchewan where she hosts *Eternity* on Access7 television.

BOOKS BY SUSAN HARRIS

General Books:
Little Copper Pennies: Celebrating the Life of the Canadian One-Cent Piece 1858-2013. (2012,
  2014). Borealis Press, Ottawa.

Picture Books:
Little Copper Pennies for Kids (2012, 2014). Borealis Press, Ottawa.
Alphabet on The Farm (2014). Borealis Press, Ottawa.
L'alphabet à la ferme (2016). Borealis Press, Ottawa.
Christmas A to Z (2016). White Lily Press, Saskatchewan.
An Alphabet of the First Christmas: A Christian Alphabet Book
(2016). White Lily Press,
  Saskatchewan.

Inspirational books:
Golden Apples in Silver Settings (2011). White Lily Press, Saskatchewan.
Remarkably Ordinary: 20 Reflections on Living Intentionally Right Where You Are (2014).
  White Lily Press, Saskatchewan.
10½ Sketches: Insights On Being Successful Right Where You Are (2015). White Lily Press,
  Saskatchewan.

Co-written books:
My Garden of Eden (2016). White Lily Press, Saskatchewan
To Aïda With Love (2016). White Lily Press, Saskatchewan
ABCs of Compassion/ L'ABC de la compassion (2017). White Lily Press, Saskatchewan
Snippets of a Country Girl (2018). White Lily Press, Saskatchewan

Connect with Susan at:
https://www.susanharris.ca
https://www.facebook.com/SusanHarris
https://twitter.com/SusanHarris20
https://www.amazon.com/Susan-Harris/e/B007XMP4QS/

~

*If you enjoyed any of my books, would you please
leave a review on any online forum.
Thank you and God bless. I hope to see you in Eternity
Your friend,
Susan*

Made in the USA
Middletown, DE
10 March 2020